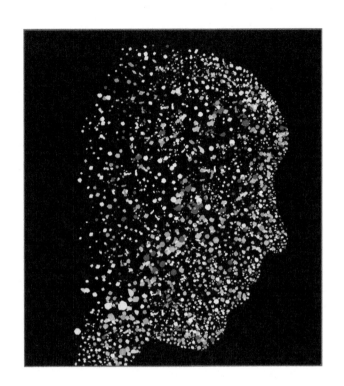

AS Level
WJEC Psychology

Nicola Taylor and Kirsty White

Edited by Nigel Holt and Rob Lewis

Crown House Publishing
www.crownhouse.co.uk

First published by
Crown House Publishing Ltd
Crown Buildings, Bancyfelin, Carmarthen, Wales, SA33 5ND, UK
www.crownhouse.co.uk
and
Crown House Publishing Company LLC
6 Trowbridge Drive, Suite 5, Bethel, CT 06801, USA
www.crownhousepublishing.com

An extension of this page appears on page 198.

British Library of Cataloguing-in-Publication Data

A catalogue entry for this book is available from the British Library.

Print ISBN 9781845909758

LCCN 2015948488

contents

AUTHORS: NICOLA TAYLOR AND KIRSTY WHITE

Nicola Taylor is subject leader for social science at Monmouth Comprehensive School. She has extensive experience of teaching AS and A level psychology, and has worked as an AS and A level psychology examiner for many years. Nicola has particular interests in counselling and therapy, and is also a qualified practitioner.

Kirsty White is a psychology graduate from Cardiff University and is trained to teach in both further and secondary education. She works as a social science teacher at Monmouth Comprehensive School, with particular responsibility for teaching psychology. She also has experience working with individuals with mental health and personality disorders, and has a keen interest in the fields of clinical and forensic psychology.

EDITORS: NIGEL HOLT AND ROB LEWIS

Nigel Holt works in the Department of Psychology at Aberystwyth University and Rob Lewis works in the School of Education at Cardiff Metropolitan University. They are always happy to hear from students and teachers so if you have any questions or would just like to say hello, please feel free to get in touch – their email addresses can be found on their respective institutional websites.

ACKNOWLEDGEMENTS

This is for my mum, who would have been so proud. (Nicola)

This book is dedicated to my family, Ali and Rich, who have been always been there for me. (Kirsty)

Nicola and Kirsty would also like to thank Rob for his good humoured editing and support in writing this book. They would also like to acknowledge the inspiration provided by Jonesy and Albie, particularly in the behaviourist approach chapter. Thank you to Olivia for lending us her photography skills and putting up with our constant book-induced stress. This book is for our students, who are an unending source of motivation and inspiration.

Nigel and Rob would like to take this opportunity to thank Nicola and Kirsty, two excellent teachers in a marvellous social science department in an exceptionally caring and dynamic school, which we have had the pleasure of visiting on several occasions.

INTRODUCTION

From 2015, AS and A level psychology in Wales will, for the first time, be different from their counterparts in England and Northern Ireland. The WJEC has grasped the opportunity to demonstrate their individuality by developing an AS specification which is unique in approach and content, as well as being appropriately challenging for advanced level study.

WHAT IS PSYCHOLOGY?

Psychology is the scientific study of mind and behaviour. It is one of the most popular subjects to study in schools, colleges and universities in Britain. Some people will tell you that psychology is just 'common sense', and it could be argued there is an element of truth to this in some aspects of psychology. What really distinguishes psychology, however, is the foundation of research that it shares with the other sciences. We live around and observe other people every day, yet they are still hard to understand. Studying behaviour scientifically can be relatively straightforward, but it can also be a very difficult undertaking indeed. It can sometimes seem as though the findings of research raise more questions than they answer. This is because human beings are very complicated and their behaviour is subject to many influences – from the actions of tiny brain cells to the impact of being amongst others in a large crowd. It is only through scientific research, where there are carefully controlled observations and tests, that we can determine, with any kind of confidence, why people behave the way they do. You will notice that there is a major focus on research throughout this book, not only in the section on research methods but in all the sections, where the material presented is largely derived from scientific methods and the theories are developed from scientific evidence.

Knowledge of how psychologists gather information through research is vital to your own success at AS level, and we cannot stress enough how important it is to have a sound understanding of research methods. The specification requires that you not only develop your own psychological research skills, but also that you are able to apply your knowledge so that you can evaluate the evidence on which theories are built. You will notice as you progress through the book that frequent reference is made to the methods used by psychologists in their research, and in order to deepen your understanding we would recommend that you regularly refer to the section on research methods. In this way, your knowledge of research methods will slowly grow and your appreciation of psychology will deepen.

We hope that AS level psychology will give you a taste for psychology and that you will continue to study further at A level and beyond at undergraduate level.

Nigel and Rob

© Mike Baldwin / Cornered

'The research proves tall rats are more confident than short rats. At least I think it does. I've never been good at this.'

Unit 1
Psychology: Past to Present

WHAT YOU NEED TO KNOW ☑

The biological approach ☐

Evolutionary influences ☐

Localisation of brain function ☐

Neurotransmitters ☐

Evolutionary influences on the formation of relationships ☐

Drug therapy **OR** Psychosurgery ☐

Classic research: Raine et al. (1997) ☐

The psychodynamic approach ☐

The unconscious mind ☐

Tripartite personality ☐

Influence of childhood experiences ☐

The influence of childhood experiences on the formation of relationships ☐

Dream analysis **OR** Group analysis psychotherapy ☐

Classic research: Bowlby (1944) ☐

The behaviourist approach ☐

Blank slate ☐

Humans and animals learn in similar ways ☐

Behaviour learned through conditioning ☐

The formation of relationships between pets and their owners: behaviour learned through conditioning ☐

Aversion therapy **OR** Systematic desensitisation ☐

Classic research: Watson and Rayner (1920) ☐

The cognitive approach ☐

Internal mental processes ☐

The computer analogy ☐

Schemas ☐

Internal mental processes and the formation of relationships ☐

Cognitive-behavioural therapy **OR** Rational emotive behaviour therapy ☐

Classic research: Loftus and Palmer (1974) ☐

The positive approach ☐

Acknowledgement of free will ☐

Authenticity of goodness and excellence ☐

Focus on 'the good life' ☐

'The good life' and the formation of relationships ☐

Mindfulness **OR** Quality of Life Therapy ☐

Classic research: Myers and Diener (1995) ☐

The Biological Approach

WHAT YOU NEED TO KNOW ☑

The assumptions of the biological approach ☐

Evolutionary influences ☐

Localisation of brain function ☐

Neurotransmitters ☐

Evaluation of the biological approach ☐

Strengths ☐

Weaknesses ☐

Comparison with the four other approaches (see page 82) ☐

Application: formation of relationships ☐

How the approach can be used in ONE therapy: ☐

EITHER: Drug therapy

Evaluation:

Effectiveness ☐

Ethical considerations ☐

OR: Psychosurgery

Evaluation:

Effectiveness ☐

Ethical considerations ☐

Classic research (Raine et al., 1997) ☐

Aim ☐

Method and procedure ☐

Findings ☐

Conclusion ☐

Evaluation ☐

Ethical issues ☐

Social implications ☐

INTRODUCTION

Biology influences behaviour. We know this from the way that changes in brain chemicals affect moods, and from how brain trauma can radically alter the ways in which we think and act. Also, behaviour influences biology. This can be seen in the stressful effects the environments we find ourselves in have on us, the way that mood influences immune system functioning, and the effects of the recreational drugs that we choose to take, such as tobacco and alcohol, on our psychology and physiology. Clearly, biology and behaviour are inextricably interwoven. Changes in one bring about changes in the other, and we cannot truly understand either without some understanding of both.

THE ASSUMPTIONS OF THE BIOLOGICAL APPROACH

1. Evolutionary influences

The basic premise of *evolution* theory is rather simple and elegant. Animals produce many more young than could possibly survive. Offspring are often very slightly different from either parent and these variations (or mutations) sometimes enable animals to cope better with environmental demands and reach maturity. The ones that do reach adulthood are the strongest of their generation, and when they breed they pass on to their young the characteristics that helped them survive. Those with traits that help them survive are more likely to reproduce themselves (i.e. they are selected by the process of evolution for their 'fitness'), and so the cycle continues. As many generations go by, the traits (or *adaptations*) that have aided survival and reproductive fitness are passed on and become widespread in the population. Such a process involves changes to both physiology and behaviour, so that the end result can be an animal that bears little resemblance to its ancestors in looks or behaviour. This is the principle of *natural selection*. A special kind of natural selection is *sexual selection*. This theory says that the characteristics of an animal that increase mating success are more likely to result in reproduction, passing on that characteristic to offspring, and thus also increasing their chances of mating success. A consequence of this is often exaggerated characteristics which appear, on the face of it, to disadvantage an animal in terms of survival chances – take the male peacock's tail for example. The more flamboyant the display, the more likely a male is to attract a female.

The male peacock's tail is an example of exaggerated physical characteristics evolving in order to increase chances of reproductive success.

2. Localisation of brain function

This assumption of the *biological approach* draws on research which has shown that particular areas of the brain are specialised for certain functions or tasks. The brain has two hemispheres (or halves). Each hemisphere has regions specialised for particular things (i.e. they have *localised* functions). The cortex of each hemisphere consists of four areas called lobes. The large *frontal lobes* are involved in higher functions e.g. thinking, speech and motor control and coordinating information from other lobes. Behind the frontal lobes sit the *parietal lobes* which receive and interpret sensory information. Visual information is received and processed at the back of the brain by the *occipital lobes*. Finally, at the sides of the brain are the *temporal lobes* which process auditory information and are also important for memory. The areas of the cortex directly responsible for sensory information are called *primary areas*. All other cortical areas are collectively known as *association areas*. The *neurons* in the association areas appear to be less specific in what they do,

are more flexible in their functions and adapt to experience, much more so than neurons in the primary areas. This makes some sense in that they are involved in integrating and using information from the primary areas in high level functions such as perception, decision making and planning.

Language is a good example of localisation of function. In 1861, physician Paul Broca exhibited the brain of a patient who, before dying the year before, had lost the ability to say anything other than 'tan'. The brain showed clear damage to the left frontal cortex, an area now called Broca's area, which is important for guiding the muscles in the mouth into the right shapes to make speech sounds. In 1874, Carl Wernicke described a patient who, following damage to the left temporal cortex, had great difficulty understanding speech. This area is now known as Wernicke's area. Since then a number of other locations have been discovered in the brain that are important for language, and for the vast number of people these are in the left hemisphere.

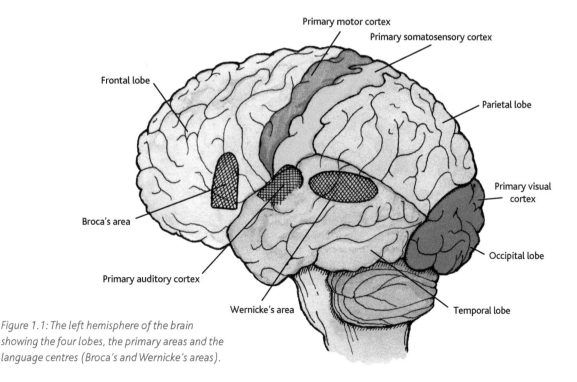

Figure 1.1: The left hemisphere of the brain showing the four lobes, the primary areas and the language centres (Broca's and Wernicke's areas).

3. Neurotransmitters

The brain is made up of billions of cells called neurons. These communicate with one another using electrical and chemical signals. The chemical used in this communication is called a neurotransmitter. When a neuron receives messages from others neurons, it is stimulated to pass messages on to other neurons with which it is associated. These messages occur at synapses – tiny gaps between neurons used for communication (see Figure 1.2). A neuron sends molecules of neurotransmitter across the synapse to another neuron. This communication causes either *excitation* or *inhibition* in the receiving neuron. Excitation occurs when neurotransmitter messages make it more likely that receiving neurons will themselves send the message on to other neurons. As the name suggests, inhibition makes passing the message on less likely to happen. This process occurs in the brain many millions of times every second, resulting in the regulation of thinking and behaviour.

There are many different kinds of neurotransmitters, and research into these substances has told us a great deal about the origins of both normal and abnormal behaviour. For example, reduced levels of the neurotransmitter dopamine lie behind the symptoms of Parkinson's disease, and increasing levels of dopamine can help reduce these

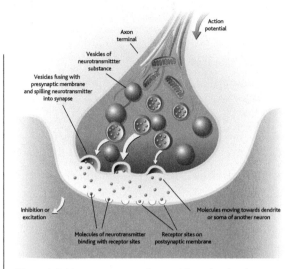

Figure 1.2: Neurons communicate with each other by releasing neurotransmitters into a synapse (a small gap between neurons).

symptoms. Increased levels of dopamine are associated with schizophrenia, and antipsychotic drugs can help some individuals by reducing these levels and thus controlling symptoms.

Neurotransmitters are made up of quite simple chemicals and are readily manufactured by the body. For example, acetylcholine is produced from choline-rich foods such as egg yolks and vegetables, serotonin from tryptophan-containing foods like bananas and gamma-aminobutyric acid (GABA) from natural protein foods. Mechanisms in the brain ensure that the amount of neurotransmitter available for use is always, in the normally functioning brain, limited to just the right amount.

NEUROTRANSMITTER	FUNCTION
Dopamine	Increases addictive effects of reinforcement, contributes to control of movement; linked with schizophrenia, Parkinson's disease, addiction.
Serotonin	Associated with mood, eating, arousal (including sleep); linked with depression, aggression, OCD, eating disorders.
Noradrenaline	Increases arousal, attentiveness, sexual behaviour; released as a hormone during stress; linked with depression.
GABA	One of the most widespread neurotransmitters in the brain, it contributes to motor control and helps regulate anxiety.

Table 1.1: Some behaviours associated with neurotransmitters.

Have you ever felt better after a cup of coffee? Lots of things that we eat and drink contain chemicals that affect neurotransmitters. Caffeine, for example, blocks the effects of adenosine, a neurotransmitter that not only makes us sleepy but also influences other major neurotransmitters, such as dopamine, serotonin and noradrenaline – three neurotransmitters closely associated with mood.

EVALUATION OF THE BIOLOGICAL APPROACH

	STRENGTH	WEAKNESS
Scientific research methods can be used	A person's biology can be studied scientifically, so this approach is perhaps the most objective way to investigate human behaviour.	It is not always clear that behaviour is determined solely by a person's biology; it is not always clear whether biology influences psychology or whether psychology influences biology.
The biological approach is reductionist	Lots of research indicates that behaviour can be explained in terms of altered neurochemistry, hormones and changes to brain structure.	Reducing behaviour to biological origins runs the risk of underestimating the importance of things like social and cultural influences on behaviour.
The use of animals in research	Using animals in research to test the effect of altering certain biological systems or processes means that we do not have to do this to humans. It protects individuals from harm but also allows us to develop an understanding of our own biology, and therefore further psychology and medicine.	Although animals do share some similar body systems, it is not known if these systems always work in the same way as they do in humans. Therefore, the findings and conclusions from research on animals may not be generalisable to humans.

EVOLUTIONARY INFLUENCES ON THE FORMATION OF RELATIONSHIPS

Evolution theory attempts to apply the principles of evolution to understanding human behaviours, including the formation of relationships. According to this approach, both males and females are seeking to produce healthy offspring in order for their genes to survive into the next generation. Consequently, sexual partners will be sought who can produce and provide for healthy children, although males and females do look for different things in their partners.

Females produce few eggs in comparison to the millions of sperm produced by males and they also invest heavily in the nine months of pregnancy, the childbirth, lactation and child dependency period. Clearly, the male contribution to the reproductive process is minor in comparison. Females are limited in the number of children they can produce during their reproductive years whereas males can produce a seemingly unlimited number of offspring throughout their lives. These biological differences have led males and females to develop different strategies and tactics to maximise their chances of reproductive success.

Females are programmed to mate with carefully chosen partners with plentiful resources, whereas males are programmed to maximise their chances of producing offspring by mating frequently and 'sowing their seed' with as many partners as possible. Promiscuity for males is a way of increasing their chance of reproducing, whereas monogamy is a more appropriate strategy for females, who may seek older, reliable males for long-term relationships who can provide good resources for a potential family. Males may seek younger, attractive females who are likely to be more fertile and produce healthy offspring. Table 1.2 is a summary of some findings from research.

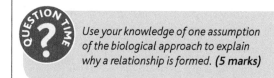

Use your knowledge of one assumption of the biological approach to explain why a relationship is formed. **(5 marks)**

STUDY	FINDINGS	EXPLANATION
Buss (1989)	Males: valued physical attractiveness more. Females: valued earning potential and occupational status more.	Males: attractiveness could be an indicator of fertility. Females: earning potential indicates the ability to provide for offspring.
Singh (1993)	Men prefer women with a low waist-to-hip ratio, indicative of higher conception rates.	Males: prefer this body shape as it indicates higher conception rates and more offspring. Females: their shape is a signal to 'fit' males.
Montoya (2007)	Both sexes interested in body parts predictive of health (e.g. eyes, skin, complexion). Males preferred body parts predictive of fertility (e.g. hips). Females preferred body parts predictive of strength and overall fitness (e.g. muscle tone).	Males: seek partners who are more likely to produce offspring. Females: strength indicates the ability to protect offspring.

Table 1.2: Some findings from research into evolutionary explanations for the formation of relationships.

THERAPY – DRUG THERAPY

The focus of *drug therapy* is either to increase or decrease the effects of neurotransmitters in the brain. Because behaviour originates with minute chemical changes in the brain, the assumption is that deliberately altering this brain chemistry with drugs should change unwanted behaviour (drugs that have psychological effects are known as psychoactive drugs). Many of the first drugs for treating psychological disorders were discovered accidentally. For example, in the 1950s it was found that lithium salt made animals quiet and calm. Lithium was then trialled as a treatment for depression and became the main psychoactive drug for depression until the introduction of safer and more effective alternatives.

The beneficial impacts of drug therapy are not always due solely to the psychoactive effects of the drug. There is a cultural belief in the benefits of drug treatments and so there is a great expectation of recovery. This means that there is a strong *placebo effect* with some psychoactive drugs – patients unknowingly

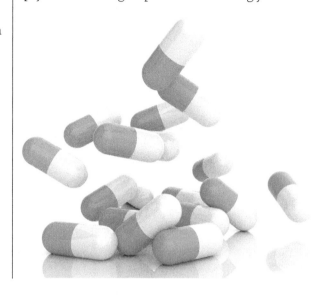

DISORDER AND POSSIBLE CHEMICAL CAUSE	DRUG THERAPY	EFFECT ON NEUROTRANSMITTERS
Schizophrenia: an excess of dopamine	Conventional antipsychotics (e.g. chlorpromazine) or atypical antipsychotics (e.g. clozapine)	Antipsychotic drugs reduce the effect of dopamine in the brain, thus reducing the symptoms of schizophrenia.
Depression: low levels of serotonin	Selective serotonin reuptake inhibitors (SSRIs, e.g. Prozac)	SSRIs maintain levels of serotonin in the synapse, thus increasing its effects.
Depression: low levels of noradrenaline	Tricyclic antidepressants: (TCAs) or monoamine oxidase inhibitors (MAOIs)	TCAs and MAOIs both increase the amount of noradrenaline in the brain.
Anxiety (as the main symptom): low levels of serotonin	Anxiolytic antidepressants: SSRIs	SSRIs used to treat depression also work with anxiety disorders.
Anxiety (with strong physical symptoms): susceptibility to the effects of the fight-or-flight hormone adrenaline	Anxiolytics: benzodiazepines (BZs, e.g. Valium)	BZs enhance the activity of the neurotransmitter GABA which 'quietens' the neurons in the brain by making it harder for them to be stimulated by other neurotransmitters. A person therefore feels more relaxed.

Table 1.3: Some disorders and drug therapy treatments.

given non-active (neutral) medication show improvements because they believe that drug therapy will work. This undoubtedly improves the effectiveness of drug therapy for many individuals, and shows not only that the brain affects the mind but also that the mind affects the brain.

Evaluation of drug therapy

Effectiveness

▸ Drugs are cheap, quick, easy and effective ways of managing the symptoms of psychological disorders. Whilst this is their greatest strength, it is also their greatest weakness. They treat the symptoms rather than the cause, so do not provide a 'cure' as such. They are a convenient alternative to the lengthy and expensive process of psychological therapy and this has led to their over-prescription. There is a risk of both physiological and psychological dependency with drug therapy. There are also a great number of side effects from medication, depending on the dosage and type of drug taken.

▸ Many psychologists argue that psychological treatments are more appropriate than drug treatments. Greist (1998) compared the effectiveness of psychological therapy to that of drug treatments for anxiety. Greist found that psychological therapy was just as effective as drugs and did not have the side effects and high relapse rates associated with drug therapy. This has led some to argue that drug therapy should never be the sole treatment and there should always be an associated or alternative psychological treatment available.

▸ Elkin et al. (1989) conducted a large-scale study comparing cognitive-behavioural therapy (CBT), interpersonal therapy, drug therapy and placebos for treating depression. They found that the use of drugs generally provided quicker effects than the other therapies, especially for those with severe cases of depression. However, when individuals had mild cases of depression they experienced little reduction in the symptoms compared with those undergoing the other treatments, or even taking the placebo.

Ethical considerations

▸ As with all drug treatments, psychoactive drugs cause side effects. For example, TCAs can cause drowsiness and numerous other side effects, MAOIs can be fatal if consumption is mixed with certain foods, BZs can cause memory problems and conventional antipsychotics can cause involuntary movements of the mouth and tongue.

▸ Drugs are non-invasive ways of treating disorders: the patient does not have to undergo surgery, which could lead to irreversible changes, and can be weaned off the mediation if and when medical professionals feel it is safe to do so. Where possible, medical professionals will use drug therapies that have less severe side effects (e.g. SSRIs are the most common drug treatment for depression as the side effects are less serious than those of MAOIs) or when non-drug treatments are not suitable (e.g. CBT; see the section on the cognitive approach).

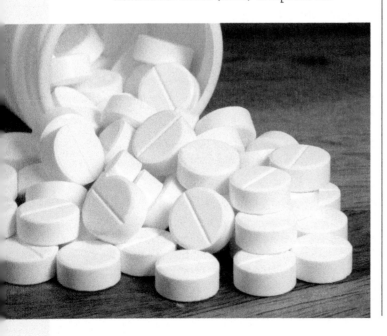

THERAPY – PSYCHOSURGERY

Psychosurgery is a biological approach to abnormality which sees abnormal behaviour as a symptom of an underlying physical problem originating in the brain. Surgically altering the physical state of the brain therefore should bring about change in the unwanted abnormal behaviour. Psychosurgery specifically aims to alleviate the symptoms of mental illnesses by destroying areas of the brain or interrupting the flow of information between particular brain areas that may be the cause of these behaviours.

Trepanning

Evidence for the basic principle of psychosurgery can be seen in fossils dating back to prehistoric times. Skulls have been found with large holes cut into them through a process known as 'trepanning'. This is where an instrument has been used to cut away circular sections of the skull. Historians have surmised that the purpose of this was to cure abnormal behaviour by releasing evil spirits. It is likely that these unfortunate individuals suffered a great deal before they died prematurely.

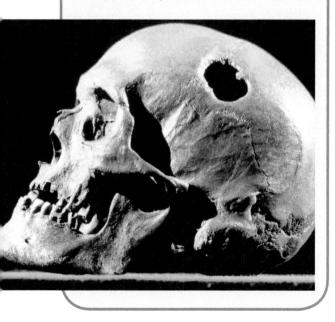

Prefrontal lobotomy (leucotomy)

In the 1930s Egan Moniz developed a surgical procedure known as a *leucotomy*. This involved drilling two holes on either side of the skull and inserting through these a tool which was rotated to separate the frontal lobes from the rest of the brain. This idea came from the discovery that when aggressive monkeys had the frontal lobe area of their brain removed they became subdued and calm. Reports of lobotomies on schizophrenic patients claimed near miraculous outcomes, so that previously aggressive and unpredictable individuals were now quiet and docile. In the 1940s Walter Freeman developed a much quicker procedure called the *transorbital lobotomy*, which involved separating the frontal lobes by inserting a large needle into the brain through the eye socket. This quick and easy procedure meant that in the United States alone over 50,000 people received lobotomies. Lobotomies fell out of favour in the 1950s with increasing reports of fatalities and negative side effects and the development of drug therapies.

Over time much more precise surgical procedures were developed. Stereotactic psychosurgery, for example, involves destruction of very specific areas of the brain. Areas for surgery are targeted by using brain scans; measurements are taken so that neurosurgeons are able to insert probes with great precision to particular locations in the brain. Electrical currents to the tip of the probe ensure that only small sections of brain tissue are destroyed, with little or no damage to surrounding healthy tissue. However, such surgical procedures are now carried out only as a last resort with severe cases of disorders such as depression and obsessive-compulsive disorder (OCD).

D'Astous et al. (2013) evaluated an operation called bilateral anterior capsulotomy (surgical damage to a part of the brain called the internal capsules). Nineteen patients were studied up to seven years following their operations and almost half had responded well to surgery.

Whilst there were no deaths, two patients had permanent complications as a result of the brain surgery. A new surgical procedure trialled by Jung et al. (2015) uses ultrasound to destroy the anterior internal capsules. Follow-up assessments of four patients showed gradual improvement in symptoms. As this is a non-invasive procedure there were none of the side effects or complications associated with invasive neurosurgery.

Evaluation of psychosurgery

Effectiveness

» The lobotomy eventually began to fall out of favour with those working with patients with mental disorders and illnesses. Side effects such as unresponsiveness, decreased attention span and blunted or inappropriate emotions led to the conclusion that this treatment produced effects that were worse than those caused by the disorder in the first place. Furthermore, there was a fatality rate of up to 6%, with severe side effects including brain seizures (Comer, 2006).

» Kim et al. (2002) investigated the long-term effects of various stereotactic psychosurgeries in patients with aggression, OCD, depression and anxiety disorders and concluded that

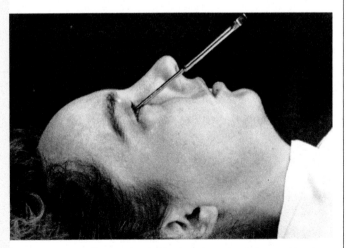

A quick procedure taking less than ten minutes and leaving no scars other than black eyes, some surgeons claimed to be able to do several dozen transorbital lobotomies in a day.

they are safe and effective for some mental disorders and illnesses. Different scales to measure the severity of symptoms were used for each disorder. During follow-ups years after the surgery, all patients showed significant decreases in their symptoms.

» Even though psychosurgery has come a long way there are still risks involved in the procedure which could reduce the effectiveness of the treatment. In some cases treatment can impact on a person's ability to lead a normal life as side effects can include memory loss, seizures and changes to personality.

Ethical considerations

» Nowadays, psychosurgery is used only as a last resort when other therapies or treatments have been ineffective. Medical professionals and psychologists will always seek to try less extreme measures to help those with mental illnesses or disorders, to minimise the risk of harm. Drug therapy is always preferable to psychosurgery and its effects are often not as severe or long term.

» Patients who could undergo psychosurgery would do so because they have a serious psychological disorder or illness. Therefore, it is questionable whether they can give fully informed consent. Their disorder could make it difficult for them to fully understand the consequences of their decision, particularly as these therapies can cause irreversible damage. At certain times, the patient may not have the choice of whether to undergo the surgery or not; medical professionals may have made a judgement that they are incapable of making a decision and have prescribed this as the best course of action. In these instances the surgery may be administered against the will of the patient. This was commonplace in the first decades of using psychosurgery, but occurs less often today due to our understanding of its effects.

CLASSIC RESEARCH
– RAINE ET AL. (1997)

Raine, A., Buchsbaum, M. and LaCasse, L. (1997). Brain abnormalities in murderers indicated by positron emission tomography. *Biological Psychiatry*, 42(6), 495–508

Aim

Raine et al. wanted to investigate whether criminals who had committed murder and pleaded not guilty by reason of insanity (NGRI) had brain structures different from those who had not committed murder.

Method and procedure

Raine et al. used a *matched pairs design* in their *natural experiment*. In the experimental group (NGRIs), there were 41 criminals (39 males and 2 females) who had committed murder and pleaded NGRI. Those in the control group were matched by age, sex and diagnosis but none had committed murder. Participants in both *conditions* stopped taking any prescribed medication two weeks before the study began. This allowed the researchers to rule out the effect of this medication on the brain. On the day of their positron emission tomography (PET) scan, all participants were injected with a glucose tracker and completed a target-recognition task for 32 minutes. They were then given a PET scan, allowing researchers to monitor activity across the brain.

Findings

Compared to the control group, NGRIs were found to have less activity in their prefrontal and parietal areas, more activity in their occipital areas and no difference in their temporal areas. They were also found to have less activity in the corpus callosum (the part of the brain that joins the two hemispheres) and an imbalance between the two hemispheres in terms of

Positron emission tomography (PET)

A small amount of harmless radioactive material is injected into a vein, which bonds to glucose (a form of energy readily used by brain cells). The areas of the brain which are most active use more of it. The glucose is broken down but the radioactive material remains and emits positively charged particles called positrons which are picked up by the scan. This information produces coloured images of the level of activity occurring throughout the brain – the brightest areas showing greatest activity.

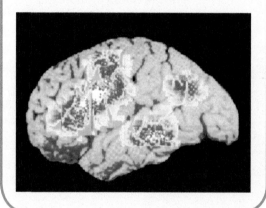

activity in the amygdala (less activity in the left side and more in the right), the hippocampus (less activity in the left side and more in the right) and the thalamus (more activity in the right side but no difference in the left side).

Conclusion

Raine et al. concluded that individuals who have committed murder but plead NGRI did have significantly different levels of activity in various areas of the brain, and these brain areas may be related to the violent behaviour for which they were convicted. The study highlights several important points:

1. The amygdala is important for processing emotions, so the findings could support theories

METHOD	NATURAL EXPERIMENT
Participants	Experimental group: 41 criminals (39 males and 2 females) who had committed murder and pleaded NGRI Control group: matched on age, sex and diagnosis
Design	Matched pairs
Independent variable	Whether or not participants had committed murder (a naturally occurring independent variable)
Dependent variable	PET scan results

Table 1.4: Summary of the key features of the Raine et al. study.

that violence is due to unusual emotional responses (e.g. lack of fear).

2. People with a damaged corpus callosum have been found to have difficulties controlling emotions, which fits with the nature of their violent crimes.

3. The differences in activity in the prefrontal cortex may be important because rational thinking takes place here.

Evaluation of Raine et al. (1997)
Internal validity
Raine et al. increased the validity of their study by ensuring that they controlled for possible factors that could have contributed to the participants' violent behaviour (other than brain activity), such as *individual differences*, by using a matched pairs design and stopping medication.

Demand characteristics
One strength of the study was that they used a biological measurement which cannot be affected by *demand characteristics*. The participants would not have been able to alter their brain activity to fit in with what they may have thought the researchers wanted to find. This increases both validity and reliability.

NGRI

Beheading killer not guilty by reason of insanity
BBC, 23 June 2015

A man who beheaded an elderly woman in North London will be detained indefinitely in a secure hospital after being cleared of murder by reason of insanity.

Nicholas Salvador, 25, was suffering from a severe psychiatric illness when he attacked 82-year-old Palmira Silva in her garden in September last year.

'Not guilty by reason of insanity' (NGRI) is a plea made in court that, whilst a person charged with a crime did actually do it, a mental disturbance meant that they lacked the capacity to *intend* to do it. 'Insanity' is a legal term, it does not exist in clinical psychology or as a medical term in psychiatry. Not all people with mental health problems meet the criteria for insanity. To be NGRI a person's mental state at the time of the crime must be proven to be such that they would not have known the true nature and quality of their behaviour. This is not at all straightforward and because of this NGRI is a relatively rare verdict.

Cause and effect

The data appear to show that there is a relationship between two *variables* (activity in the brain and violent behaviour). However, this does not allow us to establish cause and effect. We will never know if the brain activity caused the violent behaviour, or if the violent behaviour caused the brain activity. There may be other variables involved too that were not controlled for in this study. Therefore, the results have to be treated with caution.

Ethical issues

The medication of all participants was stopped prior to the study. This could have put the participants and those around them at risk of harm – remember that a lot of them had disorders that were likely being controlled by medication. A PET scan was used, which is a relatively non-intrusive method of observing activity in the brain and only carries a small risk (because of the injection of a radioactive substance). It does not involve any surgery and it allows researchers to observe the activity of the living brain. This is helpful in informing our understanding of certain disorders, and therefore allowing the development of useful treatments.

Social implications

Studies like this raise the possibility that one day technology will allow us to predict whether individuals are likely to commit crimes, and whether those convicted of crimes are likely to re-commit. For example, Aharoni et al. (2013) scanned the brains of 96 male prisoners just before their release from prison and followed the lives of the ex-criminals for four years. They found that those with low activity in a particular part of the brain called the anterior cingulate

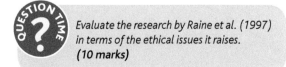

Evaluate the research by Raine et al. (1997) in terms of the ethical issues it raises.
(10 marks)

Free will and determinism

When explaining behaviour in biological terms, especially behaviour that has real-world social and moral implications, the extremely important issue of free will versus determinism arises. Some argue that by attributing behaviour solely to our biology (i.e. behaviour is determined by biology) we are in essence excusing behaviour for which a person should really be held accountable. This determinism has implications for society. The legal system operates on the basis that adults have the free will to choose whether to do right or wrong. For example, someone who commits murder has engaged in a deliberate and controlled act. If, however, behaviour is determined by factors outside of an individual's control, can or should they be held responsible for it? There are also repercussions for the way people think about their own behaviour. Research suggests that what a person believes about their own free will influences their attitude towards their own moral behaviour. If we believe we have little or no control over our behaviour then we are less inhibited from doing things that we know we shouldn't. We have in effect a ready-made excuse for it: 'it wasn't my fault, it was my biology'. Psychologists clearly need to very carefully consider the implications of the conclusions they draw about the origins of behaviour and how this is likely to be interpreted by the wider, non-scientific community.

cortex were more likely to be arrested and arrested sooner.

Even if this becomes a reliable test of the likelihood of reoffending, however, there are many further social implications to consider. For example, criminals may be able to argue for diminished responsibility because of their biology, or individuals may be irrevocably labelled as criminals regardless of whether they do actually commit further crimes.

The Psychodynamic Approach

WHAT YOU NEED TO KNOW ☑

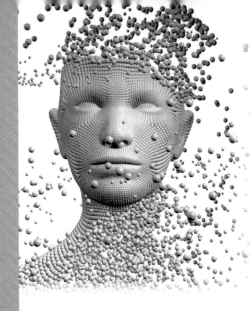

INTRODUCTION

The *psychodynamic approach* was developed by Sigmund Freud and others towards the end of the 19th century. The word 'psychodynamic' is used because this approach sees the mind (or *psyche*) as being influenced by powerful, active (*dynamic*) unconscious forces. This approach has had a major influence on psychology, and whilst many of its theoretical elements have been rejected by most mainstream psychology, ideas like the assumption of behaviour being guided by things which we are not consciously aware of are now generally accepted. Indeed, the principal value of the psychodynamic approach to contemporary psychology is its place in the history of psychology and the contribution it has made to our approach to understanding mind and behaviour.

THE ASSUMPTIONS OF THE PSYCHODYNAMIC APPROACH

1. The unconscious mind

Freud likened the structure of our mind to an iceberg. The tip of the iceberg, which sits above the water, represents our conscious mind. Our conscious mind is the part of ourselves that we are aware of – the self we can describe. The unconscious part of the mind contains our deepest thoughts, feelings and desires of which we are unaware. It is constantly influencing our behaviour, particularly with urges to seek pleasure. Sometimes this unconscious pleasure-seeking may manifest itself through our dreams or through 'slips of the tongue' that unconsciously reveal what we really think. The unconscious also contains repressed thoughts and emotions from our childhood which, if they became conscious, would be painful and unpleasant and disrupt our normal day-to-day functioning. For example, Freud believed that repressed memories of early traumatic events in our lives could appear later in adulthood as depression, phobias and obsessions.

Consciousness

Unconsciousness

Freud compared the mind to an iceberg.

2. The tripartite personality

Freud claimed that the mind (or 'psyche') has three components: the id, ego and superego. These appear at different times during our childhood. They are dynamic forces, always competing for dominance of the psyche (an example of how they interact can be seen in the box 'The tripartite personality at work'). It is important however that they are kept in balance, otherwise one may dominate, leading to psychological and behavioural problems. For example, if the id is powerful and the superego weak then antisocial behaviour might emerge, or if the id is weak and the superego strong then a person may feel intolerable guilt and shame. Abnormal behaviour can be seen as a sign of unconscious conflicts between the id, ego and superego.

Id: The id is present from birth. This part of the psyche is unconscious and operates on the 'pleasure principle'. This is where the pleasure-seeking drive in the unconscious mind originates. Freud described babies as all id as they seek satisfaction at any cost and are not capable of either logical thinking or morality.

Ego: At around the age of 2 the ego develops to meet the demands of the id in a socially acceptable way. The ego is the conscious part of our personality – the part of ourselves of which we are aware. It operates on the 'reality principle'.

Superego: The superego emerges at about 5 years of age. The superego is also unconscious and operates on the 'morality principle'. It acts as the individual's conscience and ego ideal, guiding behaviour with a sense of what is right and wrong, and thus generates a sense of guilt or pride in response to our behaviour.

> ### The tripartite personality at work
>
> As an adult your decisions about how to act in certain situations may be influenced by the three parts of your personality. For example, if you find a purse lying in the street your id will drive you towards keeping it and any money it may contain for yourself. However, your superego – acting on the morality principle – will push you towards handing in the purse at the nearest police station. If you satisfy the demands of the id, and keep the purse, you risk feeling guilty and shameful as the conscience within the superego punishes you for acting immorally. The decision you make is down to the ego which tries to balance the demands of the selfish id and the moral superego. You may do the right thing by handing in the purse but selfishly hope to get praise or a reward for doing so, thus satisfying both the moral and pleasure-seeking sides of your personality.

*Analyse the strengths and weaknesses of the psychodynamic approach. **(10 marks)***

PART OF THE PERSONALITY	AGE OF DEVELOPMENT	KEY PRINCIPLE	AREA OF THE MIND
Id	Present from birth	Pleasure	Unconscious
Ego	Emerges around age 2–3	Reality	Conscious
Superego	Emerges around the age of 5	Morality	Unconscious

Table 1.5: The development of the tripartite personality.

3. Influence of childhood experiences

For Freud, childhood experiences are a crucial element in the formation of our personality and the way we behave as adults. The stages of psychosexual development are especially important. At each stage we find pleasure and gratification from a different part of our body – our erogenous areas. Our experience of these erogenous areas can cause fixations – unconscious preoccupations with that particular psychosexual stage which can be expressed in adult behaviour. During the oral stage the focus of pleasure is the mouth and fixations result from oral gratification. After the first year the erogenous area moves to the anus, and in particular controlling bowel movements. Fixations arise from experiences during toilet training. By the age of 5 years most children are in the phallic stage, where the erogenous area is now the genitals. The child begins to have unconscious sexual desires for the opposite sex parent. This causes psychological conflict because the child fears punishment if discovered. In boys this is called the Oedipus conflict, and is resolved by the boy identifying with and becoming like the father. Girls experience the Electra conflict. Girls unconsciously believe that their feelings have already been discovered and they have been castrated as punishment. This leaves them with a sense of inadequacy and inferiority, which Freud referred to as penis envy. Girls resolve the Electra conflict by identifying with the same-sex parent, although more weakly than boys. It is this identification which results in the emergence of the superego. A period of psychological rest called latency follows. This ends with the genital stage, where once again the genitals become the erogenous area. The fixations of the first five years re-emerge, making this a time of storm and stress for some adolescents.

PSYCHOSEXUAL STAGE	EROGENOUS AREA	HEALTHY RESOLUTION OF THE STAGE
Oral stage 0–1 year	Mouth: satisfaction gained from putting things in the mouth so feeding is very important.	Trusting, able to give and receive affection and form healthy relationships.
Anal stage 1–3 years	Anus: pleasure gained from going to the toilet. Conflict arises when parents demand child learns to use the potty.	Can deal with authority figures appropriately.
Phallic stage 3–5 years	Genitals: child has unconscious sexual desires for the opposite-sex parent and fears punishment from the same-sex parent for their desires. This causes psychological conflict.	The values and behaviour of the same-sex parent are internalised to resolve the conflict, leading to the development of morals and gender identity.
Latency 5–12 years	This is a period of consolidation and rest. Sexuality lies dormant and the child is busy learning their gender roles, social rules and developing self-confidence.	The individual becomes a well-adjusted adult.
Genital stage 12 years+	Genitals: the individual becomes interested in the opposite sex.	

Table 1.6: Stages of psychosexual development.

The Rat Man

In 1909, Freud saw a patient in his late twenties (he later referred to him as 'Rat Man' to protect his identity), who suffered obsessions about punishment and torture. The pseudonym came about because of his fear of rats. For example, he made references to a torture he had heard about involving rats. Rats would be put into a pot and the pot then turned upside down on the buttocks. To escape their trap the rats would gnaw a way out through the anus. He obsessed that this may happen to him or his loved ones, such as his fiancée or father (even though his father had been dead for years). During psychoanalysis, Freud discovered that as a child he had been allowed by his governess to explore her genitals. For Freud, this lay at the root of Rat Man's obsessional neurosis. He unconsciously feared that his father would find out about this sexual relationship and punish him (an Oedipal conflict). These hostile feelings were disguised and showed themselves later as concern for his father and fiancée. The obsession with the rat torture was a sign of repressed sadistic urges due to a fixation at the anal stage.

EVALUATION OF THE PSYCHODYNAMIC APPROACH

	STRENGTHS	WEAKNESSES
Can the psychodynamic approach be tested?	Fisher and Greenberg (1996) claimed that whilst the theory as a whole cannot be tested, specific hypotheses can. They found evidence to support Freud's oral and anal personalities. Personality questionnaires have been devised that indicate a correlation between adult personality and childhood experience.	Concepts such as the unconscious and the id, ego and superego are not tangible structures, therefore they cannot be tested scientifically to prove whether they exist or not.
Freud's psychodynamic theory is deterministic	Freud's theory provides an explanation for abnormal behaviour as being rooted in traumatic childhood experiences. This has led to the development of psychodynamic therapy which is still used today to treat a wide range of mental health problems.	Freud viewed behaviour as governed by innate forces and childhood experiences, and our adult personality as something that is determined by forces outside of our control. This implies that as adults we have no free will or choice in how we behave and cannot, therefore, be blamed for any negative behaviour or criminal activity.
Freud's theory is based on his case study evidence	Freud conducted case studies of adults such as the Rat Man, which provide rich and detailed information about the behaviour of individuals and are still referred to in psychodynamic therapy today.	Freud's case studies were comprised of a narrow sample of adults, mainly women who were his patients and, therefore, suffering from mental health problems. This sample is unrepresentative and lacks generalisability. Freud is also criticised for potential research bias – only focusing on information from case studies that support his theory and ignoring any contradictions.

THE INFLUENCE OF CHILDHOOD EXPERIENCES ON THE FORMATION OF RELATIONSHIPS

John Bowlby (1958) applied Freudian principles to his theory of *attachment* formation, particularly the assumption of the influence of childhood experiences on the adult personality. However, his ideas are different from Freud's, as he believes in the impact of the reality of the child's world more than that of fantasy and unconscious drives.

For Bowlby, one of the most important events during the first years of a child's life is the development of attachments. An attachment is an emotional bond between a child and their primary caregiver. This means that there is mutual affection, a desire to remain close to one another and distress on separation. From a psychodynamic point of view, the formation of the infant–caregiver relationship is important for healthy psychological development and in establishing the pattern for the formation of relationships later in life, especially future romantic relationships. Bowlby believed that the bond with the mother is a special one which is different from any other attachment that the infant might develop. The quality of this bond is important for healthy psychological development through childhood and into adulthood. He called this special bond to the mother 'monotropy'.

Bowlby also saw attachment as reciprocal (i.e. a two-way process between mother and infant). It is in an infant's nature to engage in behaviours that encourage the main caregiver to stay close and provide for all its needs, and also encourage the caregiver to respond to it and, in turn, support the growth of the bond between them. These behaviours are called 'social releasers' and they include crying, smiling and gurgling. The kind of emotional relationship that an infant has with its mother provides it with a set of expectations about relationships that stay with the baby throughout life. This is called 'an internal working model' and provides the infant with a template for all future relationships. This is known as the 'continuity hypothesis'. For example, a strong, secure relationship in infancy establishes a pattern for secure romantic relationships; an insecure bond in infancy may lead to an adult who is jealous and insecure in romantic relationships.

Bowlby believed that attachments develop in a fixed sequence.

According to Bowlby, the critical period for the attachment bond to form is during the first three years of life. If this bond is broken (or never develops) there will be serious consequences for the social and emotional

STAGE	NAME	DESCRIPTION
0–3 months	Non-focused orienting and signalling	Child is 'indiscriminate' – it will smile and cry for the attention of whichever adult is present. Prefers the company of people to being alone and is easily comforted.
3–6 months	Focus on one or more figures	Starts to recognise those who provide care most often. Starts to direct behaviour more towards caregivers than complete strangers.
+6 months	Secure base behaviour	Directs behaviour more towards the main caregiver. Demonstrates *separation anxiety* when apart from the caregiver and seeks close proximity to them when they are around. Shows stranger fear and suspicion when somebody unfamiliar approaches.

Table 1.7: The sequence of attachment development according to Bowlby.

Infant emotional bonds and adult mental health

Evidence for the relationship between infant bonds and adult psychological health can be seen in a study conducted by Massie and Szajnberg (2002). Using a longitudinal study, they followed 76 people from birth to the age of 30. Data were collected using a range of methods including films of mother–child interaction, interviews with parents and children and questionnaires. At 30 years of age, the adults who had received better quality care in infancy were more psychologically healthy than those who had received poorer nurturing. Good quality parental care was characterised by maternal empathy, consistency, control, thoughtfulness, affection and management of *aggression*. The researchers also found a relationship between multiple early traumas and psychological health at age 30. Those who had experienced two or more traumas before adulthood were significantly less psychologically healthy than those who had not experienced trauma.

development of the child. If, on the other hand, there is consistent, responsive and sensitive care, and a secure bond develops, then there will be long-term benefits for the child. They will be more socially competent and independent and the positive effects will continue to show themselves throughout life. The level of self-sufficiency and independence displayed by an individual in adulthood is also largely due to the sense of security created by the caregiver as the child develops. If the growing infant feels supported, safe and able to rely on their caregiver, they are more likely to feel able to explore their environment and develop greater independence. This is called the 'secure base hypothesis'.

THERAPY – DREAM ANALYSIS

Dream analysis is a technique used in psychoanalysis to help treat mental abnormalities. Freud cited dreams as the 'royal road' to the unconscious, and believed that through dreams a person could freely express what is repressed in the unconscious part of the psyche (mind). He believed that dreams had two parts to them: the manifest content and the latent content (see Figure 1.3).

The most important aspects of a dream do not appear literally but in symbolic form, and the symbols are often a representation of unconscious desires and wishes which the conscious mind cannot tolerate. There are many different dream symbols, an example of which can be seen below.

Dream analysis – a psychoanalytic technique

Psychoanalysis is a therapy based on psychodynamic ideas. It makes the assumption that mental health problems are caused by past experiences, emotions and desires which are buried deep within the unconscious part of the mind. This is called repression. A key aim of psychoanalysis, therefore, is to unlock unconscious memories and bring them into conscious awareness so that the patient gains insight into the reasons for their behaviour. Once insight is achieved the patient can face up to these memories, rather than bury them, when they cause problems. Repression uses up a lot of mental energy. By not having to use mental energy to do this, a sense of release or 'catharsis' is experienced, leading to the mental energy being invested in better ways of coping. The psychodynamic approach also assumes that abnormalities in adulthood have their root cause in the experiences of childhood. Maternal deprivation experienced in the sensitive period can have lasting consequences for the mental health of an individual, so another aim of psychoanalysis is to explore the early relationship with the primary caregiver and uncover any traumatic experiences that could explain abnormal adult behaviour.

Manifest content:
The reported event in the dream (e.g. I had a dream about kings and queens)

Latent content:
The underlying meaning behind the dream (e.g. the kings and queens are parents in symbolic form)

Figure 1.3: The manifest and latent content of dreams.

DREAMWORK PROCESSES	DESCRIPTION	EXAMPLE
Condensation	A number of elements are combined into one in the dream so the dream becomes more compact. One image may have several associations or be made up of a combination of images.	Freud once dreamed of a person who was made up of different elements of a range of people he knew.
Displacement	The emotion centred on something or someone is detached from that object or person and moved onto another, perhaps less significant, object or person.	A person who is angry with his boss may dream of kicking the cat.
Symbolisation	Abstract concepts are represented in a symbolic form.	A fear of authority may be represented by a powerful figure such as a king.
Secondary revision	The creation of a narrative to give the dream coherence and structure.	A logical storyline is created whereby you dream about a sequence of events.

Table 1.8: Dreamwork processes.

An example of dream interpretation

Megan has just started going to see a psychotherapist. She completed her first session of psychotherapy and went home. That night she had a dream:

I was getting into my car to travel on a long journey. I felt frightened because I didn't know where I was going. The map I had didn't seem to make sense and I was worried about getting lost. When I got into my car I couldn't find my car keys and had to hunt around on the floor and retrace my steps until I found them. Finally, I started the car and began to drive. The road became bumpy and I had to keep swerving around piles of bricks and rocks. Sometimes I felt as if I was driving too fast and had lost control of the car. Eventually it became very dark and I couldn't see where I was going because the lights on the car wouldn't work, and then I woke up.

Interpretation: the car journey is a symbolic representation of the journey she is about to undertake into therapy. Secondary revision has helped Megan to create a story about travelling somewhere in her car. The fear she feels about starting therapy has been displaced in the dream into a fear of getting into her car to travel into the unknown.

The process of transforming a latent desire into manifest content takes place while we are sleeping and is called *dreamwork*. Freud identified four processes in dreamwork (see Table 1.8).

A therapist may ask a patient to keep a dream diary to record their dreams as they recall them on waking. The dreams can then be recounted in therapy, if the patient chooses, and the therapist will try to work with the patient to make sense of the underlying meaning behind the dream. The therapist is interested in the dreams a patient can remember as most dreams are forgotten. The therapist will want to know what it is about the dream that makes it significant enough to be remembered. They will offer suggested interpretations of the dream and allow the patient to consider whether that seems acceptable to them.

A patient needs to develop a trusting relationship with the therapist to reveal their private dreams and take on board the interpretations. The relationship between the patient and therapist is of paramount importance to the success of psychoanalysis. The way the patient behaves in their relationship with the therapist often offers clues about how they are in relationships with significant others in their life. The therapist attempts to be neutral and imparts very little personal information to the patient to encourage a process called transference. This is where unresolved conflicts and feelings about past relationships, often to do with the patient's mother or father, are projected on to the therapist. This offers the therapist an opportunity to help the patient work through the unresolved issues from their past.

Evaluation of dream analysis

Effectiveness

» Dream analysis is just one technique used in psychoanalysis which is designed to find the underlying cause of abnormal behaviour. This may be seen as a positive criticism, especially compared with other therapies such as drugs that do not treat the cause of behaviour. Freud thought that if the cause of behaviour was revealed then the patient would be cured.

» Finding the underlying cause of behaviour can mean that the treatment takes a very long time. In classical psychoanalysis, treatment may involve attending therapy sessions three to four times a week over a period of two to five years. As well as being time consuming, this is also costly for the patient.

» Eysenck (1952) claimed that psychoanalysis (of which dream analysis is a technique) provides no benefits to a person beyond those that could naturally occur over time without treatment (i.e. spontaneous remission). He compared the results of 24 studies to see if psychoanalysis was more likely than other forms of therapy to result in positive mental health changes. He found that patients did recover but the rate of recovery was comparable to the rate of recovery without treatment, and therefore that psychoanalysis was less effective than behavioural therapies.

Ethical considerations

» Grünbaum (1993) considers the power the therapist has in the relationship with the patient. He says any apparent benefits of psychoanalysis are the result of a placebo effect; it is the action of being treated itself that cures the patient rather than the use of techniques such as dream analysis. The reason why psychoanalysis may lead to a cure is because the patient is in a powerful relationship with the therapist. Part of the power the therapist has is that they can never be wrong. For example, if the patient challenges the therapist in their interpretation of a dream, the challenging behaviour could be interpreted as a symptom of their abnormal behaviour. This means that the patient is under strong pressure to conform to the therapist's expectation.

» Psychodynamic therapists cannot always gain fully informed consent from their patients before beginning treatment. They cannot tell the patient too much about the approach or what they may be agreeing to because explaining the treatment is very difficult. The patient needs to experience psychoanalysis in order to fully understand it. This again means that the therapist is the expert in the relationship and therefore in a position of power over the patient.

THERAPY: GROUP ANALYSIS PSYCHOTHERAPY

The origins of group psychotherapy can be traced back to the United States in the early 1900s when Dr Joseph Pratt speculated that the patients he was treating for tuberculosis would benefit from meeting in groups to support one another. The idea of group support was then developed by a number of psychiatrists and psychotherapists, who recognised that the benefits of psychodynamic techniques were not confined to a therapist–client relationship but could also happen between group members.

Group analytic psychotherapy (as it is sometimes referred to) combines the principles of psychoanalysis with an understanding of how the individual functions socially. The main premise behind it is that the individual, as part of a group, will gain insight into themselves and how they function in their social circles, such as their family, friendship groups and community.

The structure of the analytic group

A typical group consists of around eight people and a group therapist or 'conductor', who meet together once or twice a week for about an hour. The group may be made up of individuals who have a range of emotional issues, the key criteria being that all will benefit from therapeutic work so the dynamics of the group are very important in ensuring that all members benefit simultaneously. In constructing the group, the aim is that it represents the wider norms of society and generates stimulating conversation and interaction between group members. The group is fluid, with members moving on and leaving and new members joining, although the group should not exceed the optimum eight members at any one time.

The process of group therapy

The group provides a nurturing and safe environment where relationships develop that reflect the relationships an individual has outside of the group. This means that an individual's patterns of behaviour in normal life are recreated in group therapy. Foulkes (1964) claims that the stronger the sense of community within the group, the more an individual grows in their individuality.

Individuals see themselves from the perspective of others in the group and this can help them to identify negative attitudes and destructive patterns of behaviour which can then be discussed and analysed within the group. Through group interactions an individual can learn more about themselves, and as they

---

Group analysis psychotherapy: a type of psychoanalysis

Psychoanalysis is a therapy based on psychodynamic ideas. It makes the assumption that mental health problems are caused by past experiences, emotions and desires that are buried deep within the unconscious part of the mind, causing problems. This is called repression. A key aim of psychoanalysis, therefore, is to unlock unconscious memories and bring them into conscious awareness so that the patient gains insight into the reasons behind their behaviour. Once insight is achieved the patient can face up to these memories rather than bury them. Repression uses up a lot of mental energy. By not having to use mental energy to do this a sense of release or 'catharsis' is experienced, leading to the mental energy being invested in better ways of coping. The psychodynamic approach also assumes that abnormalities in adulthood have their root cause in the experiences of childhood. One aim of psychoanalysis is to explore the early relationship with the primary caregiver and uncover any early traumatic experiences that could explain current problems.

become supported and comfortable they grow in confidence and feel able to share their deepest fears and personal experiences with other group members. They may be able to reveal past traumatic experiences and have enough trust within the group to explore these to help them change and grow as a person. The individual also benefits from the opportunity to support others through their problems and issues.

According to Yalom (2005), a number of factors bring about individual change in group analysis psychotherapy. Some of these are summarised in Table 1.9.

The role of the therapist

In group therapy the most important relationships the individual has are with other group members: they act as therapists for one another. However, the therapist still has a role to play in managing the group. In the early stages the therapist will be responsible for helping to create a group contract, which includes the

THERAPEUTIC FACTOR	DESCRIPTION
Information giving	Sharing of information about a common problem (e.g. depression).
Altruism	The process of helping others can improve self-esteem.
Interpersonal skills	The group can help to improve each other's social skills.
Catharsis	Sharing of long repressed painful experiences can bring a sense of relief.
Correcting past family experiences	Individuals may unconsciously identify others in the group as members of their family. This may provide the opportunity to re-enact any negative relationships experienced in childhood and put them right.

Table 1.9: Some therapeutic factors that bring about change in group analysis psychotherapy.

necessity for confidentiality and keeping social contact with each other outside of the group to a minimum.

Once the group is established the role of the therapist is to act as a facilitator rather than a leader, managing the group effectively, encouraging openness and honesty and providing direction if the group moves away from their own agreed goals. An important part of the therapist's role is in building confidence through reinforcing positive behaviours and complimenting individuals on their support of others. The therapist also helps to build a sense of group identity by observing and expressing anything that members of the group have in common with one another.

Evaluation of group analysis psychotherapy

Effectiveness

- Group analysis psychotherapy does not only address traumatic life experiences and deal with negative and abnormal behaviour, it is also concerned with uncovering the undeveloped aspirations and creativity of group members. Individuals may discover talents and attributes they did not know existed and go on to make major changes to their life, such as in their career or education.
- Group therapy has been criticised for focusing more on the analysis of the group process than on the issues of individual group members. This means that the reason why an individual is recommended for therapy in the first place may not be addressed.
- Like other forms of psychoanalysis, group therapy aims to uncover the deepest repressed thoughts, fears and aspects of the personality from the unconscious mind and therefore can take a long time. Individuals can expect to be a part of the group for at least a year.
- For individuals who are emotionally fragile and who find it difficult to listen to criticism group therapy may be a negative experience.

If a group member is struggling and finding communication difficult, it is up to the therapist to recognise this and try to make them feel less isolated and alone. Failure to do so could result in the individual leaving therapy with a sense of failure and causing damage to the whole group.

Ethical considerations

- The therapist must not allow the participation of any individual who is abusive or causes upset to any other group member. Group participants must never feel degraded or humiliated during the session by either the therapist or other group members. It is up to the therapist to ensure that the group values equality and tolerance and to manage any conflicts that arise between individuals in an appropriate manner.
- Before an individual begins group therapy the therapist must advise the potential group member of the risks and their rights and obligations as a member of the group. They must also be advised of the expectations and limits of confidentiality so that they are giving their fully informed consent before taking part in any therapy. Confidentiality should continue to be maintained even once an individual has left the group.
- Group meetings are built on trust. Individuals may reveal intimate and personal information about themselves and those close to them. It is therefore essential that all this information remains confidential. Group members are asked not to meet each other outside of the group to avoid discussing the details of each other's lives. The group therapist must also ensure that any notes made during therapy sessions are confidential. There are exceptions to this, however. If a group member indicates that they may be in danger of harming themselves or putting others at risk then the therapist is obliged to refer this information to the appropriate agency.

CLASSIC RESEARCH
– BOWLBY (1944)

Bowlby, J. (1944). Forty-four juvenile thieves: their character and home-life. *International Journal of Psychoanalysis*, 25, 19–52

During the 1930s and 1940s, John Bowlby spent a lot of time working with children, particularly those with social, emotional and behavioural issues. Through his work he recognised a link between childhood trauma and subsequent negative behaviour in adolescence. He supported the Freudian idea that traumatic childhood experiences can shape our adult personalities. He believed that one of the most traumatic events a young child can experience is separation from the primary caregiver during the critical period. According to Bowlby, an infant must form an attachment to its mother before the age of 3. If this process of attachment formation is disrupted by separation from the carer, the child would suffer emotionally and socially later in life. Bowlby called this the 'maternal deprivation hypothesis'.

Aim
Bowlby conducted the 'Forty-four juvenile thieves' study to support his maternal deprivation hypothesis by asking whether early separation from the mother could be related to behavioural problems later in life.

Method and procedure
Over a period of three years, Bowlby investigated 88 children who had been referred to a London Child Guidance Clinic for social and emotional issues. Of the 88 children, 44 were referred to the clinic for stealing and were the 'thieves' group. The other 44 children were referred for issues other than theft and acted as the control group. The children in each group ranged in age from 5 to 16 years and were matched on intelligence through an IQ test. All the children, along with their parents, were involved in a series of *interviews* to find out about their early experiences. More in-depth information on the children was also gathered using school reports and evidence from court records, if the children had been convicted of theft or any other antisocial behaviour. After all the evidence had been gathered, the children were categorised into behavioural types including normal, depressed, hyperactive and affectionless psychopaths.

Findings
Out of the 44 thieves, 14 were diagnosed as affectionless psychopaths and 12 out of these 14 children had experienced early and prolonged or even permanent separation from their mothers. The separation mainly consisted of spending their early years in residential care or hospital with few visits from their family. None of the children in the control group were diagnosed as affectionless psychopaths and only two out of the 44 had experienced prolonged separation from their mothers in the first five years of life.

Conclusion
Bowlby concluded that there was a relationship between early separation and developing an affectionless character leading to antisocial behaviour such as thieving. The findings support Bowlby's maternal deprivation hypothesis and his belief that early relationships were crucial for the child in helping them to develop mental health: 'Maternal care in infancy and early childhood is essential for mental health. This is a discovery comparable in magnitude to that of the role of vitamins in physical health, and of far-reaching significance for programmes of preventive mental hygiene.' (Bowlby, 1951)

STUDY SUMMARY	
Method	Correlational research with data gathered through intelligence tests, clinical interviews and content analysis of reports.
Participants	88 children aged 5–16 with social and emotional issues.
Sample type	Opportunity sample of children from the Child Guidance Clinic.
Co-variables	Early separation and juvenile delinquency.

Table 1.10: Summary of the key features of the Bowlby study.

Evaluation of 'Forty-Four Juvenile Thieves'

Reliability

Information about early separation was collected from the parents and children retrospectively (i.e. after the event). This could make the information unreliable as over time memories can become distorted and reconstructed, so it is difficult to know how accurate the information was regarding the time, duration and severity of the maternal deprivation experienced by the children.

Sample

The sample may have been biased as it was relatively small and consisted only of children who were referred to the clinic where Bowlby worked. The sample was also predominantly male with at least 30 in each group being boys. Although Bowlby did attempt to match the participants on age and IQ, more could have been done to ensure the population validity of the sample was more generalisable. For example, Bowlby could have included a control group of children who had not been referred to a clinic for social and emotional issues to see if any of them had experienced early separation.

Ethical issues

Bowlby's research took place many years before guidelines on the ethics of research were introduced. We can assume however that his research was governed by some kind of code of conduct used by the London Child Guidance Clinic where he worked. The participants were referred to the clinic for behavioural reasons and in the parents consenting to their child attending the clinic there may have been assumed consent that they would be used in research. There was a lack of full informed consent and an element of deception too – parents would not have been aware of Bowlby's aim to link maternal deprivation to delinquency.

Social implications

Studying the effects of early attachment on later behaviour poses a socially sensitive issue. Bowlby's research stresses the link between maternal deprivation and social and emotional issues in a child, thus implying that the neglect of the child by the parent is to blame for the child's negative behaviour. When published, the findings of Bowlby's research implied that the mothers of the juvenile delinquents had been neglectful, and this could have impacted negatively on their views of themselves as parents and caused concern for the future of their children. There are also implications that go beyond the research – for example, for parents, particularly mothers, who may want to return to work soon after their child is born. The study suggests that prolonged separation from the primary caregiver in the early years of life could have long-term consequences for the child's social and emotional development.

The Behaviourist Approach

WHAT YOU NEED TO KNOW ☑

The assumptions of the
behaviourist approach: ❑

Blank slate ❑

Humans and animals learn in similar ways ❑

Behaviour learned through conditioning ❑

Evaluation of the
behaviourist approach: ❑

Strengths ❑

Weaknesses ❑

Comparison with the four other
approaches (see page 82) ❑

Application: formation of relationships ❑

How the approach can be used in
ONE therapy: ❑

EITHER: Aversion therapy

Evaluation: ❑
    Effectiveness ❑
    Ethical considerations ❑

OR: Systematic desensitisation

Evaluation: ❑
    Effectiveness ❑
    Ethical considerations ❑

Classic research
(Watson and Rayner, 1920): ❑

Aim ❑

Method and procedure ❑

Findings ❑

Conclusion ❑

Evaluation ❑

Ethical issues ❑

Social implications ❑

INTRODUCTION

The behaviourist approach was the most prominent in psychology from the 1920s to the 1950s. It was the first approach that presented psychology as a science, emphasising the importance of empirical data obtained through careful and controlled observation and measurement of behaviour. The approach revolves around the notion that all human behaviour is learned from the environment, and only behaviour which can be observed and measured (rather than internal events like thoughts and emotions) is important. Since a person's behaviour is determined by their environment, people have no free will as such. The person we will grow up to become is entirely dependent on our environment and experiences; genetics and other biological factors play no role in shaping who we are.

THE ASSUMPTIONS OF THE BEHAVIOURIST APPROACH

1. Blank slate

According to the behaviourist approach we are born *tabula rasa*. This literally means '*blank slate*'. Newborns have the most basic drives (e.g. hunger) but we are not born with any innate characteristics, traits or behaviours. We do have the mental capacity to learn new things, however, so as we grow up we learn from our environment, and thus experience shapes our behaviour and personality. We are, then, blank slates 'written on' by our experience. Basically, within the constraints of our biology (i.e. someone 6 ft 7 is not going to become a jockey!), as long as we have the right environment, we could grow up to be anything.

> 'Give me a dozen healthy infants, well-formed, and my own special world to bring them up in, and I'll guarantee to take any one at random and train him to become any type of specialist I might select – doctor, lawyer, artist, merchant-chief, and, yes, beggarman and thief.' (Watson, 1913)

2. Humans and animals learn in similar ways

There is a *continuity* between humans and animals – that is, the theory of evolution establishes that humans and animals have common origins, and the only real difference between them is their evolutionary history. This means that many behavioural and biological principles which apply to humans also apply to animals. The study of animals is therefore a legitimate way to understand the things that we have in common. Most behaviourist research has been conducted on animals like rats, pigeons and pigs.

3. Behaviour learned through conditioning

The behaviourist approach assumes that all behaviour, no matter how complex, can be explained in terms of conditioning history – life's accumulation of all conditioning experiences. The two principal types of conditioning are *classical conditioning* and *operant conditioning*.

Classical conditioning

Classical conditioning was first observed by Ivan Pavlov (1897). Pavlov noticed that when his laboratory dogs heard the researchers' footsteps, bringing them food, they would begin to salivate. Salivation is a normal reflex in response to food but an animal should not salivate to the sound of footsteps. Pavlov thought that the dogs must have learned to associate the sound of footsteps with food, so they salivated in anticipation of the food they had learned was coming. Pavlov set up an experiment to explain this learning. He presented food to a dog which (naturally) produced salivation. This is natural reflexive behaviour so we call it *unconditioned*. This unconditioned stimulus brings about the response.

> Food (unconditioned stimulus, UCS)
> ➜ salivation (unconditioned response, UCR)

Pavlov then introduced a neutral stimulus, something that would not bring about a salivation response in a dog. He chose a bell. He wanted to see if the dog would learn to associate the bell with the food, so he rang the bell shortly before the food was presented.

> Bell (neutral stimulus, NS) + food (UCS)
> ➜ salivation (UCR)

After several pairings of the bell and food, Pavlov rang the bell without presenting food and found that the dog salivated to the sound of the bell. The dog had learned something new – it had learned to associate the bell (now the conditioned stimulus) with the food, resulting in salivation (now the conditioned response).

> Bell (conditioned stimulus, CS)
> ➜ salivation (conditioned response, CR)

In further experiments Pavlov discovered other things about what became known as classical conditioning. This association learning is passive and involuntary – that is, it happens to us. We cannot stop it, no more than we can stop a blink when something comes at our eye. The CR is not necessarily permanent – if the NS is never again paired with the UCS then the CR will gradually fade in strength and disappear. This is called *extinction*. But it is not necessarily gone forever, as the CR can suddenly reappear again – this is called *spontaneous recovery*. One other thing Pavlov noticed is that the dogs would not only salivate to the sound of the original bell but also to other bells which sounded like it – this is called *generalisation*.

Operant conditioning

Operant conditioning is the process of learning through reinforcement and punishment. The first psychologist to study this was Edward Thorndike, although B. F. Skinner is often thought of as the founding father of operant conditioning. Thorndike (1911) tested cats in a 'puzzle box', which offered the reward of a piece of fish if the cats were able to escape. In order to escape, the cats had to press a latch; at first, they only escaped when the latch was accidentally knocked. Eventually, the cats became quicker at pressing the latch to escape and earn the reward, implying that they had learned to press the latch. Thorndike termed this conditioning the 'law of effect': a positive outcome to a situation results in that behaviour being repeated more often (in the case of the puzzle box, the opening of the latch). If an outcome is undesirable (e.g. if the cats had been punished for leaving the box), the behaviour becomes less frequent.

Skinner (1948) extended Thorndike's ideas to include the term *reinforcement*; a reinforcer is anything that increases the likelihood of a behaviour occurring again. Giving a dog a treat after it has fetched a stick increases the likelihood of the dog fetching the stick in future – the treat is a reinforcer. Whilst behaviours that are reinforced are strengthened and are more likely to be repeated, those that aren't are likely to be weakened and die out (or become extinct). In operant conditioning, an animal must do

---

something before it learns (i.e. it learns as a consequence of behaviour).

Skinner also used animals in his experiments. He invented the 'conditioning chamber' (which became more commonly known as the 'Skinner box') to demonstrate operant conditioning. Skinner would place a rat in the box, and if the rat accidentally hit a lever, a food pellet would drop into the container. The rat would quickly learn that pressing the lever would result in food being dispensed – the food being the reward (reinforcer) for lever pressing. This kind of reinforcement, where there are pleasant consequences, is called positive reinforcement. Skinner extended this experiment to include giving the rats a slight electric shock. To stop the shock, the rats again had to press the lever and, again, the rats eventually became faster and faster at returning to the lever in order to stop the electric shock. Skinner called this negative reinforcement; the likelihood of a behaviour being repeated was again increased but this time in order to get rid of something unpleasant.

Another aspect of operant conditioning is punishment. A punisher is anything which weakens or eliminates a response rather than increasing it. For example, if, having learned to press the lever to get food, the rat then gets a shock, lever pressing will reduce and even stop entirely.

EVALUATION OF THE BEHAVIOURIST APPROACH

	STRENGTHS	WEAKNESSES
The learning approach is scientific	Its methods seek to be as objective as possible and so focus on behaviour that can be measured and observed rather than internal 'mental' processes.	Many important behaviours (e.g. memory) are not observable or measurable in the way this approach expects so would not be a topic of investigation.
The learning approach is reductionist	Studies have demonstrated that humans can learn via conditioning and these principles have useful applications (e.g. developing effective therapies).	Behaviour is explained by reducing it to simple conditioning processes. It underestimates the complexity of behaviour – for example, by ignoring important 'mediating' processes such as thinking and social influences.
The learning approach often relies on research with animals	Research supports the idea that humans and animals learn by conditioning. This allows researchers to study animals when, ethically, they might not be able to study humans.	Humans have complex thoughts and feelings far beyond any other animal, and these have a major effect on behaviour. Assuming that humans only learn like other animals underestimates the complexity of human behaviour.
Humans learn in similar ways to animals	Classical and operant conditioning has been shown to work in humans as well as in animals, so the assumption that humans learn in similar ways to animals appears a sound one.	Whilst there are similarities, when human learning is explained nowadays it is much more likely to be in terms of cognition (especially higher-level, complex learning). Classical and operant conditioning can only explain some relatively simple aspects of human learning.

THE FORMATION OF RELATIONSHIPS BETWEEN PETS AND THEIR OWNERS: BEHAVIOUR LEARNED THROUGH CONDITIONING

Over half the households in the UK own pets, and over 90% of pet owners consider their pet an important part of the family. Pets are clearly an important part of life for many people. However, it is less clear why we keep pets. It is possible to conjecture that before they became pets, some animals which were domesticated to perform important functions. Ancient Egyptians, for example, were known to keep cats to protect their grain stores from vermin. Dogs may have been domesticated for protection and assistance with hunting. Whilst they still can still serve this function, nowadays most cats and dogs do not.

Operant conditioning can be used to explain the attraction of keeping pets and the strong attachment that can form between pets and owners. Pets behave in ways that are appealing to potential owners. Dogs, for example, show signs of affection and attachment to their owners, such as licking and seeking comfort when they are frightened. These behaviours are positively reinforcing for owners. There is also an element of negative reinforcement. Many cat and dog owners report that in addition to unconditional love their pets provide company and stave off the unpleasant effects of loneliness.

Once developed, these relationships can have a range of additional benefits, further reinforcing the bonds between owners and their pets. For example, it has been found that university students who live with at least one dog or one cat or a combination of the two are less likely to feel lonely and depressed. Survey research suggests that owners believe their pets make contributions to their own health and well-being. Indeed, research shows that having a pet dog increases the chances of survival after recovery from a heart attack. Some psychologists even

A dog is not just for Christmas. Pets and owners mutually reinforce each other and in the process modify one another's behaviour.

argue that pets are better buffers against the effects of life stress than friends and loved ones, since pets unconditionally accept you for what you are and are not critical or judgmental.

Of course, animals also find the relationship with humans reinforcing. Cats appear to like being stroked and petted by their owners, even though they are generally more independent than dogs. We then treat these animals with behaviours that the animal finds rewarding, such as giving treats or stroking them. The animal soon learns that certain behaviours are likely to receive a positive response from their owner, making them more likely to receive rewards – so an attentive dog is more likely to receive a reward that one that is less attentive.

THEREPY – AVERSION THERAPY

One of the main assumptions of the behaviourist approach is that humans learn via classical conditioning by forming stimulus–response associations. The aim of *aversion therapy* is to unlearn existing associations by creating new ones that replace the existing undesirable behaviour.

Undesirable behaviours develop because in the past there has been an association between this behaviour and something pleasant. The task of the aversion therapist is to undo this by creating a new association – between the undesirable behaviour and something unpleasant. For example, aversion therapy for alcohol misuse might involve a person being injected with a drug which reacts violently with alcohol. When a person drinks any alcohol they are sick, so that now alcohol is associated with something unpleasant (being immediately and violently sick) and so becomes aversive – alcohol is avoided. By pairing the unwanted behaviour with an unpleasant consequence, aversion therapy can be used to treat many problem behaviours – for example, smoking, gambling and violence.

Aversion therapy has also been used to treat unwanted behaviour in children particularly, in recent times, nocturnal enuresis (bedwetting). The inability to control the bladder throughout the night-time is a distressing problem for children and their parents particularly when the problem persists into adolescence. The most common form of treatment involves the use of a bed device containing a urine alarm. The device is made up of two foil pads, one of which is perforated, which are placed between the child's bed sheets. Activation of the device occurs when the child urinates and contact with moisture causes the device to emit an unpleasant buzz or vibration which wakes the child. Waking to an unpleasant buzz or vibration is unconditioned behaviour. The pairing of the buzzing with the feeling of having a full bladder teaches the child to associate having a full bladder with waking up. After conditioning, the child has then learned to wake up at the feeling of a full bladder and can take control by going to the toilet rather than wetting the bed. Thus, the feeling of having a full bladder has become the conditioned stimulus and waking up the conditioned response.

Evaluation of aversion therapy
Effectiveness

» Aversion therapy is unpleasant; it uses things that people would rather avoid, such as electric shocks and nausea-inducing drugs. It is not surprising, therefore, that there tends to be a very high drop-out rate. Bancroft (1992) reports that up to 50% of patients drop out of or refuse even to start aversion therapy. There is also evidence to suggest that the relapse is high; not only is the drive to engage in the unwanted behaviour great but there can also be extinction of the new conditioned response – once there is no more pairing of the unpleasant stimulus and the undesirable behaviour, the conditioning weakens and people go back to the old undesirable behaviour.

» There is research to suggest that aversion therapy can be successful. Smith (1988) reported success in a study where 300 smokers underwent aversion therapy; 52% of those who were treated using electric shocks still hadn't smoked a year later. Smith et al. (1997) found that alcoholics treated with aversion therapy abstained from alcohol up to one year longer than those who received counselling alone. Fawley and Smith (1990) conducted a study into the effect of aversion therapy on two groups of individuals – one group who were addicted to cocaine and one group who were addicted to cocaine and alcohol. Eighteen months later, 38% of those addicted to cocaine had been totally abstinent and 50% of the cocaine/alcohol group had been totally abstinent.

- Controlled trials of the bedwetting device show that the use of this type of aversion therapy is superior to drugs in changing bedwetting behaviour. According to Butler (2004) controlled evaluation of the urine alarm showed a 65–75% success rate on a 5–12 week programme of treatment with only a 15–30% relapse rate 6 months after treatment.

Ethical considerations

- The unpleasantness of some of the conditioning procedures means that there is some degree of harm involved, but the experience of therapy and the likely side effects will have been explained fully beforehand. The therapy can be a very unpleasant experience so this technique should never be used without first gaining full informed consent.
- As people enter therapy voluntarily, they will always have the right to pull out. The drawback of this, however, is that the therapy requires a great deal of motivation and drive on the part of the client – a lack of which is often part of the problem to begin with. This contributes to the high drop-out rates seen in aversion therapy.
- Care must be taken when using aversion techniques to control bedwetting behaviour in children. The child needs to be evaluated thoroughly to rule out any biological cause for their bedwetting. The child's age, level of development and motivation must also be considered as the child needs to be physiologically and psychologically ready for the treatment in order that it may be successful and not cause harm. It is recommended that girls should be at least 5 years old and boys 7 before the bed device is employed and that the child shows willingness to accept the use of the device. Parents also need to agree to the use of the technique and are asked to agree not to punish or

> ### Case study of aversion therapy
>
> In 1962 an army captain called William Clegg-Hill was arrested and tried on suspicion of homosexual practices. He was sent to a military psychiatric hospital in Southampton where he was subjected to treatment using the vomit-inducing drug apomorphine. The drug was injected into him as he was subjected to images of naked men. His family fully supported the treatment as they felt ashamed of his behaviour and hoped that William would be cured of his homosexuality. Unfortunately during his treatment William Clegg-Hill died as a result of convulsions and eventual coma brought about by the drug. His death was covered up and it was claimed that he had died of natural causes. It wasn't until 34 years later that the truth behind his death was revealed.

verbally criticise the child for their bedwetting behaviour.

- During the 1950s and 1960s aversion therapy was applied to the treatment of behaviour viewed by society at the time as deviant, including overeating, transvestism and homosexuality (see box). The first recorded use of aversion therapy being administered to a homosexual male is from 1935. The patient received electric shocks as he was asked to fantasise about men. In later reported treatments, nausea inducing drugs were given to homosexual men as they viewed images of naked men. It is thought that these kinds of treatment were given to hundreds of homosexual men in Britain and America throughout the 1950s and 1960s.

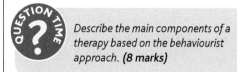

*Describe the main components of a therapy based on the behaviourist approach. **(8 marks)***

THERAPY: SYSTEMATIC DESENSITISATION

Systematic desensitisation works by creating a new, more pleasant learned response to that which causes fear. It is used to treat people with phobia, most commonly specific phobias (see Table 1.11).

The therapy begins with the client being given relaxation training. This step is very important because of *reciprocal inhibition* – this is where one response is inhibited because it is incompatible with another. In this case, fear involves tension and tension is incompatible with relaxation – one cannot be relaxed and fearful at the same time! A key component of desensitisation is the *anxiety hierarchy*. Developed in discussion between the therapist and the client, this is a list of specific situations and factors that influence anxiety level – for example, someone with a fear of spiders might list all the things about spiders they don't like and the situations in which they might encounter spiders. These are then ranked from the least to most frightening. This list is crucial

Step 1
Relaxation training

Step 2
Anxiety hierarchy

Step 3
Desensitisation sessions

as it provides a structure for the therapy. The therapist moves the client up the hierarchy, at each point associating relaxation rather than anxiety with the feared object or situation, until the highest point in the hierarchy can be reached in a state of relaxation. How long this takes before treatment is considered successful depends very much on the individual and the nature of the phobia. The therapy often involves imagining the phobic object or

TYPE OF PHOBIA	DESCRIPTION
Specific phobias	Fears of particular objects or situations, often divided into four types: natural environment type (a fear of something naturally occurring in the environment, e.g. fire, heights); animal type (a commonly occurring phobia, e.g. a fear of spiders); situational type (a fear of particular situations or events, e.g. fear of flying); and medical type (fear of medical procedures and illnesses, e.g. blood, injection or injury phobia).
Social phobia	Fear of performing some kind of action in the presence of others (e.g. using public transport, eating/drinking in public). Most sufferers fear only specific social situations, although those with what is known as generalised social phobia have this irrational fear of most social encounters.
Agoraphobia	Fear of being incapacitated by a panic attack in a situation where escape would be difficult or embarrassing or where help would be unavailable. As a result of this fear sufferers avoid public and unfamiliar places. Although the least frequent of the three classes of the condition, agoraphobia is the most commonly seen by clinical psychologists since it has such a debilitating effect on the life of the sufferer and their family.

Table 1.11: Three types of phobia treated with systematic desensitisation.

situation – known as *in vitro* desensitisation. It has been suggested, however, that the more realistic the situation, the more effective the therapy, which has led some therapists to use *in vivo* desensitisation, where the feared object or situation is encountered from the very start.

Evaluation of systematic desensitisation

Effectiveness

Paul (1966) showed that clients who received systematic desensitisation showed greater improvement compared with those receiving other treatments, and this improvement was still evident two years later. Choy et al. (2007) carried out a meta-analysis of studies using systematic desensitisation *in vitro* (imagination-based), *in vivo* (real-life) and using virtual reality. They appeared to differ in effectiveness depending on what they were applied to – for example, using virtual reality for height or flying phobias is reasonably successful, but less so for specific animal phobias or social phobias.

Systematic desensitisation may be more appropriate for some types of phobia than others, possibly because of their different underlying causes. For example, if a fear of public speaking originates with poor social skills, then phobia reduction is more likely to occur in a treatment which includes learning new and more effective social skills rather than systematic desensitisation alone.

Ethical considerations

It would be impossible to carry out desensitisation therapy without fully informed consent as it is important that the client fully understands the nature of the treatment and the importance of each stage in order for it to be effective. The client can opt out at any point in the proceedings. They are fully involved in creating the anxiety hierarchy with the guidance of their therapist and are not forced to move on to the next stage until they are completely relaxed at the current stage.

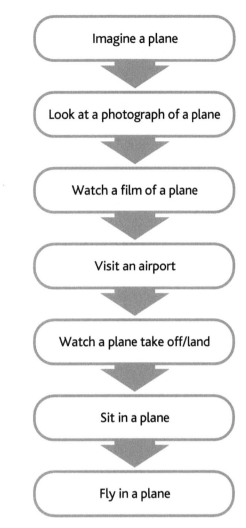

Fear of flying (aerophobia) is one of the most common phobias treated with systematic desensitisation. The next most important step after relaxation training is to create an anxiety hierarchy. Gradually, and with support from the therapist, the phobic is taken through the hierarchy.

Choy et al. (2007) found a very high level of drop-out with *in vivo* desensitisation, possibly due to the levels of stress involved in the therapy. This has important implications. Discontinuation of a treatment part way through may actually do more harm than good – individuals have been exposed to the object of their phobia and experienced high levels of anxiety, thus their existing fear has been reinforced.

CLASSIC RESEARCH – WATSON AND RAYNER (1920)

> Watson, J. B. and Rayner, R. (1920). Conditioned emotional reactions. *Journal of Experimental Psychology*, 3(1), 1–14

Aim

Watson and Rayner conducted what became one of the most famous studies in psychology in order to demonstrate the application of classical conditioning to human behaviour, specifically to create a phobia in someone for whom there was previously no phobia.

Method and procedure

Watson and Rayner conducted a *laboratory experiment* on a 9-month-old infant given the pseudonym 'Little Albert'. Before conditioning he was described as 'stolid' (calm) and 'unemotional'. Before beginning the classical conditioning, Little Albert's reactions to certain stimuli were tested. He was presented with a white rat, a dog, a monkey, a rabbit, masks, cotton wool and burning newspapers. He showed no fear to any of these stimuli. However, Little Albert did show fear to a loud noise made when the experimenters struck a metal bar with a hammer behind his head – he would cry and raise his arms. Having established that the loud noise created a fear response, Watson and Rayner set about conditioning Little Albert. They presented him with a white rat, and when Little Albert reached out to touch it they would strike the hammer against the metal bar, which would scare him. This pairing was done several times in each session and was repeated over a period of time.

Findings

Even after just a few pairings of the rat with the loud noise, Little Albert would show a conditioned fear response when the rat alone was presented – for example, by crying and trying to crawl away. He had learned to associate the white rat with fear:

Loud noise (UCS) ➜ fear (UCR)

White rat (NS) + loud noise (UCS) ➜ fear (UCR)

White rat (CS) ➜ fear (CR)

Watson and Rayner wanted to see if Little Albert would generalise his fear to objects other than the white rat. A month after they stopped the conditioning of the rat and loud noise, Little Albert was presented with a dog, a rabbit, a Santa Claus mask, a fur coat and Watson's hair (which was white). He showed the same fear response. With regard to the latter, it seemed to be the colour that scared him as he would readily play with other people's hair.

Conclusion

From their findings, Watson and Rayner concluded that classical conditioning could be used to teach an infant to fear certain stimuli. They also concluded that this fear can last for an extended period of time and that it can generalise to other objects.

METHOD	QUASI-EXPERIMENT
Participant	Little Albert, a 9-month-old infant
Independent variable	Conditioning
Dependent variable	Learned fear

Table 1.12: Summary of the key features of the Watson and Rayner study.

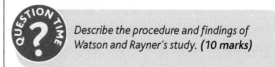

Describe the procedure and findings of Watson and Rayner's study. **(10 marks)**

Evaluation of Watson and Rayner (1920)

Internal validity

The Watson and Rayner study was not a carefully constructed experiment. There was a lack of control of variables and the measures they used were unreliable. For example, there was no objective way of assessing Little Albert's reactions following conditioning, and the researchers relied instead on subjective interpretations of Albert's behaviour.

External validity

A second criticism relates to the external validity of the study. It was carried out in a controlled laboratory setting, and it is questionable whether phobias actually develop in this kind of way in real life. It is possible that Little Albert might have reacted in a different way in a more familiar and natural environment.

Restricted scope

By focusing solely on conditioning principles, Watson and Rayner overlooked possible cognitive contributions to the development of phobias. For example, it has been shown that people with phobias experience all sorts of cognitive distortions so that threats are exaggerated – a person with a fear of spiders may perceive the spider as huge or as having something against them personally. None of this was considered a possibility by the researchers, so measures were not taken to observe and record such things.

Ethical issues

Watson and Rayner's study would not be allowed to take place today. Even for its day, many years before the introduction of ethical guidelines, it raised a number of ethical issues. Watson and Rayner deliberately tried to cause Little Albert harm

by inducing a phobia. They were aware that the noise scared him and repeatedly subjected him to this noise in order to condition him. His fear generalised to objects other than the rats, and we do not know the long-term impact on Little Albert as he was lost to the scientific community. However, Watson and Rayner did justify their choice of Little Albert: they described him as unemotional and said that they 'felt that we could do him relatively little harm by carrying out such experiments'. In part, this was because they were convinced that the induced phobia would naturally die away (extinguish). We know now, however, that this does not occur in the way that Watson and Rayner presumed.

Social implications

The 'Little Albert' study is one of the most cited pieces of research and is used in a wide range of disciplines. The knowledge gained from this study has been beneficial to our understanding in many areas, such as child development, abnormal behaviour and therapies. It has created debate about the ethics of research, including the role of children in research and considerations of costs versus benefits. It has been argued, for instance, that whilst there are many problems with this study, its benefits to knowledge and society far outweigh the costs of conducting it.

The Cognitive Approach

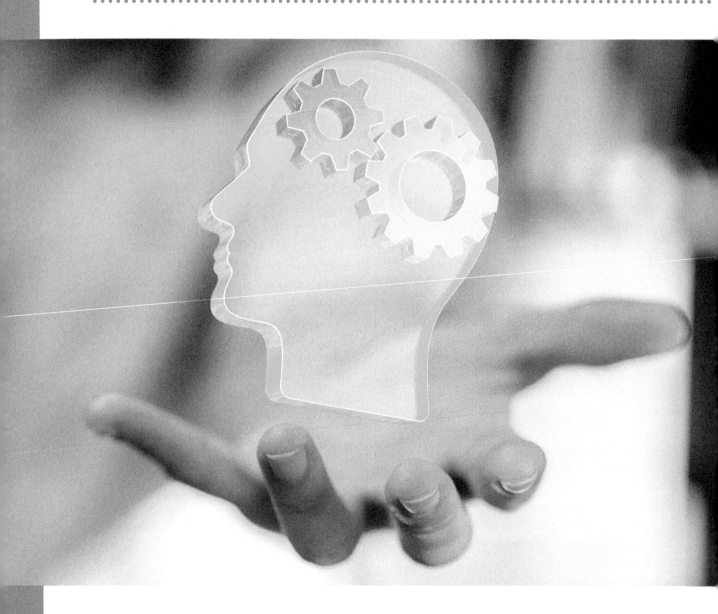

WHAT YOU NEED TO KNOW ☑

The assumptions of the cognitive approach: ☐

Internal mental processes ☐

The computer analogy ☐

Schemas ☐

Evaluation of the cognitive approach: ☐

Strengths ☐

Weaknesses ☐

Comparison with the four other approaches (see page 82) ☐

Application: formation of relationships ☐

How the approach can be used in ONE therapy ☐

EITHER: Cognitive-behavioural therapy (CBT):

Evaluation: ☐

    Effectiveness ☐

    Ethical considerations ☐

OR: Rational emotive behaviour therapy (REBT):

Evaluation: ☐

    Effectiveness ☐

    Ethical considerations ☐

Classic research (Loftus and Palmer, 1974): ☐

Aim ☐

Method and procedure ☐

Findings ☐

Conclusion ☐

Evaluation ☐

Ethical issues ☐

Social implications ☐

INTRODUCTION

When psychologists refer to 'cognition' they are referring to mental processes. It follows then that cognitive psychologists are interested in the thought processes, such as consciousness, memory, perception and learning, that help us to understand and act in the world. Whilst psychologists have always been interested in such topics, it wasn't until the development of computer science in the 1950s that cognitive psychology really took off. The *cognitive approach* makes a number of assumptions when trying to interpret and understand human behaviour.

THE ASSUMPTIONS OF THE COGNITIVE APPROACH

1. Internal mental processes

The mental skills we need to allow us to process information about the world around us are called cognitive skills. The basic assumption of the cognitive approach is that in order to understand behaviour we have to understand these internal processes of our mind. According to cognitive psychologists, these processes work together to help us make sense of the world around us and to operate effectively within it. For example, imagine you are in a bakery solving the problem of trying to decide which cake to buy. You focus your attention on one cake in particular and perceive it as a round shape with a certain colour and texture. You use your memory to recall the name of the cake, a doughnut, and your problem solving skills to consider the virtues of the doughnut over other cakes on display. You can then use language to ask to purchase the doughnut.

Internal mental processes can sometimes go wrong and result in abnormal behaviour. Depression, phobia and eating disorders can all be explained by thought processes that have become irrational or distorted. Two examples of abnormal thought processes are cognitive deficiencies and cognitive distortions (Kendall, 1993). Cognitive deficiencies are when an individual does not think or plan sufficiently, leading to negative behaviours. Cognitive distortions are a result of the cognitive system inaccurately processing information (i.e. it distorts the information so it is perceived in a different way to reality).

Attention	Focusing on one task at a time or dividing our attention between a number of tasks.
Memory	Encoding, storing and recalling information in memory.
Perception	Taking in and interpreting information from our environment via our senses.
Language	Using words and images to communicate with others and understanding the communications of others.
Problem solving	Manipulating information to reach conclusions, make decisions and judgements.

Table 1.13: Internal processes of interest to cognitive psychologists.

Cognitive deficiencies can offer an explanation for the symptoms of depression (e.g. a lack of motivation). Individuals who do not fully think a problem through may come up with an inappropriate solution. An example is when a student fails an exam and so gives up rather than trying again with a different approach to learning.

Cognitive distortions can explain the thought processes of individuals, for example, with an eating disorder, such as anorexia nervosa. Anorexics perceive themselves to be overweight, but when other people look at them they see someone who is severely underweight – the accurate perception of the individual. However, the information the individual with anorexia has received by looking at themselves in the mirror has become distorted and they alter their eating behaviour, resulting in an eating disorder.

2. The computer analogy

According to the cognitive approach the human mind can be compared to a computer. We take in information (via our senses), process it and then generate output in the form of behaviour – a process that is referred to as input, storage and retrieval. We cannot directly see the processes taking place but we can assume that the way a

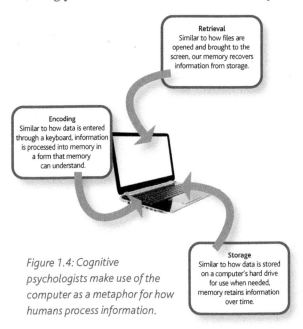

Figure 1.4: Cognitive psychologists make use of the computer as a metaphor for how humans process information.

person behaves is a reflection of these processes working in the background. In the previous example, if your friend observed you buying a doughnut, she could assume that you are thinking about how much you like doughnuts and enjoy eating them.

3. Schemas

The *schema* is a very important concept in the cognitive approach and helps us to understand how we make sense of our world. A schema is best described as a 'collection of ideas' and we have schemas for a vast number of people, places and activities. For example, when we make a cup of tea we have a routine that we follow each time: filling the kettle with water, putting it on to boil, placing a tea bag in the cup and pouring on the boiling water. This would be our 'making a cup of tea' schema. A schema often starts out as a basic and simple structure that becomes more complex through experience. Your 'making a cup of tea' schema may become more complicated once you experience different types of tea and individual preferences for the addition of milk, sugar or lemon.

A schema can also help us to make sense of new experiences. You may be learning to drive at the moment and your very first lesson will be a brand new experience. But you have other schemas that will help you to make sense of your new driving experience – for example, you may be able to ride a bicycle and therefore understand something about gears, brakes and directions. Your existing 'riding a bicycle' schema will help you to make sense of the new 'driving a car' schema.

 Consider the strengths and weaknesses of the cognitive approach. (4 + 4 marks)

 Describe the cognitive assumption of schemas. (4 marks)

EVALUATION OF THE COGNITIVE APPROACH

	STRENGTHS	WEAKNESSES
The cognitive approach lends itself to scientific testing under laboratory conditions	A high level of control can be achieved and the independent variable can be isolated so researchers can establish the cause and effect of a particular aspect of behaviour.	Studies of cognitive processes conducted in laboratories can lack ecological validity – for example, it may be difficult to generalise results of a memory test to real-life experience of memory.
Laboratory testing of behaviour uses scientific equipment	Equipment used to scan the brain is improving knowledge of internal mental processes, such as how the memory works.	By using scientific measuring equipment to measure human behaviour researchers are in danger of assuming all human behaviour is a result of information processing, and not allowing for the influence of social and cultural factors on individuals.
The cognitive approach is reductionist	The idea that complex behaviour, such as depression, can be explained through negative internal thought processes has led to the development of cognitive therapies which are effective in treating a wide range of disorders.	The cognitive approach takes a narrow focus and assumes that humans operate like computers, and ignores social and emotional factors which may impact upon the way a person processes information.

INTERNAL MENTAL PROCESSES AND THE FORMATION OF RELATIONSHIPS

The cognitive approach to the formation of relationships focuses on the internal mental processes that take place which somehow influence whether or not two people will form a relationship. One well-known cognitive explanation for the formation of relationships is social exchange theory.

Developed by Thibaut and Kelley (1959), this theory suggests that choices about relationships are essentially economic decisions – that is, relationships involve the exchange of resources, so, before we even form a relationship, we consider its possible present and future benefits and costs. Basically, we are more attracted to those who offer us more benefits than costs and less attracted to those where the potential costs outweigh the benefits. Thibaut and Kelley proposed that we engage in a 'minimax' strategy. We are motivated to minimise the costs of a relationship whilst at the same time trying to maximise the benefits. The relationship is more

Beliefs about a relationship are important – perceived costs should not outweigh benefits.

likely to form and be maintained as long as the benefits outweigh the costs.

In addition to this simple 'benefits minus cost' calculation, how people feel about a relationship also depends on their beliefs about what they expect to get out of a relationship in terms of costs and benefits. This is known as the comparison level. Some people, for example, have high expectations for a relationship, and if the reality doesn't compare favourably to this expectation then they may become unhappy and dissatisfied with it. Feelings about a relationship are also influenced by beliefs about whether there is an alternative relationship available which will satisfy these expectations. This is known as the comparison level for alternatives. For example, someone with a low comparison level for alternatives will possibly stay in an unsatisfactory relationship because they think that, whilst what they have right now may not be great, it is better than they are likely to get elsewhere. Alternatively, someone with a high comparison for alternatives will think that there is bound to be someone else out there who will provide them with what they expect from a relationship, in which case they are more likely to move on to a new relationship.

BENEFITS: PLEASANT	COSTS: UNPLEASANT
Gaining access to money	Financial costs
Receiving attention	Emotional pain
Status	Disappointment
Gratification	Embarrassment
Pleasure	Putting up with bad habits
Similarity: beliefs, values, background, age	Dissimilarity: beliefs, values, background, age

Table 1.14: Some potential benefits and costs of beginning a relationship.

Using an assumption from the cognitive approach, explain the formation of a relationship. (6 marks)

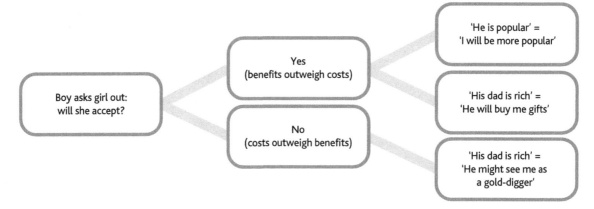

Figure 1.5: *How we might weigh up the costs and benefits of entering into a relationship.*

THERAPY: COGNITIVE-BEHAVIOURAL THERAPY

According to the cognitive approach (Beck, 1976), negative thought processes are the cause of dysfunctional behaviour and emotional distress. The main aim of cognitive-behavioural therapy (CBT), therefore, is to help an individual to identify negative and irrational thoughts and replace these with more rational ways of thinking. In turn, this should lead to more functional behaviour and positive emotional responses. Typically CBT takes place over about 20 one hour sessions with a therapist, but the duration of CBT is flexible and tailored to the needs of the client. Most CBT practitioners follow three distinct phases: case conceptualisation, skills acquisition and follow-up. During the first phase of CBT, as part of the initial assessment of the client's issues, it is common practice for a client to be asked to complete a *self-report questionnaire*. Questionnaires such as the Beck Depression Inventory (BDI) can indicate how a client is feeling and allow them to express the extent to which their issues are affecting their day-to-day life. Completing the same questionnaire periodically throughout the course of the treatment can be useful to indicate the success of the treatment and monitor progress. Comparing the results of the questionnaire completed at the end of the treatment with those acquired at the start will also help the client and therapist to see how much the client has improved.

Part of the initial process of CBT also involves the client and therapist working collaboratively to identify the client's self-defeating beliefs (e.g. 'I must be excellent at absolutely everything otherwise I am worthless'). Once these irrational beliefs have been uncovered they are challenged by the therapist by questioning the client as to why not excelling at everything makes them worthless. The client will also be required to practise certain optimistic statements which challenge their negative cognitions (e.g. 'I am a worthwhile person even though I am not excellent at everything'). Over

PHASE	DESCRIPTION
Case conceptualisation	The client needs to understand the nature of CBT.
	The therapist creates a list of problems experienced by the client using self-report and questioning.
	Set initial goals and a treatment plan.
Skills acquisition and application	Work with client on intervention techniques including teaching new skills.
	Ongoing evaluation and assessment of success of techniques and skills.
	Set goals and targets.
	Refine intervention techniques.
Ending and follow-up	Final assessment of progress using self-report and questioning.
	Discuss ending treatment and maintenance of changes.
	End treatment – client and therapist agree when this is appropriate.
	Top-up sessions can take place three or six months after completion of treatment.

Table 1.15: The three phases of CBT.

time these challenges result in changes to a person's cognition, leading to a shift in their dysfunctional behaviour.

During the skills acquisition phase, the therapist uses techniques such as questioning, designed to challenge maladaptive thoughts, and relaxation techniques such as breathing and guided imagery to relieve stress in anxious clients (see Table 1.16). Homework assignments are considered an essential aspect of CBT throughout all phases of the treatment. Homework should be tailored to the ability and needs of the client but typically consists of reading, monitoring behaviour through keeping a diary of thoughts, feelings and actions or practising new skills. Completing work outside of the therapy room helps clients to integrate what they have learned into their daily lives.

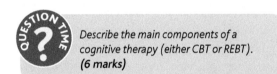

Describe the main components of a cognitive therapy (either CBT or REBT). (6 marks)

Importance of the relationship with the therapist

The three phases show the flexibility of CBT and the importance of ongoing assessment of progress, which then allows for review of goals and targets and the development of new skills and techniques for challenging irrational thoughts. Although CBT is structured and goal directed, its success is also dependent upon the relationship between the client and the therapist. If the client trusts the therapist, builds a good rapport with them and is able to work with them as an equal, then the therapy is more likely to have a positive outcome.

Evaluation of CBT
Effectiveness

A study by DeRubeis et al. (2005) demonstrates the effectiveness of CBT in treating depression. The researchers studied three groups of participants who all suffered from depression. Group 1 were treated using CBT, group 2 were given *antidepressants* and group 3 acted as the placebo (they were

TECHNIQUES USED IN CBT

Questioning	Questioning can be used to challenge clients' irrational beliefs. For instance, if a client states 'Nobody likes me' then a therapist may ask why they think that or ask them what evidence they have that this is the case. Answering these questions helps the client to see that their claim is irrational and encourages them to modify their thought to 'Lots of people like me'.
Breathing	The type of relaxation technique taught to the client may depend upon personal preferences. Some clients prefer breathing techniques and a focus on muscle relaxation. Stressed clients can be taught to identify tension in certain muscle groups and to recognise the different feelings between tense and relaxed muscles. Questioning from the therapist helps the client to express what they are feeling as they practise the breathing techniques.
Guided imagery	Some clients prefer guided imagery as a relaxation tool, with the therapist acting as a guide. The created image can be relative to the client's issue – for instance, a client with a fear of public speaking could be asked to imagine giving a successful speech. Again, questioning from the therapist helps the client to explore their thoughts and feelings.

Table 1.16: Some techniques used by therapists in CBT.

given a pill that had no effect). After eight weeks, 43% of the CBT group had improved compared with only 25% of the placebo group. The greatest improvement after an eight week period was for those participants taking the antidepressants; 50% showed signs of improvement. However, conclusions drawn from this study need to be viewed with caution since it only shows what happened after eight weeks of treatment.

Drugs may only offer a 'quick fix' in terms of improving the symptoms of depression. Hensley et al. (2004) state that the relapse rate for CBT is relatively low compared with that for antidepressants. It is estimated that 50% of those treated for depression with antidepressants will relapse within two years, whereas persevering with CBT offers the individual long-term benefits with a lower chance of relapse.

Blackburn and Moorhead (2000) found the effects of CBT on symptoms of depression to be significantly superior to antidepressant drug treatments, especially over periods of more than one year.

Evans et al. (1992) found that CBT was at least as effective as antidepressant drugs in the treatment of depression and preventing relapse in sufferers over a two year period. However, the most effective method, according to Kupfer and Frank (2001), is a combination of CBT and antidepressants.

CBT has been shown to be effective when applied to the treatment of mood disorders (e.g. depression). However, the active nature of CBT means that it will not be suitable for all clients with this disorder. The time commitment required to attend weekly sessions and the energy and motivation needed to complete homework assignments may be daunting for some, especially since depression is characterised by a lack of motivation.

Ethical considerations

The relationship between the client and the CBT practitioner may raise negative ethical issues. CBT states the importance of equality in the relationship between the client and the therapist as good ethical practice. This is only achievable once the client fully understands the nature of CBT, however, so in the first instance the therapist is in a position of power over the client and is considered an 'expert' in the client's issues. The equality of the relationship becomes more obvious once therapy is established and client and therapist are working together to establish the goals of the treatment.

The focus on the teaching and learning of skills in CBT may also raise ethical issues because the therapist could be seen as the 'teacher' and the client as their 'pupil', again leading to an imbalance of power. However, the teaching and learning element could be seen as positive from an ethical point of view as the clients are actively involved in their own treatment, and the control they take in relation to their treatment can help them to feel more positive. Homework, for example, can be motivational and lead to a sense of achievement.

What can CBT be used to treat?

Depression, anxiety disorders, phobias, OCD, lack of assertiveness, low self-esteem, relationship issues, eating disorders, insomnia, alcohol misuse.

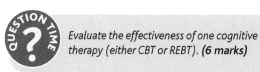

Evaluate the effectiveness of one cognitive therapy (either CBT or REBT). (6 marks)

THERAPY: RATIONAL EMOTIVE BEHAVIOUR THERAPY

The key concept underlying rational emotive behaviour therapy (REBT) is that people are not upset by an event but by their perception of the event (i.e. the way they think about it). Therefore, their perception needs to change in order for their response (behaviour) to change. The aim of REBT is to replace irrational cognitions with rational thoughts so that behaviour can change in the long term.

From his work, Ellis (1962) was able to identify a number of common irrational beliefs such as, 'I should always be loved and approved of by everyone' and 'I must be good at everything to be considered a worthwhile person'. These irrational beliefs are often characterised by the words 'should' and 'must'. As part of REBT individuals are taught what is known as the ABC model to help them understand patterns in their thoughts and behaviour so they are then able to challenge their irrational beliefs (see Figure 1.6). Clients are first of all asked to identify activating (A) events and how they felt as a consequence (C). They are then directed by the therapist to consider their beliefs (B) about the event that have triggered the negative feelings and actions. They are encouraged to recognise and challenge their 'should' and 'must' beliefs. This challenging is known as the D part of the model which stands for disputing (or arguing against) the irrational beliefs. If this is successful then the individual should achieve the E part of the model which stands for effect. There should be a new effect or outcome on the client's feelings and actions as a result of changing irrational beliefs to rational beliefs.

Importance of the relationship with the therapist

REBT is a highly active and directive approach, but it is still reliant upon the client's relationship with the therapist as a vehicle for other techniques to bring about change. Ellis agreed with the famous therapist Carl Rogers who said that clients should be given unconditional positive regard (UPR) by their therapists. This means that whatever their clients have done, and whoever they are, they must be accepted by the therapist in order that they learn to accept themselves. The relationship between the client and the therapist should also be one of equality, with the therapist even going so far as to disclose their own personal experiences to the client if they think that sharing this information might help.

A	**ACTIVATION**	Sian's friend Rhiannon says she would rather spend time alone than go with Sian to the cinema
B	**BELIEFS**	Sian believes Rhiannon does not want to be friends with her anymore
C	**CONSEQUENCE**	Sian feels rejected and stops speaking to Rhiannon
D	**DISPUTE**	Rhiannon has made a reasonable response – maybe she was not feeling well or really didn't fancy the cinema
E	**EFFECT**	Sian feels positive that Rhiannon and herself can plan future activities together and still be friends

Figure 1.6: The ABC model (including D and E!).

TECHNIQUES USED IN REBT

Using humour	Ellis supports the use of humour as a therapeutic tool. He believes that humour can help clients to take a step back from their dysfunctional beliefs and perhaps even come to laugh at themselves and the way they sometimes behave. Humour is a very tricky tool to use and relies on the skill of the therapist to judge the timing and appropriateness.
Giving clients homework	Clients may be given homework tasks to do as part of REBT. Homework should be tailored to the ability and needs of the client but typically consists of reading REBT self-help books, monitoring behaviour through keeping a diary of thoughts, feelings and actions or practising new skills. Completing work outside of the therapy room is designed to help clients integrate what they have learned into their daily lives.
Role play and modelling	Role play allows a client to practise new skills in a safe environment. For example, if a client had a fear of public speaking and had to give presentations as part of their job, they could practise with the therapist acting as the audience. The client may also use modelling in the role play situation by thinking of someone they admire who has the skills they desire and then incorporating the desired attributes into their own behaviour.

Table 1.17: Techniques used by therapists in REBT.

Evaluation of REBT

Effectiveness

A study carried out in Romania by David et al. (2008) compared the effectiveness of REBT with other treatments for depression. Some 170 participants were randomly allocated to one of three conditions; REBT, cognitive therapy (CT) or antidepressants. Each treatment was administered over a 14 week period with patients receiving up to 20 therapy sessions lasting around 50 minutes each. They also received three 'top-up' sessions over a follow-up period of six months. After the initial 14 weeks of treatment there was no significant difference between the improvement of patients in each condition. Improvement rates were similar for REBT, CT and drugs, with around 60% of patients in each condition making positive progress. Assessment of patients after the six month follow-up period did show a significant difference between drugs and REBT, with a higher relapse rate for those taking the antidepressants. The researchers concluded that in the long term REBT was significantly better than drugs at treating the symptoms of depression.

Gonzalez et al. (2004) carried out a meta-analysis of 19 studies of REBT conducted on children and adolescents. They found that all the studies in their analysis showed improved outcomes for children and teenagers receiving REBT compared with control groups receiving no intervention. The most pronounced impact of REBT was seen with children who displayed disruptive behaviour in the classroom. They also found that REBT was equally effective for youngsters both with and without a specific identified problem. This suggests that REBT can be used not only to support children with problems but also for the prevention of problems with a wide range of students. Gonzalez et al. also demonstrated that participants showed greater improvement when the REBT techniques were delivered by teachers and members of staff rather than health professionals. This has implications for practice in schools, with more children able to access the care they need within their school rather than seeking external support.

REBT can be effective when used as a model for group therapy. The advantage of using REBT in a group is that each client can contribute to disputing other's irrational beliefs. The group members can also support each other in learning the ABC model. The opportunity to take on the role of teacher in supporting others helps clients to feel more independent and in control, which are often attributes lacking in individuals suffering from depression or anxiety. Seeing change occurring in other group members is also encouraging. As REBT can be used in small or large group situations, it could be used to treat a family or even a couple experiencing relationship difficulties.

Ethical considerations

Some therapists feel that empathy is difficult in REBT even though it is an ethical consideration in accordance with British Association for Counselling and Psychotherapy guidelines (see box 'How do therapists keep their practice ethical?'). Empathy can be problematic in REBT since it is important for a therapist to remain detached enough from the client to be able to identify irrational beliefs. Empathising with a client who has irrational thoughts may lead to collusion with negative thought patterns and an inability on the part of the therapist to separate themselves from the client's irrational views.

Some clients feel threatened by the active approach taken by REBT. If irrational beliefs are challenged by the therapist too vigorously too early on in the therapeutic relationship then the client may leave the therapy no better than when they started.

> ### What can REBT be used to treat?
>
> Anxiety, panic attacks, depression, relationship issues, eating disorders, anger, OCD, phobias, stress.

> ### How do therapists keep their practice ethical?
>
> The British Association for Counselling and Psychotherapy (BACP) publish an *Ethical Framework for Good Practice* to guide and inform the practice of therapy and counselling in the UK. The framework guides practitioners in appropriate principles, values and personal moral qualities. The guidelines describe empathy as 'the ability to communicate understanding of another person's experience from that person's perspective'. Therapists are strongly encouraged to aspire to this personal moral quality and to demonstrate through their practice that they are able to 'walk in another person's shoes' and see things as they would see them.

Another ethical issue is derived from the relationship between the client and the therapist. If a client is working in a one-to-one situation with a therapist, then they have only the therapist's view as to what constitutes 'rational' beliefs and behaviour. This puts the therapist in a position of power, especially when working with clients who lack self-belief and have low self-esteem, who are more likely to believe the views and ideas of an 'expert' therapist.

Describe the main components of a cognitive therapy (either CBT OR REBT). **(8 marks)**

Evaluate a cognitive therapy (either CBT or REBT). **(6 marks)**

CLASSIC RESEARCH
– LOFTUS AND PALMER (1974)

> Loftus, E. F. and Palmer, J. C. (1974). Reconstruction of automobile destruction: an example of the interaction between language and memory. *Journal of Verbal Learning and Verbal Behaviour*, 13, 585–589

Loftus and Palmer conducted two experiments to investigate the effect of leading questions on the recall of events by eyewitnesses. Leading questions are questions that somehow, by the way that they are worded, suggest the answer that should be given.

Experiment 1

Aim

In this experiment, Loftus and Palmer investigated the effect that leading questions have on eyewitnesses' ability to recall information.

Method and procedure

Forty-five American college students watched seven films of traffic accidents, ranging from 5 to 30 seconds in duration. The participants filled in a questionnaire giving a general account of what they had seen and answering specific questions about the accident. The critical question (the one Loftus and Palmer were really interested in) asked the participants about the speed of the vehicles. The participants were asked, 'How fast were the cars going when they _____ each other?' Only the verb changed.

Findings

Table 1.18 shows the mean speed estimates given for each of the verbs. 'Smashed' generated higher mean speed estimates (40.8 mph) and 'contacted' generated the lowest (31.8 mph).

VERB	MEAN SPEED ESTIMATE (MPH)
Smashed	40.8
Collided	39.3
Bumped	38.1
Hit	34.0
Contacted	31.8

Table 1.18: Estimated speed for each verb used.

Conclusion

Loftus and Palmer concluded that the form of a question – and just changing a single word – can markedly and systematically affect a witness's answer to that question. Not only are people poor judges of speed but their recall of an event is greatly influenced by the wording of the question.

Loftus and Palmer speculated that their findings could be due to two factors:

1. A response-bias: the participant is unsure whether to say 30 mph or 40 mph and the verb used biases the estimate (i.e. 'smashed' causes a bias towards a higher estimate).

2. The leading question changes the participant's memory of the event – for example, the verb 'smashed' causes the participants to 'see' the accident as being more severe than it actually was. If this is the case, other details may be remembered that did not actually occur.

Experiment 2

Aim

In this experiment, Loftus and Palmer wanted to investigate whether leading questions distorted eyewitnesses' memory of an event.

Method and procedure

One-hundred-and-fifty US college students were shown a short film of a multiple car crash. The participants completed a questionnaire asking them to describe the accident and answer a series of questions. The critical question asked about the speed of the vehicles. One week later the participants returned and, without viewing the film again, answered a series of 10 questions about the accident. The critical question was, 'Did you see any broken glass?', which the participants answered by ticking 'yes' or 'no'. There was no broken glass in the accident, but since broken glass is highly likely to occur in a high-speed accident Loftus and Palmer expected participants in the 'smashed' condition to answer 'yes' to the question. Their schemas would 'fill in' this information.

Findings

Table 1.19 shows the responses to the critical question, 'Did you see any broken glass?' Those in the 'smashed' condition were more than twice as likely as those in the 'hit' and control conditions to say 'yes' to the critical question.

Conclusion

Loftus and Palmer concluded that the verb used in a leading question has an effect not only on speed estimates but also on information recalled a week later.

	'YES' RESPONSES OUT OF 50
Smashed	16
Hit	7
Control	6

Table 1.19: Responses to the question, 'Did you see any broken glass?'

Evaluation of Loftus and Palmer (1974)

Internal validity

A laboratory experiment was used in both studies which allowed the experimenters to manipulate the independent variable (verb) and objectively measure the dependent variable (answers to critical questions). This high level of control increases the internal validity of the experiments as the experimenters were measuring what they set out to measure. The second experiment tested this.

External validity

A laboratory experiment is often lacking in ecological validity, making it difficult to generalise to the real world. Questions in a courtroom, where the answers given by an eyewitness could lead to the prosecution of an individual, would not be asked by questionnaire. Also, the shock and emotional

	EXPERIMENT 1	EXPERIMENT 2
Method	Laboratory experiment	Laboratory experiment
Participants	45 American college students	150 American college students
Design	Independent measures	Independent measures
Independent variable	Change of verb	Change of verb
Dependent variable	Speed estimate	Recall of broken glass (yes or no)

Table 1.20: Summary of the key features of the Loftus and Palmer study.

impact of witnessing a car accident in real life cannot be recreated under laboratory conditions.

Demand characteristics

Another limitation of a laboratory experiment is that participants know they are in an experiment. This could lead to demand characteristics – for example, they probably suspected they would be asked about the film clips (or why watch them?) and may have altered their answers to fit in with what they believed the experimenter was looking for.

Ethical issues

Deception

The participants did not know what the aim of the experiment was or that there were other conditions in the experiment. They were not aware of what the experimenter was actually looking for (i.e. the answers to the critical questions). However, the level of deception in these experiments is both necessary and acceptable. It was necessary to minimise the effects of demand characteristics as far as possible, and it was acceptable because it was not a high level of deception.

Protection from harm

Although Loftus and Palmer did show clips of real car accidents to their participants, most of the clips were staged. While this reduces psychological harm to some extent, the participants could still have experienced strong emotional reactions to these clips. For example, it is unknown whether any of the participants had been in a car accident themselves (what effect could this have on someone?).

Social implications

The findings of Loftus and Palmer's study have important implications for our understanding of the testimonies given by eyewitnesses to a crime. The consideration of eyewitness testimony is important because the statements given by witnesses are used as evidence in court and could be key pieces of information on which a jury makes their decision about whether a person is guilty or not. The consequences of inaccurate information can be catastrophic. Innocent people may go to jail, or even be put to death in some parts of the world, just because inaccurate eyewitness statements have been made. The research by Loftus and Palmer shows, first, that our memory is reconstructive and that people may not even be aware of it. New information is stored as a memory (or alters an existing one), meaning that we will recall something that may not have actually happened. Therefore, when questioning eyewitnesses, interviewers must avoid using leading questions that could affect the accuracy of recall. Second, the study shows that even in the absence of *misleading information*, witnesses can still make errors (e.g. six participants said 'yes' to seeing broken glass in the control group). The error in recall stems from their schema for road accidents and the expectation that there must be broken glass even if they didn't actually see any. Therefore, eyewitness testimony must be used with caution. It seems that memories are not an accurate representation of events, but according to Loftus (2003) they are a sum of what people have thought, what they have been told and what they believe.

Describe the method and findings of Loftus and Palmer's study. (6 + 6 marks)

'Loftus and Palmer's research has many social implications.' Discuss this statement with reference to the procedures and findings of the research. (6 + 6 marks)

The Positive Approach

WHAT YOU NEED TO KNOW ☑

The assumptions of the positive
approach: ☐

Authenticity of goodness and excellence ☐

Acknowledgement of free will ☐

Focus on 'the good life' ☐

Evaluation of the positive approach: ☐

Strengths ☐

Weaknesses ☐

Comparison with the four other ☐
approaches (see page 82)

Application: formation of relationships ☐

How the approach can be used in ☐
one therapy:

EITHER: Mindfulness:

Evaluation: ☐

    Effectiveness ☐

    Ethical considerations ☐

OR: Quality of Life Therapy:

Evaluation: ☐

    Effectiveness ☐

    Ethical considerations ☐

Classic research
(Myers and Diener, 1995): ☐

Aim ☐

Method and procedure ☐

Findings ☐

Conclusion ☐

Evaluation ☐

Ethical issues ☐

Social implications ☐

INTRODUCTION

Positive psychology was founded in 1999 by Martin Seligman at the University of Pennsylvania. Seligman pointed out that other approaches for explaining human behaviour were based on the 'disease model' – focusing on trying to find out what is wrong with people and making them less miserable. Instead, Seligman believed that psychology should aim to understand what makes people happier and develop ways to achieve a more positive state of mind. The *positive approach* also extends beyond the individual to look at the strengths and virtues that enable groups and communities to thrive and flourish.

THE ASSUMPTIONS OF THE POSITIVE APPROACH

1. Authenticity of goodness and excellence

If something is authentic it is genuine, real and believable. Positive psychology assumes that goodness and excellence in human beings is authentic and therefore should be studied by psychologists in as much depth as human disorders and inadequacies. Peterson (2006) agrees with Seligman when he observes that psychology has focused too much attention on negative aspects of human behaviour and ignored what people do well. This has led to a distorted view of the human condition. Our distorted view of human behaviour can lead us to make predictions about how we will react to major life events that contradict reality. For example, young people are often poor judges of how long they will feel sad after the break-up of a relationship. Most predict that they will feel sad for months when in reality they manage to get on with their lives and feel unhappy for far less time than they imagined. Peterson believes that 'some of the true miracles of human activity receive scant attention from psychologists' (2006, p. 11). He quotes examples of these 'miracles' as children learning language with negligible explicit instruction, people's ability to recover from trauma or having the ability to give up smoking with little help. Positive psychology believes that these abilities should be explored and understood further to create a more complete picture of human behaviour.

2. Acknowledgement of free will

Positive psychology has its roots in the humanistic approach which focuses on happiness and fulfilment. Humanistic psychologists such as Abraham Maslow and Carl Rogers believe that, given the right conditions, an individual can demonstrate *free will* in making choices that lead to self-actualisation – being the best they can be in all areas of their life. Positive psychology goes hand in hand with the notion of free will as it is about taking control and working on your strengths to change your life. Individuals who report feeling in control of their life choices are less stressed and physically healthier than those who do not feel in control. The acceptance of free will goes against the idea that human beings are victims of circumstance and that antisocial behaviour can be explained through a bad upbringing or negative past experiences.

3. Focus on 'the good life'

Seligman (2002) identifies three types of life that he describes as 'happy' lives: the pleasant life, the meaningful life and the life of engagement that is also known as 'the good life'.

THE PLEASANT LIFE	THE MEANINGFUL LIFE	THE LIFE OF ENGAGEMENT
Involves generating as much positive emotion as you can and learning the skills to make this happen. The pursuit of pleasure.	Involves knowing your key strengths and using them in the service of something larger than yourself (e.g. an institution such as religion or education).	Involves engagement in all aspects of your life including relationships, parenting, work and leisure. Time becomes distorted and an activity becomes autotelic and an end in itself.

Table 1.21: Seligman's three types of 'happy' life.

Positive emotions can improve our mood when we are under stress and counteract the effects of stress-related illnesses. However, life that involves only pleasure has drawbacks. Individuals can habituate to pleasure – we don't get the same amount of pleasure from the same thing constantly. Seligman uses the example of ice cream: the first spoonful is amazing but after six spoonfuls the intensity of the pleasure has passed. Seligman describes the life of engagement, or good life, as one which has a balance between pleasure and 'flow'. When we are in a state of 'flow' we are at one with what we are doing. The demands of the environment are completely balanced with available resources and the ability to meet these demands. This leads to a state of absorption, complete concentration and a loss of self-awareness. Time either seems to stand still so that seconds can feel like hours or time can seem to pass very quickly if you are fully engrossed in what you are doing. Activities that encourage a state of flow include playing sport, dancing and listening to music; conversely, flow is inhibited by watching television and generally being apathetic and idle. Seligman claims that individuals can work towards a good life by identifying personal strengths and then remodelling life to build on these strengths, which will then lead to an increased experience of flow.

Playing a sport such as tennis can induce a state of flow. The individual is so absorbed in what they are doing that time seems to pass very quickly.

EVALUATION OF THE POSITIVE APPROACH

	STRENGTHS	WEAKNESSES
Free will	The concept of free will is supported by our justice system. We expect people to be responsible for their actions and to be held accountable for any wrongdoings.	Diener and Biswas-Diener (2008) claim that we have a happiness set point that is genetically determined. Diener and Biswas-Diener say that 20–50% of our happiness is outside of our control, so no matter how hard we try we are only able to reach a certain level of happiness. We are not able to exercise complete free will over our happiness.
Happiness can be measured	Happiness can be tested scientifically. Neuroscientific evidence from brain imaging shows that the prefrontal cortex is more active when we are happy. This method offers a reliable and objective measure of happiness.	Many studies that measure happiness are based upon self-report and may not be accurate as memory distorts the recall of experience. Measures such as questionnaires and interviews may therefore not offer the most reliable source of data to measure happiness. They are more likely to be subjective.
Cultural bias	The positive approach identifies the contributions an individual can make to their community as important in enhancing well-being. These qualities are celebrated in collectivist cultures where success is measured by the contributions an individual can make to the group.	Qualities such as individuality and autonomy are identified as important in leading a 'good life'. These qualities are particular to Western individualist societies where success is judged on individual achievement.

Our mood fluctuates throughout the day; we may laugh, feel sad or worry about something. Despite these ups and downs some scientists believe that we have a happiness set-point which is a fixed or average level of happiness suggesting that some people have a natural tendency to be happier than others.

'THE GOOD LIFE' AND THE FORMATION OF RELATIONSHIPS

According to the positive approach, a 'good life' is one where you experience engagement in all areas of your life, including relationships. According to Myers and Diener (1995), individuals who can name several close friends, whom they can confide in, rely on and share their feelings with, are happier, healthier and more likely to live longer than people who have few or no intimate friends. This suggests that we form relationships in order to buffer ourselves against the stresses and strains of everyday life.

A study conducted by Diener and Seligman (2002) found that people judged as 'very happy' spent less time alone and more time socialising than individuals rated as 'average' or 'very unhappy'. The 'very happy' group also rated their social relationships as being of good quality. It seems that the more and better quality friendships people have, the happier and more satisfied with life they feel, supporting the idea that a search for happiness underpins the drive to create and maintain friendships.

Another reason for the formation of friendships is that they can help us to get the most out of positive events in our lives (Langston, 1994). This happens when an individual shares good news with close friends, who respond positively to the good news, thereby increasing the happiness gained from the news and maximising its benefits. For example, it is common for good friends to celebrate a pregnancy with a 'baby shower', where presents are bought and excitement about the forthcoming birth is shared. Such events increase the happiness and well-being not only of the individual concerned but of all involved.

Research indicates that a sense of independence has a positive effect on our well-being. Forming friendships can help us feel more independent, for example, having others we can turn to for guidance, support

Being fully absorbed in a romantic relationship enhances positive feelings and contributes to a 'good life'.

and assistance gives us the confidence to take chances and explore. This can help us to achieve more of our goals in life. Psychologists refer to this as the 'dependency paradox' (Feeney 2007): recognising that we need to depend on others for support actually helps us to be more independent! Research has shown that when close friends are able to support each other's independence through equally offering support that is mutual and balanced, the friendship is seen to be of high quality and related to improved psychological well-being.

Seligman describes 'the good life' as one which involves experiences of 'flow.' Many of the activities encouraged by our friends may contribute to being able to access this state of absorption e.g. joining a dance class or taking up a sporting activity. We may also become absorbed in the relationship especially when it is a romantic relationship with which we are fully engaged, leading to an enhanced sense of a 'good life.' Friendship formation could therefore be seen as a means to enhance opportunities for 'flow'.

THERAPY – MINDFULNESS

Mindfulness is a therapy based on the art of meditation and has its origins in Buddhist practices. Jon Kabat-Zinn brought mindfulness into mainstream therapy with the launch of his Mindfulness Based Stress Reduction (MBSR) programme in 1979. The main aim of mindfulness is to develop a sense of 'here and now', so the focus of a person's attention is on what is happening in their mind and environment in the present moment. Individuals are taught to tune in to the present moment and tune out any thoughts of the past or future. Links to the positive approach can be seen through the benefits of mindfulness in improving cognitive functioning and inducing an improved sense of well-being in an individual, as well as enhancing relationships with friends, family and peers. Ultimately, developing a mindfulness approach can help us to lead a better life.

The two main components of mindfulness are self-regulation of attention and orientation to the present moment.

Self-regulation of attention

This involves learning to focus on the here and now and to sustain focus over long periods

---

Meditation – a simple breathing exercise

Sit in an upright position on the floor or on a straight-backed chair. Focus on your breathing – listen to and feel as you breathe in and out. Notice any thoughts that come into your mind but do not dwell on them. Accept the thought for what it is but do not judge your thought, add meaning or react in any way. Let the thought go and refocus on your breathing. Repeat this process every time a thought enters your head.

Using mindfulness to treat anxiety

When suffering from anxiety, an individual experiences certain bodily sensations such as an increased heart rate and breathing. Mindfulness encourages them to focus on the sensations and experience the full symptoms of anxiety rather than try to pretend they are not happening. Opening up to distressing thoughts and sensations seems like an odd thing to do if you are feeling anxious, but experiencing the anxiety fully means that the anxious person learns to respond to negative thoughts and let them go. Symptoms of anxiety are not removed; instead the person develops a different relationship with their anxiety provoking thoughts, behaviour and emotions.

---

of time. Breathing exercises can help by bringing the focus back to the present (see box 'Meditation – a simple breathing exercise'). Any thoughts that occur should be acknowledged and not ignored but should not be elaborated upon. We should not allow a thought to capture our attention to the point where we are considering further thoughts, feelings and sensations in relation to that thought. This should lead to an acceptance of things as they are without adding our own judgements or beliefs into the mix. For example, if you suddenly start to think ,'I'm going to fail this exam', don't dwell and start to brood about past failures, what your parents might say or how anxious this makes you feel. Instead, acknowledge the thought, 'Here is that thought about failing the exam again', and then let go of it.

Orientation to the present moment focuses on increasing emotional awareness by developing curiosity about where the mind wanders and what is happening in the present. All thoughts, feelings and bodily sensations should be noticed and accepted without trying to change them or force a state of relaxation. Even painful and unpleasant emotions and thoughts should be recognised rather than avoided or repressed. The aim is to see thoughts and feelings as passing moments in time rather than permanent characteristics of ourselves. Recognising painful thoughts and feelings for what they are should lead to them becoming less unpleasant and threatening. The thoughts are not changed, but what is changed is the relationship between a person and their thoughts (see box 'Using mindfulness to treat anxiety').

Kabat-Zinn advocates the use of a range of techniques that can help to improve

Body scan		Clients are asked to scan their bodies working from their head down to their toes. As they do this they are asked to be aware of any sensations they are experiencing. If a client feels pain or an area of tension or discomfort, they should acknowledge it but not try to change or control the sensation.
Raisin exercise		Clients are encouraged to use all of their senses to experience a raisin. They start by looking carefully at the raisin and examining its shape, colour and contours. They then experience how it feels, smells and, finally, tastes. The exercise is designed to develop a sense of the here and now.
Walking meditation		This exercise focuses on sensations experienced as each step is taken. Clients develop a sense of how their foot feels as it leaves and then reconnects with the ground. Initially this can be practised over a short distance of about 10 steps. It is designed to build awareness and appreciation of something we do every day.
Loving-kindness meditation		This form of meditation encourages a client to focus on feeling more acceptance and compassion towards themselves, which is then extended to feeling more compassionate towards loved ones, people you both like and dislike and, eventually, all human beings.

Table 1.22: Techniques used in MBSR training.

mindfulness. His Mindfulness Based Stress Reduction programme involves attending a weekly group session to learn mindfulness techniques. Between sessions clients are given 'homework' and expected to practise meditation and exercises to improve their learning.

Kabat-Zinn claims that most of us live our lives as if on autopilot and we do not stop to build our awareness. Past fears and insecurities develop into automatic responses to situations that do not enhance our well-being. He claims that there are certain attitudes (see Figure 1.7) that need to be adopted by a client learning mindfulness for the therapy to be successful.

Relationship with the therapist

Mindfulness therapy is different from many other therapies because the therapist is both teacher and practitioner. Research suggests that this develops in therapists greater levels of empathy towards their clients and therefore helps to foster positive therapeutic relationships. Research by Tang et al. (2007) found that therapists who practised mindfulness meditation scored higher on measures of self-reported empathy than therapists who did not meditate.

Evaluation of mindfulness

Effectiveness

Davidson et al. (2003) conducted a study into the effects of mindfulness meditation on brain function and the immune system. They offered an eight-week Mindfulness Based Stress Reduction programme to a group of 25 healthy employees in a work-based environment. They measured the participants' brain activity before

Figure 1.7: Attitudes for mindfulness practice.

What can mindfulness interventions be used to treat?

Anxiety, stress, post-traumatic stress disorder (PTSD) and obesity. It can also help to overcome chronic pain, boost the immune system, improve memory and focus attention.

the programme, straight after the programme and then four months later. The results were compared with 16 members of a control group who were tested at the same points but who did not do the mindfulness training. At the end of the programme all participants were also given an influenza immunisation jab. The group who had received the mindfulness training showed increased activity in areas of the brain associated with positive emotions. They also produced higher levels of antibodies in response to the flu vaccine compared with those who did not receive mindfulness training.

Some of the positive effects of mindfulness meditation are believed to be an improved ability to control stress, regulate emotions and feel empathy. Research by Hölzel et al. (2011) found that meditating for 30 minutes each day can improve the density of grey matter in the brain in areas associated with memory, stress and empathy.

Mindfulness practice has been applied in educational settings to help children who find it difficult to concentrate. A study of 123 high school girls in Philadelphia showed an increase in positive emotions, fewer physical aches and pains and an improved ability to relax. They also demonstrated better focus of attention which improved their ability to learn.

Mindfulness meditation may not be suitable for all. Participants need to already possess a degree of calm and patience to be able to meditate. They must be willing to learn and stick with a programme for at least eight weeks.

Ethical considerations

Issues have been raised regarding the level of competence of some mindfulness practitioners. Some facilitators of mindfulness-based interventions may only have completed an eight week course followed by one year's experience before they begin tutoring others. It is important for therapists to have a good understanding of mindfulness, have received formal training and be practitioners of mindfulness in order to act as suitable role models for their students. They also need to develop a thorough understanding of the range of disorders that may be treated using mindfulness-based interventions and know how mindfulness can help with these disorders. There may be an issue with obtaining fully informed consent from clients who need to be made aware of the intentions of the therapy from the start of the treatment. This is especially important when considering the religious beliefs of the client since mindfulness has its roots in Buddhist practices. Clients need to be made aware of the background to mindfulness so they can make an informed choice and not begin to pursue a therapy which may conflict with their own personal religious beliefs.

As part of their research into the effects of meditation on the brain Davidson et al. (2003) scanned the brain of the Buddhist monk Matthieu Ricard. The scan took place as Ricard was meditating on compassion. The data revealed excessively high levels of activity in the left prefrontal cortex; an area of the brain associated with positive mood and happiness.

THERAPY – QUALITY OF LIFE THERAPY

Quality of Life Therapy developed by Frisch (2006) provides a way of using the findings of the positive approach towards well-being and happiness to help clients identify and meet their goals and wishes in life (i.e. to lead a 'good life'). Successfully pursuing and achieving goals gives life a sense of purpose and direction, which in turn enhances feelings of well-being and happiness. During the treatment clients are taught strategies and skills based on meeting their needs in 16 areas of life that contribute to well-being and happiness. The therapy can be used as a form of life coaching for any individual or can be tailored to the needs of clients with specific issues or problems. The therapist aims to work collaboratively with the client, and the close working alliance begins with the therapist explaining the principles of the therapy to the client in an effort to create a common understanding.

Quality of Life Therapy uses the Quality of Life Inventory to carry out an initial assessment of the level of a client's happiness and well-being. The inventory identifies 16 factors which contribute to an individual's quality of life. These can be condensed into seven categories (see Table 1.23). After an initial assessment the therapist prescribes Quality of Life Therapy interventions that are aimed at particular areas of dissatisfaction in the client's life. Only areas of life that are valued and important to the client are targeted. The interventions suggested by the therapist will depend on which of the 16 areas the client has identified through the inventory as an area of dissatisfaction. This inventory is also used during therapy to measure progress and is completed again at the end of the therapy, so clients can see how much their life satisfaction has improved.

The results of the Quality of Life Inventory are shared with the client and clients are told that interventions will be 'prescribed' by the therapist that will target their areas of unhappiness. According to Seligman (2011), clients should also be told that the approach is supported by research that shows evidence of its success. Therapists encourage clients to put into practice the interventions that have been discussed in the therapy sessions. They may support this with the use of homework tasks designed to get clients to use the techniques learned in therapy in-between therapy sessions and after therapy is complete. The aim is to get the client to become their own therapist.

FACTORS IN THE QUALITY OF LIFE INVENTORY		
1	Health	Absence of pain or disability and being physically fit.
2	Self-esteem	Valuing yourself and accepting your strengths and weaknesses.
3	Goals and values	What matters to you in life – your purpose.
4–7	Self-enhancement	Work; play; learning; creativity.
8–11	Relationships	Love; friends; children; relatives.
12–15	Environment	Money (standard of living); home; neighbourhood; community.
16	Helping	Social service and civic action and helping those who are not friends or relatives.

Table 1.23: The Quality of Life Inventory (adapted from Frisch, 2013).

FIVE PATHS	DESCRIPTION	EXAMPLE – JOB SATISFACTION
Circumstances	Physical and social characteristics of an area of life.	Dissatisfaction with your job is centred on job security, conditions and relationships with your boss and co-workers.
Attitude	Individual perception or interpretation of an area of life.	You see your job as beneath you.
Standards	The level of standard you set for achieving your goals in a particular area of life.	The goal you set for achieving promotion may be too high and unrealistic.
Importance	How important this area of your life is to your overall happiness.	Achieving in your job may be more important to you than success in recreational pursuits or parenting.
Overall happiness	What lesser areas are there in your life that you have not considered recently but that may contribute to your overall happiness?	Focus on areas of lesser concern to improve overall well-being.

Table 1.24: The CASIO (or Five Paths to Happiness) model.

One of the interventions used by the therapist is based on the CASIO model, also known as the Five Paths to Happiness. This technique is centred on the idea that each area of your life is made up of five parts and that change to any one of these five parts can improve satisfaction within that area of your life. The client is encouraged to brainstorm ways of making changes to bring about improved satisfaction. A description of the five paths and an example of their application can be found in Table 1.24.

For 'play' (in the life area of self-enhancement), one intervention is the 'Frivolous Flow Principle'. This is where clients are encouraged to carry out an activity that is done purely for fun and in no way 'enhances our income or prestige' (Frisch, 2006). The activity should be for enjoyment but it should also challenge our skills so that it is engaging and absorbing enough to generate a state of flow (i.e. being fully focused on the activity).

A variety of interventions can be prescribed by the therapist to enhance satisfaction in the life area of 'relationships'. These include the favour bank, expert friend and the string of pearls (see Table 1.25).

Evaluation of Quality of Life Therapy
Effectiveness
Rodrigue et al. (2005) conducted a study on patients with severe lung disease who were on a transplant waiting list. The patients often had to wait years for a lung to become available during which time their health was deteriorating, leading to high levels of stress and anxiety. The Quality of Life Inventory was used to help patients to identify areas of their life where they felt unfulfilled or dissatisfied. The patients were randomly assigned to 8–12 weeks of therapy in one of two groups; traditional support or Quality of Life Therapy. For the Quality of Life Therapy group, interventions (e.g. the Five Paths to Happiness or CASIO exercises) were

Favour bank

doing favours for others so that they, in turn, will do favours for us.

Expert friend

making friends with people in similar situations to us e.g. single mums who are coping well with the challenges of the situation. These friends can offer social support and advice.

String of pearls

thinking of daily life as a series of interactions with people ranging from relatives to strangers and taking care to be kind and responsive to others. Each act of kindness is a pearl to add to your string.

Table 1.25: Interventions used in the life area of relationships.

used to boost the level of satisfaction in the areas identified by the patient. Three months after the end of therapy, 76% of those who had received Quality of Life Therapy reported improved levels of satisfaction with their lives compared with 27% of those who received traditional support.

» The effects of Quality of Life Therapy extend beyond those who are directly receiving the treatment. In the Rodrigue et al. (2005) study, the primary carers and spouses of the lung transplant patients also reported improvements in the quality of their life in relation to the patient. This included increased social intimacy and improved mood, which helped the carers to function more efficiently and therefore provide better care for their loved one.

» Frisch points out that no matter how much rigorous therapy is received there are limitations to how happy an individual can become. This is because we have a happiness 'set point' which we inherit from our parents. According to Diener and Biswas-Diener (2008), about 20–50% of our happiness is outside of our control. This contradicts the concept of free will.

Ethical considerations

» Quality of Life Therapy respects the diversity of each client and accounts for differences in the needs and values of individuals in terms of age, socioeconomic status and gender. It assumes that there are innumerable factors that determine happiness and well-being and that not everybody will want the same thing. It accepts that there may be some common factors that enhance happiness and well-being but they may not be valued to the same degree by everybody. This supports the ethical consideration of respect, particularly in relation to general standards of valuing the uniqueness of each individual.

» Frisch uses the word 'prescribe' when describing how the therapist works with the client to decide which interventions are suitable for improving life satisfaction. The word suggests the directive nature of Quality of Life Therapy which may challenge the ethical guidelines for practice that stress the importance of client autonomy and self-determination. When forming a contract with the client it is therefore important for the therapist to recognise the client's right to withdraw from or challenge the nature of the therapy offered by the therapist. The client should be advised of this at the earliest opportunity and the therapist should respect the client's wish to discontinue the therapy if that is their choice.

CLASSIC RESEARCH – MYERS AND DIENER (1995)

> Myers, D. G. and Diener, E. (1995). Who is happy? *Psychological Science*, 6(1), 10–19

Aim

The researchers aimed to find out who are the 'happy people'. They recognised that most people claim to be reasonably happy but some are happier than others. They wanted to know whether people are happier due to their gender, race, age or wealth, or whether happiness comes from having a particular job, religion or close friends. Myers and Diener accepted that theories about what happiness is have been in existence for a very long time, but they believed that a review of more recent scientific research would help to answer the question about what makes people happy.

Method and procedure

Myers and Diener considered a number of studies designed to measure an individual's subjective well-being. Most of the studies they reviewed were carried out between 1985 and 1991 and were conducted in a wide range of countries. A variety of self-report techniques were used to gather data about subjective well-being, including single questions (e.g. How satisfied are you with your life as a whole?), questionnaires with multi-item rating scales and clinical interviews. Some studies in the review also gathered data from peers and relatives of the participants so a correlation could be made between the ratings of the participants and the judgement of their friends and family as to how happy they were.

Findings

Myers and Diener found that happiness is a stable factor. Those people who rate themselves as happy at one particular point in time continue to be happy despite changes in circumstance, such as moving house or changing job. After reviewing many studies, the researchers found that consistently happy people possessed four particular personality traits: high self-esteem, a sense of control over their lives and they were optimistic and extrovert.

Friendship also emerged as a factor in happiness. Happy people reported having a network of supportive close friends whom they could confide in and rely on for support. A network of supportive relationships can also be experienced through work, and happy people report a sense of fulfilment through their job when they feel they are part of a community. A person's job can generate a sense of purpose and a feeling that they are doing something that matters, whether it is saving lives, educating others or creating a piece of art. When it is experienced as both challenging and engaging, work can induce a sense of flow – an individual becomes so absorbed in what they are doing that time seems to fly. Anything that increases flow contributes to a general feeling of well-being.

Self-esteem	They value themselves and say they are fun, intelligent and able to get on with others.
Control	They feel empowered rather than helpless and cope well with stress.
Optimism	They approach life with a positive attitude and expect to do well.
Extroversion	They are outgoing but are happy both in their own company and with others.

Table 1.26: The four personality traits of happy people.

STUDY	SUMMARY
Method	Content analysis (review) of studies that used self-report techniques to gather data.
Sample studies	A wide range of studies from both individualist and collectivist countries were included in the sample.
Sample study methods of gathering data	Questionnaires, clinical interviews.

Table 1.27: Summary of the key features of the Myers and Diener study.

Links between subjective well-being and the active practice of religion were also found by Myers and Diener. Research studies conducted in Europe and the United States found that religious people who regularly practiced their faith reported higher levels of happiness compared with those who claimed to have low spiritual commitment. Surveys conducted in North America and 14 other Western nations found a *positive correlation* between frequency of worship and happiness.

Conclusion

After considering a range of studies into subjective well-being, the researchers concluded that, beyond having enough money to afford basic necessities, wealth does not bring happiness. The age, sex or race of an individual also provides no clue to their happiness. Better indicators of happiness come from knowing an individual's traits. Happy people have strong support networks and close relationships, including those at work and through their faith; they find purpose, meaning and engagement in their work and leisure pursuits.

Evaluation

Self-report method

The research is a content analysis of a range of studies that gathered data using self-report techniques. A common criticism often levelled at self-report techniques is that they are subjective, giving only the personal views from a participant at a particular point in time which can often make the data unreliable. In this case, however, the research studies were actively seeking to explore the *subjective* well-being of an individual and therefore recognise that an individual's assessment of their own happiness should be taken seriously.

Correlational method

Many of the findings presented by Myers and Diener are correlational. One example of this is the link between personality traits and happiness. The researchers claim that this link is not fully understood, especially when considering the relationship between extroversion and happiness. It may well be that being an extrovert means you are more sociable, spend more time with friends and therefore build a bigger social support network which then contributes to happiness. On the other hand, it may be that being happy produces more outgoing behaviour in an individual and a tendency to seek the company of others. Either way, the lack of clarity in the relationship does not allow for any prediction to be made about the effect of extroversion on happiness. The positive relationship between faith and subjective well-being is also unclear and requires further exploration to discover what it is about being actively involved in religion that contributes to happiness. Myers and Diener offer a range of possible explanations, including the social support of a congregation, the explanation of life as purposeful and meaningful, and belief in an afterlife which makes death seem less terrifying.

Ethical issues

Socially sensitive research – cultural bias

The studies reviewed by Myers and Diener included research from both individualist and collectivist countries. In general, collectivist cultures reported lower ratings of subjective well-being than individualist cultures. Care needs to be taken in the interpretation of these findings as it would be easy to conclude that people living in collectivist cultures are somehow less happy. This conclusion may be inaccurate and misleading, as it does not account for cultural norms (i.e. the norm for expressing positive emotion with regards to personal happiness in individualist cultures does not translate in a collectivist culture where personal happiness is not as important as group well-being). The research serves to highlight the importance of considering the findings of research within their cultural context rather than drawing inaccurate conclusions.

Individualist and collectivist cultures – differences

In individualist cultures people value independence – the ability to be assertive and stand on your own two feet. The focus is on individual success, and being dependent on others is seen as a sign of weakness. In contrast, in collectivist cultures, the focus is on working as a group. Traits such as selflessness, helpfulness and generosity are valued and community and family come first. Examples of collectivist cultures include China, Japan and India, whereas Western European countries and the United States are individualist.

Social implications

The widely held beliefs that teenagers experience high levels of stress and adults often go through a 'midlife crisis' were not supported by the research findings. Teenagers may experience more extreme moods within a shorter space of time compared with adults but their general sense of well-being averaged over time is no different. Adults in their forties showed little evidence of 'empty nest syndrome' when their offspring left home, and were more likely to welcome the release from the stress of raising a child. In general, the review of the research showed that people do experience times of crisis but that this can happen at any age.

Myers and Diener looked at research comparing happiness in wealthy and poorer countries. They found that having basic necessities, such as food, shelter and safety, were central to a feeling of well-being, but once these were achieved increased wealth did not lead to marked differences in happiness. A better predictor of subjective well-being was a person's satisfaction with how much they earned, with only a slight positive correlation between higher earnings and increased satisfaction with life. It seems that wealth does not necessarily bring happiness. Moreover, neither does disadvantage inevitably bring unhappiness. Members of a society who are discriminated against due to their race or whose quality of life is affected by a disability or lack of wealth would be presumed to be unhappy and dissatisfied with their life. Research conducted in 1993 by Diener et al. shows that African-Americans are almost as happy as European-Americans and report lower levels of depression. Despite discrimination, Crocker and Major (1989) noted that people in disadvantaged groups maintained self-esteem by comparing themselves within their groups and focusing on their strengths.

Comparison
of Approaches

Table 1.28 summarises key points about each of the approaches to allow you to begin to make comparisons between them.

The first column in the table offers a range of issues for comparison to support you in looking for similarities and differences between each approach.

To write effective answers to questions you will need to be able to expand on the information given in the table, especially if you have to compare therapies.

Page references are included in the table to help you find out more about each point of comparison.

Example: Comparing and contrasting the psychodynamic and positive approaches

Suggested points of comparison:

Point 1: Similarity in that both consider external and internal influences affecting behaviour. External: parental influence on development during childhood is important for optimum development (positive); normal adult personality (psychodynamic). Internal: ability to achieve level of happiness could be biologically determined (positive); unconscious forces influence conscious behaviour (psychodynamic).

Point 2: Difference in the way abnormal behaviour is interpreted: psychodynamic approach assumes abnormal behaviour is driven by unconscious forces; positive approach rejects the disease model and focuses on what makes people mentally healthy.

Point 3: Difference in methods of investigation: objective measures of happiness can be made under laboratory conditions (positive); case studies are used to carry out in-depth investigations of individuals (psychodynamic) which tend to be more subjective.

Example: Comparing and contrasting behaviourist (systematic desensitisation) and biological therapies (drugs)

Suggested points of comparison:

Point 1: Differences in assumptions about the causes of abnormal behaviour: physical causes such as imbalance of neurotransmitters requires physical intervention (drugs); abnormal behaviour is learned so can be unlearned (systematic desensitisation).

Point 2: Differences in effectiveness of the treatments: systematic desensitisation is effective for the treatment of anxiety disorders such as phobia but not for psychotic disorders such as schizophrenia; drugs can be used to treat the symptoms of schizophrenia.

Point 3: Similarity in that both treatments raise ethical issues in relation to protection from harm: clients should feel protected throughout both therapies; patients should be weaned off drugs gradually; clients should be taught to relax at each stage of a fear hierarchy to prevent any negative effects from treatment.

ISSUE	BIOLOGICAL	PSYCHODYNAMIC
Interpretation of behaviour	Internal influences: Behaviour stems from physical elements that make up the human body (page 11). Behaviour evolves due to environmental demands and is passed on genetically (page 10).	Internal and external influences: Behaviour is affected by the influences of the unconscious mind (pages 24–25). Childhood experiences affect the development of the personality (page 26).
Assumption about abnormal behaviour	Behaviour is affected by damage to brain structures, genetic abnormalities and changes in levels of neurochemicals (pages 11–12).	A lack of balance between the three parts of the personality, unresolved conflicts during psychosexual development or repression of traumatic experiences into the unconscious can affect conscious behaviour (pages 25–27).
Therapeutic techniques	Drugs and psychosurgery are used to target physical abnormalities and rebalance neurotransmitters (pages 15–16 or 17–18).	Dream analysis or group analysis psychotherapy can help to unlock the unconscious (pages 30–32 or 33–35).
Methods of investigation	Biology of a person can be studied scientifically in a laboratory using PET scans (page 19).	Case studies of individuals or small groups of people such as a family. Questionnaires to gather data on personality traits (page 27).
Assumption about relationship formation	Evolution determines that we find certain characteristics attractive in the opposite sex because they increase the chances of reproductive success (page 14).	The attachments formed during early experience with caregivers influence quality of relationships throughout childhood and into adulthood (pages 28–29).

Table 1.28: Comparison of the five approaches: biological, psychodynamic, behaviourist, cognitive and positive.

BEHAVIOURIST	COGNITIVE	POSITIVE
External influences:	Internal influences:	Internal and external influences:
We are born as a 'blank slate' and all behaviour is learned through a stimulus–response process (pages 40–42).	Behaviour is a result of internal processes of the mind (page 52).	Given the right conditions an individual can grow to their full potential.
Behaviour is learned through processes of classical and operant conditioning (pages 40–41).	The mind processes information like a computer and develops schemas that help us to interpret our world (page 53).	Focuses on what makes people happy, taking control of life to change behaviour and living in the moment. (pages 68–69).
Abnormal behaviour occurs when learning is maladaptive (i.e. a person has associated fear with an object or situation) (pages 48–49).	Faulty cognition, negative thought processes and errors in logic lead to abnormal behaviour.	The focus is on what makes a person mentally healthy rather than on explaining why abnormal behaviour occurs. Rejects the idea of psychology as based on a 'disease model' (page 68).
Undesirable behaviour has been associated with a positive response (pages 48–49).	An individual's perception of themselves is distorted (page 57).	
Aversion therapy and systematic desensitisation to 'unlearn' the association (pages 44–45 and 46–47).	CBT or REBT can be used to change negative, irrational thoughts into positive, rational thoughts that then lead to changes in behaviour (pages 57–59 or 60–62).	Focus on the present moment through the use of mindfulness, meditation and self-regulation (pages 72–75).
		Identify and meet life goals through Quality of Life Therapy (pages 76–78).
Laboratory experiments are carried out, particularly with non-human animals (pages 41–42).	Laboratory experiments are carried out mainly on humans.	Self-report techniques including questionnaires and interviews.
	Processes such as memory can be studied scientifically using brain scans (page 54).	Laboratory experiments and scientific measures of brain responses in happy people (page 70).
Pets and owners form relationships through conditioning. Each finds something positively reinforcing in the other (page 43).	Humans use internal mental processes to consider the positives and negatives in current and potential relationships (page 55).	Living a 'good life' means living a happier life, creating a need for fulfilling relationships that lead to happiness (page 71).

Unit 2 Section A
Contemporary Debates

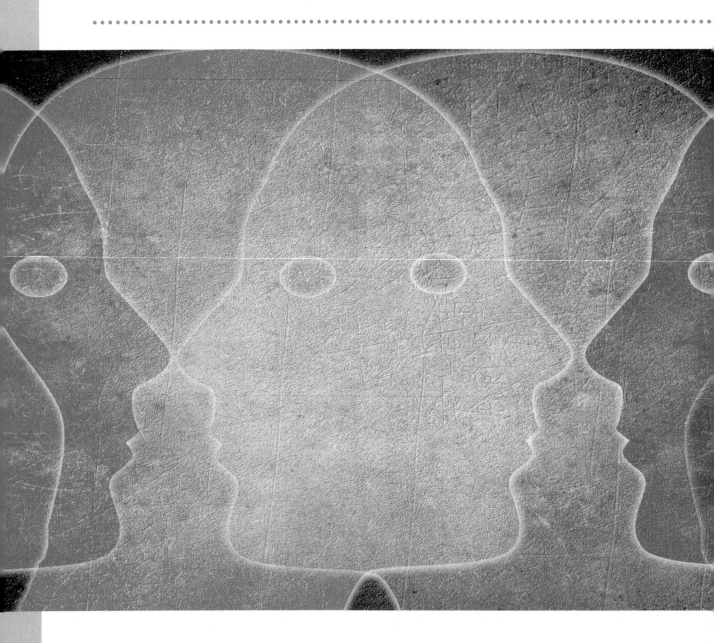

WHAT YOU NEED TO KNOW ☑

The biological approach: the ethics
of neuroscience ☐

The core of the debate ☐

Psychological studies and theories ☐

Both sides of the debate:

    Ethical implications ☐

    Economic implications ☐

    Social implications ☐

The psychodynamic approach: the
mother as primary caregiver of an infant ☐

The core of the debate ☐

Psychological studies and theories ☐

Both sides of the debate:

    Ethical implications ☐

    Economic implications ☐

    Social implications ☐

The behaviourist approach: using
conditioning techniques to control
the behaviour of children ☐

The core of the debate ☐

Psychological studies and theories ☐

Both sides of the debate:

    Ethical implications ☐

    Economic implications ☐

    Social implications ☐

The cognitive approach: the reliability
of eyewitness testimony ☐

The core of the debate ☐

Psychological studies and theories ☐

Both sides of the debate:

    Ethical implications ☐

    Economic implications ☐

    Social implications ☐

The positive approach: the relevance of
positive psychology in today's society ☐

The core of the debate ☐

Psychological studies and theories ☐

Both sides of the debate:

    Ethical implications ☐

    Economic implications ☐

    Social implications ☐

THE BIOLOGICAL APPROACH: THE ETHICS OF NEUROSCIENCE

This debate focuses on neuroscience and the potential gains made from the study of the brain and nervous system compared with the ethical costs and implications. The social and economic implications are also considered.

Neuroscience provides us with a scientific and objective way of studying human behaviour by researching what happens in the brain and nervous system when particular actions are performed. Brain scanning techniques such as functional magnetic resonance imaging (fMRI) and positron emission tomography (PET) can be used to measure activity in areas of the living and active brain, such as when we are speaking, thinking and experiencing particular emotions. Not only do we learn about the normal functioning of the brain, but such techniques can also help us to see what has gone wrong in the brain when there is abnormal behaviour.

THE DEBATE: POSITIVE APPLICATIONS OF NEUROSCIENCE

Applications to criminal behaviour

Raine et al. (1997) demonstrated what had 'gone wrong' in the brains of murderers. He found different levels of activity in the brains of people who had committed murder compared with a control group. The murderers had different levels of activity in the amygdala and corpus callosum both of which are involved in the experience of emotion and in the prefrontal cortex which is responsible for reasoning.

Ways of improving brain cell function have been explored by Raine et al. (2003) who

> ### What is neuroscience?
>
> Neuroscientists study the function of the brain and nervous system to understand the impact of these structures on our behaviour and cognition (the way that we think). They are interested in the normal functioning of these structures as well as what happens when the system goes wrong and an individual develops a psychiatric or neurological disorder.

designed an enrichment programme for a group of 83 children in Mauritius focused on nutrition, education and physical activity. This was based on research showing evidence of

Social implications

The research by Raine et al. demonstrates the effect that early intervention could have on the prevention of crime.

brain dysfunction in criminals, and support from animal research demonstrating that enrichment benefits brain structure and function. The children began the programme at the age of 3 for two years. They were educated in a special facility with a child to teacher ratio of 5:1. Each day consisted of two-and-a-half hours of organised physical activity, lessons to promote verbal, visuo-spatial and memory skills and a nutritious lunch of milk, fruit juice, chicken or fish and salad. Their progress was compared with a control group of 355 children who followed the normal community education programme with a ratio of 30:1 and basic lunch of bread or rice. Assessment at the age of 17 showed that the enrichment group scored lower than the control group for antisocial behaviour and lower for criminal behaviour at the age of 23.

Neuromarketing

Neuroscience has also made a significant impact in the world of marketing and advertising. Neuromarketing involves the use of technology such as fMRI scans to measure what consumers are really feeling when they look at products by observing the blood flow to various areas of the brain. This allows companies to understand why preferences are shown for one product over another. A study conducted by McClure et al. (2004) looked at what was happening in the brains of participants when they tasted Coca-Cola and Pepsi. The participants were first asked to taste the two colas in unmarked cups so they didn't know which was which.

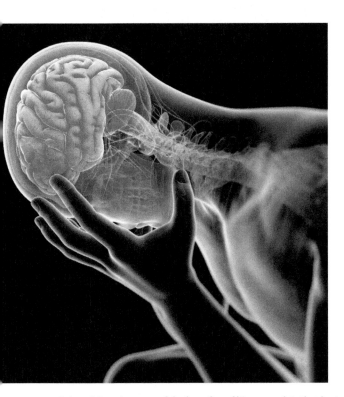

Raine claims that one of the benefits of his research is that brain deficiencies could be measured in childhood many years before an individual develops psychopathic behaviour or commits a crime.

You might have a preference for a particular product, but do you really know why you have a preference?

In this 'blind' condition preferences were equal for each cola. In a second 'semi-blind' condition the participants were presented with the same cola in two different cups but only one of them was labelled as Coca-Cola or Pepsi. In the Pepsi condition equal preference was shown for the drink when it was labelled as when it was unlabelled. With the Coca-Cola condition, however, the participants showed a much greater preference for the labelled cola over the unlabelled cola. Using fMRI scans the researchers were able to see that when drinking the labelled cola certain areas of the brain involving memory and emotion were activated. The participants were not just basing their preferences for cola on the taste, their choice was affected by what they had learned about Coca-Cola and their associations with the brand and, what is more, the effect of this learning had impacted upon the response of their brain.

Social implications

Shoppers may find in the future that they are subject to marketing strategies that are more personalised and culturally targeted, further reducing customer effort and time in making choices.

Research such as this allows marketers and advertisers a better understanding of what products are desired, and consumers can be targeted by more effective and accurate marketing. Television advertisements can be tested before they are aired so that advertising agencies can find out what is appealing to the consumer. Technology could be developed to assess consumers on entering a shop and their data combined with previously stored information about their purchases and preferences. This could then generate the display of a personalised message on a product of potential interest.

Alzheimer's disease

Another positive effect of neuroscience can be seen through research that has been conducted into diseases such as Alzheimer's. There is a growing urgency to learn more about Alzheimer's which is becoming more common with the increased average lifespan of the population. In 2004 the World Wide Alzheimer's Disease Neuroimaging Initiative (WW-ADNI) was set up to help predict and monitor the onset of the disease by sharing data across the world. The use of PET and MRI scans means large amounts of data can be gathered quickly and easily, and WW-ADNI ensures that this data is available to the scientific community at no cost. This ethical initiative involves Alzheimer's sufferers around the world and follows their progress to gain a universal picture of the disease in the hope that the information can be used to treat, prevent and slow down the progress of this debilitating condition.

Economic implication

Billions of pounds could be saved on care if progress of Alzheimer's can be delayed.

THE OTHER SIDE OF THE DEBATE: ETHICAL IMPLICATIONS OF NEUROSCIENCE

Raine's research raises questions about the accountability of murderers for their actions. The assumption drawn from the research was that the murderers were not guilty by reason of insanity (NGRI) because the differences in their brains were the cause of their actions. The murderers were unable to experience the emotions and reason the implications associated with harming another person. This challenges the notion of free will and the idea that as human beings we are responsible for our actions and should be held accountable for the decisions we make. If tendencies towards antisocial behaviour can be detected early on then there is a possibility that measures to prevent later criminal activity could be taken before any crime occurs. Neuroscientists understand the plasticity (flexibility) of the brain so interventions could be put in place with children who are at high risk of becoming psychopathic and committing a crime. However, the form that the intervention takes raises ethical issues; we cannot perform brain surgery on children who have not yet committed a crime! What can be put in place are social interventions (i.e. environmental experiences that change the brain). A study by Fontaine et al. (2011) supports the idea of early detection of psychopathic tendencies. They discovered a link between being callous and unemotional (CU) in childhood and developing psychopathic tendencies later in life. Fontaine et al. claim that ethical interventions such as behaviour modification techniques are more effective than punishment in changing the behaviour of CU children and could prevent possible psychopathic tendencies in adulthood.

Advances in neuromarketing suggest that in the future the consumer's brain could be continually monitored whilst shopping to register the impact the personalised messages were having. This kind of marketing could have many ethical issues, such as the rights to the data from brain scans, who would own them and whether data could be sold to other companies. Also, when scanning brains further information about an individual could be revealed (e.g. health issues) and consideration would need to be given to what would happen to this information.

Many positive benefits can be seen from the research conducted into Alzheimer's disease in terms of slowing progression and possible prevention. However, in order to make progress research has to be conducted on people who already have Alzheimer's. Due to the nature of the disease in relation to the effects it has in

causing confusion and memory loss, there may be issues in gaining fully informed consent from people who are already sufferers.

CONCLUDING THE DEBATE

Advances in neuroscience are challenging beliefs about criminal behaviour and consumerism, and leading to developments in preventing crime and marketing products that bring with them both benefits and ethical drawbacks. The use of neuroscientific techniques is furthering research into previously unexplained diseases with the hope of improving treatments but brings with it ethical issues regarding the testing of participants and whether the costs to a relative few serve to benefit many people in the future.

FINDINGS	POSITIVE BENEFITS	ETHICAL ISSUES
Criminal behaviour: Study: Raine et al. (1997) Brains of murderers are different in regions related to experience of emotion and reasoning.	Brain deficiencies could be identified in childhood and early interventions put in place to prevent the development of criminal behaviour.	Challenges the notion of free will as murderers may not be held accountable for their actions. Interventions can be non-invasive and ethical (e.g. behaviour modification techniques, enrichment programmes).
Neuromarketing: Study: McClure et al. (2004) There are changes in brain activity of consumers when they are choosing a product (e.g. Coca-Cola), activating areas of the brain involved in emotion and memory.	Benefits to marketers and advertisers in understanding which products are desired. Benefits consumers through accurately targeted marketing, thereby speeding up decision making and the shopping process.	Research is currently conducted on consenting volunteers to inform decisions on the marketing of products. Future use of brain scanning in shops could raise issues of personal intrusion and the use/ownership of the data gathered.
Alzheimer's disease: Study: WW-ADNI Identification of areas of the brain affected by Alzheimer's.	Global sharing of research data to enhance knowledge of the causes and progression of Alzheimer's with a view to improving treatment.	Research is conducted on people who already have Alzheimer's, so there may be issues in gaining fully informed consent from people with memory and confusion issues.

The ethics of neuroscience: debate summary.

THE PSYCHODYNAMIC APPROACH: THE MOTHER AS PRIMARY CAREGIVER OF AN INFANT

This debate focuses on whether the mother should be the primary caregiver of an infant in order to provide the best basis for healthy development, or whether other options for care could be just as good for the development of the child. The ethical, economic and social implications of the debate are considered.

THE DEBATE: THE MOTHER AS PRIMARY CAREGIVER

According to Freud, early childhood experiences are considered crucial in the formation of the adult personality. In the oral stage of development, feeding the appropriate amount at the correct time is important if the child is to develop trust in the carer and go on to form healthy relationships later in life. From a psychodynamic point of view, the formation of the infant–caregiver relationship is important for healthy psychological development. John Bowlby stresses the importance of the special bond between mother and infant (monotropy) in providing the infant with an 'internal working model' for relationships for the rest of its life. He also stresses the importance of forming and maintaining the bond for the first three years of an infant's life. If this bond is broken or never forms there will be serious consequences for the

> ### What is a primary caregiver?
>
> A primary caregiver is a person who is the main carer for an individual who is unable to take care of themselves. In relation to an infant, the person taking on this role is often assumed to be the biological mother or mother substitute. The primary caregiver is the person an infant will turn to when feeling insecure or threatened, such as by the presence of a stranger.

development of the child. If, on the other hand, there is consistent, responsive and sensitive care and a secure bond develops, there will be long-term benefits for the child; they will be more socially competent and independent throughout life. The level of self-sufficiency and independence displayed by an individual in adulthood is largely due to the sense of security created by the

As gestation occurs within the woman she can always be 100% certain that the offspring is hers. A man does not have the same certainty.

caregiver as a child develops. The emphasis is therefore on the mother to make the infant feel supported and safe and able to rely on her.

Bowlby proposed the maternal deprivation hypothesis which emphasised the negative outcomes in terms of development for a child if the attachment bond with the mother is broken in the early years. The classic 'Forty-four juvenile thieves' research supports his hypothesis by demonstrating that a high proportion of children in the study deemed to be affectionless psychopaths had experienced prolonged or even permanent separation from their mothers during the first five years of life.

Evolutionary psychologists argue that human behaviour has evolved through adaptation to

Social, ethical and economic implications

The publication of Bowlby's maternal deprivation hypothesis in 1951 was timely for the British government. During the Second World War many women had been employed in jobs traditionally held by men. After the war the government faced the problem of men returning from military service and needing to find work. Bowlby's research was used to publicise the need for women to stay at home with their children, thus leaving more jobs for men and preventing the need for government investment in childcare and nurseries.

environmental demands in order to promote the survival of the species. Buss (1995) suggests that variations in behaviour between men and women in relation to childcare are due to differences in the challenges faced by men and women when it comes to reproduction. As with all mammals, fertilisation occurs in the human female who then carries the baby for nine months until birth. The mother's investment in the baby is high compared with that of the male who, up until the point of birth, has only invested the time taken to conceive. When a woman spends time nurturing the child to whom she has given birth, she always knows that she is raising her own offspring and that the child is carrying 50% of her genes. This offers a strong incentive to be the primary caregiver. Given that mothers also produce food for the baby that is necessary for survival, it seems logical that she should be the one to take control of the child-rearing for at least the early years of the infant's life and that the role of the father is secondary to that of the mother.

Research studies support the idea that nurturing from the mother is more critical to the survival of offspring than the presence of the father (Campbell, 2002). Studies conducted with tribes living as hunter-gatherers show traditional divisions of labour between men and women, with men providing the food and women remaining in the camp to raise the children. Amongst the Ache of Paraguay, children are five times more likely to die if their mother dies compared with three times more likely if the father dies. If the mother dies before the child reaches the age of 1, the mortality rate of the infant is 100% (Hill and Hurtado, 1996). These statistics suggest that in traditional tribes the infant needs to be nurtured by the mother in order to stand the best chance of survival.

Social and economic implications

In Western cultures the presumption that the mother is the best person to nurture and raise a child has had a major impact on social policy and legislation. A mother automatically has parental responsibility for her child from birth. A father only has parental responsibility if he is married to the mother. If a couple are unmarried and have a child but then separate, the mother is automatically given custody of the child and has the right to look after the child wherever and however she sees fit. Since 2002 an unmarried father does have the right to joint custody but only if he is registered as the child's father at the time of birth or if both parents have signed a parental responsibility agreement. Regardless of whether the father has contact with his child or not, he still has a financial responsibility and the mother can claim money from him in order to support the child.

In traditional hunter-gatherer tribes, care from the mother is essential if the child is to survive beyond infancy.

THE OTHER SIDE OF THE DEBATE: THE PRIMARY CAREGIVER DOES NOT NEED TO BE THE MOTHER

John Bowlby stated that the primary caregiver does not have to be the mother, but said that continuous quality care from one individual was what was important. The deprivation hypothesis uses the word 'maternal' because mothers have traditionally been the primary caregivers. It could be argued that Bowlby reflected what he saw happening in society when naming his hypothesis rather than dictating how it should be. Schaffer and Emerson's findings (1964) directly challenged Bowlby's idea of monotropy. They found that infants became attached to other people soon after the primary attachment was formed at about 7 months. By 18 months a little over 10% of infants were attached to one person and a third had five or more attachments. Whilst fathers were rarely the primary attachment figure they were joint first attachment figure for nearly a third of infants. Research presented from the findings of tribes living as hunter-gatherers suggests that in order to stand the best chance of survival the infant should be cared for by the mother. However, it could also be argued from an evolutionary point of view that it is not necessarily a good thing that the mother is the sole caregiver. Total reliance on one person means that should anything happen to that person the infant may not survive. Having multiple caregivers maximises the chance of the child surviving. Hrdy (1999) has argued that 'humankind would not have survived if solely mothers had been infants' caretakers'.

There are many examples of caregiving environments that deviate from the Western middle class ideal of exclusive maternal responsibility for childcare. For example, Meehan (2005) described the cooperative child-rearing practices in the Aka people living in the

Cassidy (1999) suggests that infants form what she calls an 'attachment hierarchy'. Whilst most infants place the mother at the top of the hierarchy, not all infants do; some favour the father or other provider of care, such as a grandparent, as a primary attachment figure. In the absence of the preferred attachment figure, any other attachment figure is acceptable for comfort when the infant is distressed or anxious.

Congo Basin rainforest. Aka infants interact with approximately 20 caregivers on a daily basis, and whilst the mother is the primary caregiver for the first year, her role significantly reduces after this period. Keller (2003) argues that monotropy is the exception rather than the norm and only promotes survival in societies where resources are plentiful and a mother can afford to focus all her attention on her infant without worrying about where to find water or food. In support of this, Weisner and Gallimore (1977) found that across all human cultures, mothers are the exclusive caregiver of their infants in only 3% of societies and the main caregiver in only 60%.

Social implication

The Children and Families Act (2014) reflects more recent research into parenting by challenging former residency and contact orders that have existed previously for children of divorced and separated parents. The assumption of the Act is that from the outset both parents will be involved in childcare. Each parent is viewed as equally capable of both nurturing the child and providing financial support.

The Children and Families Act (2014) aims to alter the perception that one parent is more important than the other, and works on the principle that both parents should be involved in the lives of their children.

CONCLUDING THE DEBATE

It is clear from both sides of the debate that early nurturing is critical for the survival of the infant, but what remains open to discussion is whether this is best provided by the mother as primary caregiver, a parent of either sex or a group. What is best for an infant may depend upon their particular circumstances, socioeconomic status and culture.

MOTHER SHOULD BE THE PRIMARY CAREGIVER	MOTHER DOES NOT HAVE TO BE PRIMARY CAREGIVER
Bowlby: Monotropy with mother provides healthy physical, social and emotional development for infant in short and long term.	**Bowlby:** Continuous care from one person is most important for development of the infant but this does not have to be provided by the mother.
Bowlby (1951): Maternal deprivation hypothesis stresses negative outcomes for development if no bond is formed or the bond is broken in the early years.	**Cassidy (1999):** Attachment hierarchy states that in the absence of the preferred attachment figure other attachment figures can give comfort.
Study support: Bowlby (1944) 'Forty-four juvenile thieves' found affectionless psychopaths were more likely to have experienced separation from mother in critical period.	**Study support:** Schaffer and Emerson (1964) found infants form multiple attachments.
Evolution: High investment in infant prior to birth and being provider of food source after birth means the mother is best placed to be the primary caregiver to improve the infant's chances of survival.	**Evolution:** Monotropy is not the norm and only promotes survival in affluent societies. In most cultures the survival of an infant is enhanced by multiple caregivers.
Study support: Hill and Hurtado (1996) studied the Ache tribe and found 100% infant mortality within first year of life if mother died.	**Study support:** Meehan (2005) showed that amongst the Aka people infants have approximately 20 caregivers.
Ethical implications: Supports gender inequality and traditional divisions of labour between men and women.	**Ethical implications:** Supports gender equality with both parents having equal involvement in childcare.
Economic implications: Encouraging women to stay at home was timely for a post-war government which wanted returning servicemen to get back to work and to prevent investment in childcare.	**Economic implications:** Supports a mother's right to work to support herself and contribute to the economy.
Social implications: Effects on social policy and legislation supporting the rights of the mother to have custody of the children in most cases decided by family courts.	**Social implications:** Informs recent legislation challenging traditional perceptions that one parent is more important than the other.

Mother as primary caregiver: debate summary.

THE BEHAVIOURAL APPROACH: USING CONDITIONING TECHNIQUES TO CONTROL THE BEHAVIOUR OF CHILDREN

This debate focuses on the use of conditioning techniques to control children's behaviour. **Evidence for the effectiveness of these techniques and the possible negative effects and outcomes are discussed. The ethical, economic and social implications of the debate are considered.**

THE DEBATE: THE POSITIVES OF USING CONDITIONING TECHNIQUES TO CONTROL THE BEHAVIOUR OF CHILDREN

According to the behavioural approach, children and adults influence each other's behaviour in a reciprocal way: the behaviour of the adult will determine the future actions of the child, and the actions of the child in turn influence the subsequent behaviours of the adult. For example, if a child has a tantrum when they can't have what they want, a parent may respond by giving them attention for their behaviour and then giving in to their demands. The child has then learned the relationship between having a tantrum (stimulus) and getting what they want (response) so they are

> ### What is meant by conditioning?
>
> Conditioning is a process of changing behaviour through association or reward and reinforcement. Undesirable behaviour may be punished to prevent reoccurrence and positive behaviour may be rewarded to encourage repetition.

likely to repeat tantrum behaviour in the future. Behaviourists recognise this stimulus–response relationship as the way in which children develop their behaviour and personality. Everything they are is learned from their environment. Any behaviour that is rewarded or reinforced is more likely to be repeated.

The child having a tantrum is less likely to repeat the behaviour if the parent ignores them. By not giving the child attention the parent is not rewarding or reinforcing the behaviour. There is no response to the tantrum so it is less likely to be used by the child in the future. This is an example of negative reinforcement as it is based on the withdrawal of attention to prevent the repetition of unwanted behaviour.

Strategies for changing behaviour through the use of conditioning are known as behaviour modification techniques and include the use of reinforcement such as praise, behaviour shaping and punishment.

Understanding how behaviour in children can be conditioned has had positive implications for parenting. As well as helping parents to understand how behaviour is learned, the principles of conditioning can also be applied to the unlearning of negative behaviour and the repetition of desirable behaviour. For example, parents may use praise or a token economy system, which may take the form of a sticker chart where the child receives a sticker when they have done something good. On reaching a certain number of stickers the child would then be rewarded with a treat such as

Social and ethical implications

Behaviour modification approaches have helped parents to see that punishment does not work in changing 'naughty' behaviour. Parenting skills courses and self-help websites focus on teaching parents to reduce the use of punishment to control their child's behaviour and instead to use more ethical ways, which should then have long-term benefits for the child when they become parents themselves.

an outing or watching their favourite television programme. The stickers on their own are not worth anything but an accumulation of a certain number leads to something that is desirable to the child, so they provide an incentive to continue with the positive behaviour in order to achieve the final reward.

One of the advantages for parents in using behaviour modification techniques is that they provide measurable outcomes. Prior to the application of a technique the parent can observe baseline behaviour and set a goal for change. The observation stage involves creating a record of what the child is doing – for example, how many acts of antisocial behaviour a child demonstrates over the course of a day. This baseline information means that as the parent progresses with a programme of behaviour modification, they will know if things are changing and will be able to measure improvement.

Behaviour modification techniques can be used in the classroom to help teachers change the disruptive or unproductive behaviour of pupils. Teachers frequently praise their students to reinforce academic achievement and

Economic implication

The cost of setting up a token economy system could be a limitation to the effectiveness of the technique since the final reward needs to be something that is valued by the children. Schools could consider low cost alternatives such as free time or privileges such as prefect positions. Filcheck et al. (2004) found the cost of training pre-school teachers to be effective token economy practitioners was minimal – it only took four hours for the teachers to become competent.

positive behaviour or use punishment to put a stop to actions that could have unpleasant consequences. The token economy has also been used extensively across the age range from pre-school to university undergraduates.

Filcheck et al. (2004) researched the use of a class-wide token economy on a group of pre-school children described as 'out of control'. The token economy consisted of a level system made up of faces. The children were promoted up the levels from sad, grey faces to neutral faces to happy, sunny faces when they demonstrated desired behaviour. The children who gained promotion to the happy faces level took part in special activities outside of the regular class schedule and were given stickers. The researchers found that the implementation of this system led to a decrease in inappropriate behaviour across the group.

The main goal of all behaviour modification techniques is to bring about a permanent change in behaviour by applying a temporary reinforcement system. It is thought that by using extrinsic rewards like stickers, praise and privileges, a child will learn intrinsic rewards such as feeling good about themselves and having a sense of achievement on completion of tasks. This in turn should then lead to a permanent change in behaviour.

THE OTHER SIDE OF THE DEBATE: THE NEGATIVES OF USING CONDITIONING TECHNIQUES TO CONTROL THE BEHAVIOUR OF CHILDREN

The use of a token economy in classroom settings has been much debated, and research suggests that it is on the decline in schools (Doll et al., 2013). One of the reasons why a token economy may be difficult to employ effectively is due to the fact that the system on its own is not enough to elicit behaviour change. Success depends upon the ability of the teacher to communicate clearly with the pupil to set goals and expectations in relation to the desired behaviour change. Alberto and Troutman (2012) found that token economy systems do not work without clear communication between teacher and pupil. This criticism could also be applied to any behaviour modification technique. Reinforcement can only work if pupils know exactly what is expected of them and outcomes are very specific.

Another criticism levelled at behaviour modification techniques is that children may

Modern day and progressive behaviour management methods emphasise the power a teacher has over the child and are thought to be far less effective in bringing about long-term change than traditional methods based on punishment.

Ethical implications

Token economy systems in classrooms could be open to corruption. The teacher may not be consistent or fair in giving out the tokens. Removal of privileges could be considered as an alternative but this puts the teacher in a position of power that could be seen as unethical.

become dependent upon the system and only demonstrate desired behaviour when in receipt of tokens or praise. Children may only show change in the behaviour that is reinforced, and this could lead to a decrease in behaviour that is not reinforced. The hope, therefore, that the system leads to intrinsic reward and motivation may not apply to all children and the degree of effectiveness will differ across individuals. Approaches that criticise behaviour modification offer explanations as to why this might be. The positive approach suggests that whether punishment or external rewards are used to control children's behaviour, the end product is the same: pupil compliance with rules and adult authority. Brophy (1996) calls this 'grudging compliance'. Instead, the positive approach emphasises the need for self-discipline, with children choosing to inhibit inappropriate behaviour and display positive behaviour because they have internalised the beliefs and values of the adults around them. This will then generate a willing compliance because the children believe in what is right and wrong rather than just learning that some behaviours are punished and others are rewarded. Intrinsic motivation will only happen in an environment where children feel as though they are competent in what they are doing, have a sense of belonging and feel in control. The positive approach therefore advocates this approach in education as a way of preventing problem behaviour rather than placing emphasis on correcting negative actions.

CONCLUDING THE DEBATE

An understanding of the use of conditioning techniques to control the behaviour of children has had a major impact on both teachers and parents. The emphasis in controlling behaviour has moved away from punitive approaches to positive reinforcement, and from preventing unwanted behaviour to reinforcing desirable behaviour. However, the success of conditioning techniques may depend upon the quality of the communication between the adult and the child and the encouragement of self-discipline in order for reward to become intrinsic and bring about permanent behaviour change.

Positive implications for teachers in managing pupil behaviour using praise and token economy techniques

Study support: Filcheck et al. (2004) found a class-wide token economy improved behaviour in an 'out of control' pre-school class.

Ethical implication: Teacher is in a position of power and token economy systems can be corrupt and unfair.

Economic implication: Setting up token economy systems can be costly to schools, although training is relatively quick and therefore cheap.

Positive implications for parenting with measurable outcomes

Study support: Steeves et al. (2012) found behaviour modification techniques successful in reducing number of hours children spent on screen-based activities.

Social and ethical implication: Parenting skills courses advocate less emphasis on punishment of unwanted behaviour and more emphasis on rewarding desirable behaviour.

Behaviour management techniques can lead to a permanent change in behaviour when extrinsic rewards become intrinsic.

However ... Not for all children – for some it may just lead to 'grudging compliance'. Self-discipline is needed for intrinsic reward to happen.

Using conditioning techniques to control the behaviour of children: debate summary.

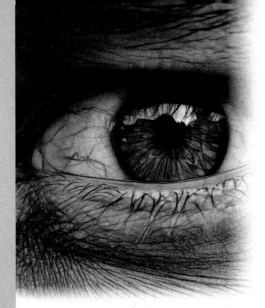

THE COGNITIVE APPROACH: THE RELIABILITY OF EYEWITNESS TESTIMONY

This debate examines some of the theory and research behind *eyewitness testimony* and considers factors that impact upon its *reliability*. The ethical, economic and social implications of the research into the reliability of eyewitness testimony are considered.

THE DEBATE: THE RELIABILITY OF EYEWITNESS TESTIMONY

When an eyewitness to a crime or an accident is describing their experience they are relying on memory to give an accurate account of everything they have observed. However, human memory is an active process and memories are constantly changing. Stored material is reorganised and transformed because of new knowledge and the passage of time. Cognitive psychologists agree that most memories are, at least in part, reconstructions of events rather than exact versions. When recalling a crime the eyewitness will retrieve some accurate fragments of information and then fill in the gaps using pre-existing expectations or schemas about crimes. Loftus and Palmer believe that the memories of eyewitnesses are prone to all sorts of influences and distortions and in many circumstances are very unreliable (see page 63).

Ceci and Friedman (2000) argued that memories of younger children (aged from 3

What is eyewitness testimony?

Eyewitness testimony is a legal term used to describe the first-hand account of an event described by someone present at the scene. The event observed by the witness may be an accident or crime. The account of the eyewitness is given under oath in a court of law and may include details of the scene of the accident or crime and descriptions of the people involved.

to 5 years) were weaker and faded faster than those of older children, which makes them more uncertain about the details of an event. This then leaves them more suggestible and their memories more vulnerable to reconstruction. Research has shown that children are more likely to be influenced by leading questions than adults. Children also have a tendency to be more compliant and answer questions in a way that they feel will please the interviewer.

This is particularly apparent when children are interviewed by an authority figure such as a police officer. They want to be helpful and tell the adult what they think they want to know rather than what actually happened.

It is important to consider the effect of anxiety on memory given that witnessing a crime or accident is highly likely to be a traumatic event. Research suggests that events that cause a great deal of trauma can be stored but remain beyond conscious recall. This means that the memory of the event is forgotten and the witness has no recollection of the crime or accident. The individual may never remember the event, or recall could be triggered spontaneously months, years or even decades later. Loftus and Ketcham (1994) describe the case of George Franklin, whose daughter claimed that she had seen her father murder her best friend when she was 8 years old – she

Ethical implications

More effective and ethical ways of interviewing children have been developed as a result of research. Advice for law students published by the European Association of Psychology and Law (2011) recommends that when interviewing a child, the interviewer should focus first on putting the child at their ease and building a rapport with them. The interviewer should also be aware of the complexity of the language used and gauge the level of understanding of the child before the interview begins.

had apparently repressed this memory for 20 years. Even though there was no other credible evidence the jury at Franklin's trial found him guilty. He served five years in prison before the decision was overturned on appeal.

It is not only adults who are called to give testimony in court; evidence from children may also be used. Research seems to suggest that children are more susceptible than adults to leading questions, and the younger the child, the more likely they are to be influenced.

THE OTHER SIDE OF THE DEBATE: WHEN IS EYEWITNESS TESTIMONY RELIABLE?

Research stressing the unreliability of eyewitnesses has often been conducted under laboratory conditions. Loftus, for example, used videos of a car crash to study the effects of leading questions on eyewitness testimony. Watching a film of a car crash is not the same as witnessing one in real life. In reality, participants would experience the shock and emotional impact of the car crash as well as the distractions and different smells and noises, all of which would add to the experience and the type of memory formed of the event. When considering the reliability of eyewitness testimony, it is therefore important to carry out naturalistic studies which examine the testimonies of witnesses to real-life events. One such study was conducted by Yuille and Cutshall (1986) who interviewed 13 witnesses to a real-life shooting incident during which someone was killed. Despite the anxiety which the experience must have caused, the accuracy of their recall was not significantly affected. The witnesses appeared to be resistant to leading questions. They stuck to their original versions of the event and there was little evidence of memory reconstruction. Contrary to findings in laboratory settings, it would seem that the testimonies of witnesses to

Economic implication

According to Geiselman et al. (1986), the cognitive interview can be used with relatively little training and still produce effective results. They found 35% more accurate information could be obtained after giving only brief guidance on how to use the technique, which indicates that it is an efficient and cost-effective way to gather information from eyewitnesses.

Social implication

Research into eyewitness testimony has led to changes in social policy designed to improve the criminal justice system. As early as the 1970s, psychological research highlighting the unreliability of eyewitnesses led to concerns being raised about the use of eyewitness testimony in convictions. In 1976 the Devlin Report was published in the UK which recommended that no individual should be convicted on the basis of eyewitness testimony alone. However, this recommendation was never made law because it could have led to criminals who are guilty not going to trial.

real-life crimes, even those involving a high level of trauma, are reliable.

Research highlighting the unreliability of eyewitness testimony has helped us to identify conditions under which testimonies are more reliable. The sooner a witness can be interviewed after the event, using techniques that avoid leading questions, the better the chance of the recall being accurate. Interviewing a witness as soon as possible helps to avoid reconstruction of the information as there will be less time for it to be rehearsed. Using questioning techniques that avoid leading questions will also prevent suggestibility and improve the accuracy of the information. These findings have led to the development of the cognitive interview technique. According to Waddington and Bull (2007), the cognitive interview is an approach to interviewing that seeks to encourage thorough and accurate recall of specific events. It does this by recognising that memories are context dependent, meaning that recall will be more effective if cues present at the time the memory was stored are reinstated. An interviewer might do this by asking the witness to think back to before, during and after the event to consider how they were feeling and what they were doing. The cognitive interview technique also acknowledges that information in memory is organised such that it can be accessed in a number of different ways. As well as recalling the event in chronological order, a witness may be asked to imagine the crime happening in reverse. They may also be asked to give an account of what happened from the point of view of another person present at the time, such as the victim. Accessing the memory using these different methods aims to increase the amount of accurate detail in an eyewitness account.

Despite the number of studies that highlight concerns about the reliability of eyewitnesses, juries continue to be persuaded by evidence from eyewitness accounts – sometimes to the detriment of the person on trial. Vollen and Eggers (2005) estimate that suspects in the United States are wrongly convicted 0.5% of the time. This amounts to approximately 11,000 innocent people currently in prison for crimes they have not committed.

The Cardiff Innocence Project

In 2005 Cardiff University Law School established an Innocence Project through which law students could work alongside solicitors and barristers representing convicted prisoners who were trying to prove their innocence. Cases are selected for review based on the maintenance by the prisoner that they are innocent and where there are issues of concern regarding the evidence for their conviction. Several of the cases cited by the Cardiff Innocence Project raise concerns about the reliability of evidence from eyewitnesses that were used in the conviction of the prisoner. One such case is that

of 'Mr F' whose conviction for murder was largely based upon the evidence of eyewitnesses but who highlights discrepancies between some witnesses who say he did commit the crime and others who could not positively identify him as the murderer. One witness has since withdrawn his statement claiming that he was put under pressure to identify 'Mr F' as the murderer during interview. In July 2010 six cases were submitted to the Criminal Cases Review Commission for re-assessment of the evidence used to convict potentially innocent men, some of whom had already served lengthy prison terms.

CONCLUDING THE DEBATE

In weighing up the evidence into the reliability of eyewitness testimony, it is easy to come to the conclusion that eyewitnesses are generally unreliable. However, extensive research conducted over the last 40 years highlights the complexity of this argument and the number of variables that impact upon the accuracy of the testimonies.

Individual variables, such as the age of the witness or amount of anxiety experienced at the time, and external factors, such as the length of time before interview and the style of questioning, can all impact on the accuracy of recall. What is most important about this research is that it can be used to inform practice and suggest steps that can be taken to improve the justice system and help prevent wrongful convictions.

Ethical issue: Juries are persuaded by eyewitness testimony even though this may lead to wrongful conviction. Study support: Miller (2000) quotes cases of wrongful conviction based on eyewitness reports.

Research shows eyewitness testimony is unreliable when ...

... memory is reconstructed using schemas and stereotypes.
Study support: Loftus and Palmer (1974).
Social implication: Devlin Report (1976).

... anxiety causes repression and forgetting.
Study support: Loftus and Ketcham (1994).

... eyewitnesses are children.
Study support: Ceci and Friedman (2000).

... eyewitnesses are asked leading questions.
Study support: Loftus and Palmer (1974).

HOWEVER, eyewitness testimony can be reliable when ...

... research is conducted in a natural environment.
Study support: Yuille and Cutshall (1986).

... appropriate questioning techniques are used on adults and children.
Study support: Fisher et al. (1990).
Economic implication: Cognitive interview can be cost-effective.
Ethical implication: Guidelines for interviewing children.

The reliability of eyewitness testimony: debate summary.

THE POSITIVE APPROACH: THE RELEVANCE OF POSITIVE PSYCHOLOGY IN TODAY'S SOCIETY

This debate considers how positive psychology may be relevant in helping people to discover what makes them happy and the benefits that this may have for society today. **The drawbacks of this approach are also considered along with the ethical, social and economic implications.**

THE DEBATE: THE RELEVANCE OF POSITIVE PSYCHOLOGY IN TODAY'S SOCIETY

Before considering the relevance of positive psychology to today's society, it is important to think about what we mean by 'today's society' and how society may have changed over the last 50 years. A 2013 survey commissioned by a well-known health food chain, Holland & Barrett, asked 4,000 people a range of questions about their lives. The *Good Life Report* found some significant differences between the responses of participants in their twenties compared with those in their fifties. When asked about life 30 years ago, the participants in their fifties quoted less stress and more 'living for the moment' than those currently in their twenties. Today's 20-somethings are more concerned about work, finances and personal appearance and face a more significant range of

> ### What is a positive psychology?
>
> Positive psychology is the scientific study of what makes people happy. The field of positive psychology was founded in 1999 by Martin Seligman, who believes that psychology should aim to understand what makes people happier and develop ways to help them achieve a more positive state of mind. The positive approach also extends beyond the individual to look at the strengths and virtues that enable groups and communities to thrive and flourish.

threats to their happiness and contentment than their parents did at their age, even though over the past 50 years incomes have risen and quality of life has improved. Martin Seligman and Ed Diener claim that despite the fact that income has climbed steadily in the United States over the past five decades, 'life satisfaction has been virtually flat. Since World War II there has been a dramatic divergence between real income and life satisfaction … and a similar pattern can be seen in the data from other nations such as Japan' (Diener and Seligman, 2004). Society may be wealthier today but, clearly, wealth does not bring happiness.

The approach taken by psychology since the 1950s has focused on what Seligman terms 'a disease model' – finding out what has gone wrong when people are suffering from mental illness and learning how to put it right. It may well be that this approach is now outmoded since, as research suggests, we are not making progress in understanding what makes people happy and therefore are focusing on prevention rather than cure. Positive psychology may be more relevant to today's society because it aims to find out what makes people happy in order that their life satisfaction may improve. The *Good Life Report* also found that young people today are taking more care of their health and fitness, eating healthier diets and smoking less than 50 years ago. These findings indicate that the current generation are listening to scientific research evidence regarding appropriate changes

Happy people have close friendships.

to enhance their physical well-being, so the time may be right for them to consider what research is telling them about how to improve their mental well-being for greater life satisfaction.

According to positive psychology, happy people have close friendships. Importance is placed on the quality not the quantity of the friendships. Diener and Seligman (2002) conducted a study with university students and found that the students who were rated highest for happiness and lowest for signs of depression reported strong ties to friends and family and a commitment to spending time with them. The importance of these findings to today's society can be seen when we consider the extent to which people conduct their relationships via social media. In 2013 Facebook published statistics on users in the UK. Figures showed that over a third of the population in Britain were accessing the site on a daily basis. The average number of friends for British Facebook users in 2013 was 130. This indicates a quantity rather than a quality approach to friendship which research suggests does not necessarily mean that a person is not experiencing loneliness. In order to experience quality in friendships, topics of conversation need to move beyond the trivial; in other words, sharing information about music, clothes and politics will not develop a quality friendship. Instead, conversation between friends should include self-disclosure and a sharing of personal information in order to reduce feelings of loneliness and hence vulnerability to depression.

As well as relevant applications to our emotional well-being and mental health, aspects of positive psychology can also be applied to the management and improvement of our physical health. As the population ages, instances of cancer diagnosis are on the increase. According to Cancer Research UK, overall cancer incidence rates have increased by more than a third since the mid-1970s – by 23% in males and 43% in females. Advances in cancer treatment mean that 50% of people diagnosed with cancer survive for 10 years or more. One area of study within the field of positive psychology is optimism and the effect that being optimistic can have on physical health. Optimists tend to view problems as opportunities and maintain an upbeat approach to life, which research has shown can boost the immune system and protect against chronic disease. There have been a variety of studies that have looked at the impact of optimism on people undergoing cancer treatment. One such study by Schou et al. (2005) looked at a group of breast cancer sufferers. They found that those deemed to have a 'fighting spirit', which is a trait found in optimists, were predicted a markedly better quality of life one year after receiving surgery for their cancer. Optimism appears to be an important factor in a patient's perception of their health and ability to fight disease.

According to Seligman, one of the key factors in happiness is to be able to experience things in the moment and savour what is happening to you currently. The practice of mindfulness complements this key idea from

Social implication

The positive approach looks beyond individual well-being to consider what makes groups and communities thrive and flourish. According to the positive approach, one feature of a thriving community is having institutions that support individuals in being better citizens. This idea is advocated by the current Conservative government, who in their aim to create a 'big society' announced in April 2015 that all companies with more than 250 employees will be required to offer three days of volunteering each year. The government claims that volunteering improves the morale and well-being of employees, which in turn will have a positive effect on the productivity of the company.

Economic implication

NHS funding could be spent on teaching patients to be more optimistic and promoting well-being to save money on expensive drug treatments and long-term care.

positive psychology as the aim is to encourage practitioners to spend more time focusing on what is happening in the 'here and now' and less time worrying about the future or evaluating the past. Research has shown positive effects from mindfulness on the immune system and improvement in the density of grey matter in areas of the brain associated with memory, empathy and stress. Most research into the effects of mindfulness has been conducted on adults but more recent research has looked at the effects that mindfulness-based training can have on adolescents. This comes at a time when questions are being raised about the role that schools play in student well-being and whether enough is being done in schools to support emotional development. Huppert and Johnson (2010) considered the effects of mindfulness training on a group of 173 14–15-year-old boys. The boys were split into a control group and a mindfulness group. Training took place during RE lessons over a four week period, with the mindfulness group also encouraged to practise outside of lessons. Both groups completed a questionnaire before and at the end of the training covering their resilience, personality and well-being. The researchers found that the more mindfulness practice the students completed, the greater their sense of well-being.

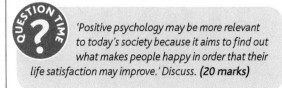

'Positive psychology may be more relevant to today's society because it aims to find out what makes people happy in order that their life satisfaction may improve.' Discuss. **(20 marks)**

THE OTHER SIDE OF THE DEBATE: ISSUES WITH THE RELEVANCE OF POSITIVE PSYCHOLOGY IN TODAY'S SOCIETY

Although there seems to be a growing body of evidence into the beneficial applications of positive psychology to today's society, much of the research needs to be approached with caution. Many studies that measure happiness and well-being are based upon self-report techniques and therefore the reliability of the data may be questionable. Questionnaires and interviews can be subjective with the participants offering personal views and opinions rather than objective scientific evidence. Surveys such as the *Good Life Report* gathered retrospective data from people in their fifties about their perceptions about themselves and their lives when they were in their twenties. This required the participants to accurately recall their feelings and attitudes from 30 years ago. Over time memory can become distorted; participants may have filled in gaps in their memory or looked back on their youth with the benefit of hindsight, perhaps painting a more positive picture than the reality of the time.

There is also evidence to suggest that positive thinking may not always lead to greater happiness and well-being. The majority of studies conducted into optimism support the conclusion that positive thinking leads to a better immune system and an improved ability to cope with adversity and longevity.

> ### Ethical implication
>
> Segerstrom and Sephton (2010) show that not everybody benefits from being more optimistic, so teaching optimism to adults should be approached with caution as we could end up doing more harm than good.

But this may not be the case for everybody. In a study conducted on first year law students, Segerstrom and Sephton (2010) found that for some individuals higher levels of optimism were associated with worse immune system functioning. A volunteer sample of 124 students were followed over a period of six months. At five different points in time they were questioned about how positive they felt about law school. Each time they were questioned they were also injected with a substance to test their immunity. Two days after each injection they returned to have the injection site measured, with a larger bump indicating a stronger immune system response. Generally the researchers found that higher levels of optimism generated larger bumps and therefore a stronger immune response. However, there was a group of students who did not show this pattern. One factor that this group of law students had in common was that they had stayed near to home. The researchers speculated that these students, whilst under pressure to do well in their studies, were also trying to juggle spending quality time with their family and friends. Given the tendency for optimists to persevere when

faced with obstacles, it may well be that these students were exhausting their resources, with negative consequences for their immune system functioning. On the face of it, the students were demonstrating positive approaches to their life, with close friendships, family relationships and meaningful study. However, in trying to do too much they were potentially affecting their health in damaging ways.

Studies carried out into the nurturing of optimism indicate that children whose personalities are still malleable can be trained into more positive ways of thinking using large-scale interventions through school. However, any research into training adults has only looked at the use of cognitive-behavioural therapy in a one-to-one counselling setting with individuals who are in need of intervention to change their negative thought patterns to help them deal with anxiety or depression. It is yet to be shown through any large-scale interventions whether adults can learn to be more optimistic, and more research into the effects of positive thinking needs to be conducted.

CONCLUDING THE DEBATE

Research into positive psychology seems to hold a lot of promise and there is an increasing number of studies exploring the benefits of the positive approach. More scientific and objective research still needs to be done, however, to convince people of its merits and make the approach mainstream.

THE RELEVANCE OF POSITIVE PSYCHOLOGY IN TODAY'S SOCIETY	ISSUES WITH THE RELEVANCE OF POSITIVE PSYCHOLOGY IN TODAY'S SOCIETY
Research shows people are making changes to improve physical health, so why not mental health?	Self-report techniques used to measure happiness are questionable in terms of reliability.
Positive psychology advocates the importance of small groups of close friends. **Study:** Diener and Seligman (2002) showed that happy university students had strong ties to family and friends.	Emphasis on friendships in today's society is on quantity not quality. **Study:** Facebook (2013) showed an average number of friends in the UK of 130.
Can help manage and improve physical health. **Study:** Schou et al. (2005) found that optimistic cancer sufferers were better able to fight the disease.	Positive thinking does not always lead to greater happiness and well-being. **Study:** Segerstrom and Sephton (2010) revealed that some optimistic law students had lower immune functioning.
Mindfulness practice in schools is an ethical way to improve well-being in children. **Study:** Huppert and Johnson (2010) proved that boys trained in mindfulness showed greater well-being.	The effects of nurturing optimism in adults is yet to be studied through a large-scale intervention so there is no convincing evidence that it will have any impact.

Positive psychology: debate summary.

Unit 2 Section B
Principles of Research

DECIDING ON A RESEARCH QUESTION

AIM OF THE RESEARCH

Psychologists get their ideas for research either from direct observation of behaviour or indirectly through background knowledge and theory. The best attribute you can have as a psychologist is a real desire to seek out the origins and motives of human behaviour. This can be anything from wondering why a teacher or a friend gets cross or reacts the way they do, to wondering why some people have the 'right' attitude and some do not, to wondering what the best way is to remember things for an exam. All of these things really interest psychologists.

Once you've decided on an idea for your research the next step is to generate research *aims*. An aim is a reasonably precise idea about the area of the study and what the study is going to try to achieve. It is important that the aim clearly describes the purpose of the proposed research. This will make it apparent early on whether or not the proposed research is realistic. An aim doesn't need to be very detailed, it just needs to say very clearly what the focus of your research is all about.

An example of an aim might be: 'To describe the effects of stress on memory'.

RESEARCH HYPOTHESIS

Once you've got your research aim you need to change it into a statement, which psychologists refer to as a *hypothesis*. A hypothesis predicts what we expect to find. The idea is to try to find evidence in your research that will 'support your hypothesis'. For example, take the research aim we used earlier:

> **Aim:** To describe the effects of stress on memory.
>
> **Hypothesis:** The more stressed we are, the worse our memory will be.

The hypothesis takes the aim and makes a testable statement of it. Our hypothesis predicts that we will find that people who are stressed will have a worse memory than people who are not stressed. The next step is to design a study that investigates this problem. The results of the study will either support the hypothesis or not. If the results do not support the hypothesis it will have to be rejected.

ALTERNATIVE (EXPERIMENTAL) HYPOTHESIS

There are different types of hypothesis and which one is used depends on the type of research being conducted. If the research is experimental then the hypothesis is an *experimental hypothesis*, often written as H_1. In other types of (non-experimental) research – for example, making observations of behaviour or collecting opinions – the hypothesis is called an *alternative hypothesis* and we use the symbol H_A to represent it.

DIRECTIONAL AND NON-DIRECTIONAL HYPOTHESES

Look at the two hypotheses below. The types of research to which they relate are very similar indeed. In fact, the tasks you might decide to investigate these two hypotheses with could be identical but the predictions they make are different:

Hypothesis 1: Stress makes your memory worse.

Hypothesis 2: Stress affects your memory.

Hypothesis 1 predicts a *direction* for the results. Stress makes your memory *worse*. This type of hypothesis is called *directional*. You may also see it described as a 'one-tailed hypothesis'. Hypothesis 2 does *not* predict a direction. It simply states that stress will *affect* your memory. It does not predict an increase or a decrease in memory capability; either may happen. For this reason, hypotheses of this type are known as *non-directional* and may also be described as 'two-tailed hypotheses'. So, which is best, directional or non-directional? The answer is: it depends. Table 3.1 outlines when to use one or the other.

NULL HYPOTHESES

To make the hypothesis complete we also write something called a *null hypothesis*. A null hypothesis (written as H_0) predicts that what we find in our research just happened by chance. It looks like the opposite of the main hypothesis. This is how we form a null hypothesis from the hypothesis we described earlier:

Null hypothesis: Our memory will not become worse as stress increases; any change is due to chance.

The null hypothesis must be included in research because psychologists can never rule out the possibility that the results gained in any investigation are due to chance. What this really means is that if the hypothesis is not supported by the research findings then the null hypothesis is probably true. Put another way, if you have to reject the hypothesis then you have to *accept the null hypothesis*. And if you accept the hypothesis because your research supports it then you must *reject the null hypothesis*.

DIRECTIONAL HYPOTHESIS	NON-DIRECTIONAL HYPOTHESIS
A directional hypothesis is generally used when a researcher is confident enough to make a clear prediction. Previous research may suggest that something quite specific will be found, or a quick study the researcher may have tried out (often called a pilot study) may have suggested a direction for the findings. If a directional hypothesis is selected then the results have to be even more convincing for it to be supported. In other words, a directional hypothesis is easier to reject than a non-directional one. However, the benefit of choosing a directional hypothesis is that, because they are harder to support, research that *does* support a directional hypothesis is more convincing.	A non-directional hypothesis might be chosen if the researcher is not terribly clear what will happen – perhaps when carrying out a study which has not been done before. For example, eating chocolate may keep people awake or it may help them go to sleep. There is no previous research to indicate what might happen one way or another, so choose a non-directional hypothesis. That way, if *anything* happens to your dependent variable (the amount we sleep) then you are bound to find it. In your next piece of research, once you have an idea of what might happen, your hypothesis may change to a directional prediction.

Table 3.1: When to choose to use a directional or non-directional hypothesis.

INDEPENDENT AND DEPENDENT VARIABLES

A hypothesis will also express the things of interest to a researcher in the piece of research – the *variables*. They are called variables because they change or 'vary' during the research. Some variables are changed by the researcher and some change *because* the researcher has changed something. This is much easier to explain with an example: for instance, the time it takes to get to the shops.

You decide to investigate whether taking different routes to the shops makes your journey time faster or slower. The variable under your control is 'the route you take'. The 'time taken to get to the shops' varies because of the route you have taken. You (the researcher) have changed the route. The time taken to get to your destination changed *because* you have changed the route. In research, a variable is a something which is observed (i.e. looked at and watched), measured (e.g. length, temperature, time), controlled or manipulated. The hypothesis should tell you how these variables will relate to each other in your research.

The variable that is manipulated by the researcher in order to see what effect this has is called the *independent variable* (IV). The variable being measured is the *dependent variable* (DV – it 'depends' on the IV). In our earlier example of stress and memory, our IV is stress level and the DV is memory. The IV can be confusing as it is sometimes naturally occurring, such as age or gender (you may want to see the difference between males and females but the researcher can't manipulate this, i.e. choose whether to make you a male or a female!). A good hypothesis must always clearly include the IV and the DV.

CO-VARIABLES

Co-variable is a term used in correlational research. They differ from IVs and DVs because they both vary and they are both measured – they are never set or manipulated by the researcher. Co-variables tend to have a relationship which is either positive or negative. (Further information on co-variables is given later in this chapter under the section on correlations on page 131.)

OPERATIONALISING VARIABLES

Operationalising variables means making them measurable. This is extremely important because we need to be clear about what it is we are studying and measuring in research and communicate this to others. Take the following hypothesis as an example:

> The greater the stress, the poorer the recall on verbal memory tests.

The dependent variable is *operationalised* – it is the recall on verbal memory tests. An alternative non-operationalised version might be, 'Stress affects memory', but this is too brief and does not communicate clearly enough what is being measured.

EXTRANEOUS VARIABLES

An *extraneous variable* is something that we haven't controlled for that could affect our DV. This is an issue because if it affects the results, and we haven't accounted for it, our results may not be reliable. There are many examples of extraneous variables – temperature, noise, time of day and weather are just a few. All of these can have an impact on our results if we do not try to control them. For example, if we are doing an experiment into how noise (IV) affects our memory (DV) and we put our participants in different environments to each other, it may actually be something else (e.g. temperature) which affects the DV rather than our IV. This can become a real problem in research.

CONFOUNDING VARIABLES

A *confounding variable* is one that interferes ('confounds') with the relationship between the two variables we want to study and can lead us to an incorrect conclusion. When we are looking at the relationship between two variables there is always the chance that there is a third variable affecting our two variables of which we are unaware. This third variable may actually be responsible for our results. Extraneous variables run the risk of becoming confounding variables if they are not controlled. In the example above, if the extraneous variable of temperature did have an effect on our DV it would become a confounding variable. Confounding variables can occur when a researcher does not or cannot randomly assign participants to groups. Some types of individual differences, such as ability or intelligence, can be confounding variables as they cannot be controlled by the researcher.

ENVIRONMENTAL FACTORS (EXTERNAL)	INDIVIDUAL DIFFERENCES (INTERNAL)
Temperature	Ability (e.g. memory)
Time of day	Intelligence
Weather	Age
Noise	Gender
Location	Personality

Table 3.2: Some extraneous variables which, if not controlled in psychological research, could become confounding variables.

Operationalising

Operationalise the following hypotheses, i.e. rewrite them in a way that makes it clear how the dependent variable will be measured.

(i) Rehearsal improves duration in short-term memory.

(ii) Stress increases the likelihood of illness.

(iii) Day care is related to aggression in children.

(iv) Leading questions influence recall.

(v) CBT is a more effective therapy than psychoanalysis.

(vi) Mnemonics improve memory.

Hypotheses

First (a) decide whether the following hypotheses are directional or non-directional and then (b) identify the IV and the DV.

(i) The more stress a person experiences the more risk there is of a heart attack.

(ii) Stressful unemployment can influence the functioning of the immune system.

(iii) The risk of coronary heart disease is affected by feelings of hostility.

(iv) Stress management techniques improve the functioning of the immune system.

(v) Stressful life events increase the likelihood of illness.

(vi) The more complex the question the more likely a child is to give an inaccurate response.

METHODOLOGIES

EXPERIMENTS

A good experiment is one in which:

- Findings are *generalisable* – the findings can be said to apply to others outside the sample.
- Procedures are *replicable* – the experiment can be reliably repeated.
- Findings are *reliable* – if the experiment was done again, the results would be the same or similar.

A great deal of psychological information has been acquired from experimental research – it is the prime method of enquiry in science. The experiment is a method of studying human behaviour that, through careful measurement, looks to uncover causal relationships – that is, factors which cause us to act in certain ways. It differs from other methods in that it involves the deliberate control and manipulation of variables. There are a number of types of experiment.

Laboratory Experiments

Laboratory experiments, or lab experiments for short, are those carried out in carefully controlled conditions. The logic of the experiment is straightforward – if we have two groups of people all doing the same task, except that one of the groups does *one* thing differently, then any change in behaviour between the two groups must be due to that one thing. For instance, if we had two identical tennis balls and dropped them using an identical dropping machine from an identical height, except that one ball was wet and one was dry, then if they hit the floor at different times, the thing that is different (the wetness) must have been the thing that caused the change in the speed at which they fell to the ground. See – simple!

The thing that is different between the two groups is the *variable that we manipulate*, and this is called the independent variable (IV). In the example we've just used, the independent variable is whether the tennis balls were wet or dry.

What we *measure or record* as a change in behaviour is another variable, and we call this the dependent variable (DV) (because it 'depends' on the independent variable). In our tennis ball dropping example, the dependent variable is 'how long it takes for the balls to fall to the ground'.

An experiment is perhaps best understood through looking in detail at an example. You may have noticed that some people like to revise for exams with music playing in the background or on their personal music systems. Some of these individuals are absolutely certain that they must have music otherwise they can't concentrate. Other people prefer to work in silence and are equally as sure that silence is best. As a psychologist you might ask yourself which is best – music or silence? We can't just take a person's preference as evidence of what is best, since we know from other areas of life that what people prefer is not necessarily what is best for them! We need an *objective assessment* of which is best, and this is where an experiment is most useful. We need an aim for the study. An aim is a general idea of what the study is going to try to achieve. For example:

The aim: To investigate whether or not having some kind of noise in the background (e.g. music) affects the retention (memory) of something we have learned.

We also need to formulate a hypothesis. The results of our experiment will either provide support for our hypothesis or they will lead us to the conclusion that our hypothesis must be rejected. A straightforward hypothesis might be something like: 'music affects memory'. This is not quite enough however. Whilst the hypothesis includes our independent variable and our dependent variable (the IV is the music, the DV is a measure of memory), it is not clear how the variables are being measured or operationalised. An example of a better hypothesis might be:

The hypothesis: Music played during learning will influence recall performance on a memory task.

There are a couple of ways we could conduct this experiment. One way would involve having two *conditions*, each containing a selection of *participants* chosen at *random* to be in one condition or another. Remembering the logic of the experiment, all participants would have the same experience except for one thing – the independent variable. The group in which the IV appears would be called the *experimental condition*. The other group would be in the

EXPERIMENTAL CONDITION (MUSIC)	CONTROL CONDITION (SILENCE)
P1	P6
P2	P7
P3	P8
P4	P9
P5	P10

Table 3.3: In research, P stands for 'participant'. In our experiment, participants 1 to 5 are in the experimental condition and participants 6 to 10 are in the control condition.

control condition, against which the scores of the experimental condition would be compared.

Assuming that all participants have the same experience except for one thing (the IV), any difference in task performance between the two conditions could only be due to the one thing that varies – whether or not participants listen to music whilst performing the memory task.

We now need to give our participants some kind of task to do. Since we are interested in memory, an important component of learning (which is what revision is all about!), we could give the participants something from a French textbook to learn, perhaps a list of verbs. How well the participants learn these verbs in a given time would be what we measure (this is the dependent variable).

Alas, things in psychology are rarely as simple as this. In order to ensure that the experience of participants differs *only* in terms of the IV, we must go to great lengths to ensure that we control the experience of the participants. For example, we have given a French verb learning task. Have we controlled for the linguistic ability of participants? Are some of the participants studying French? Indeed, are all the participants students? How do you know whether any of them are French? Have you checked?

What we need is a task which asks the same of all participants. In psychology, *word lists* are often used in these circumstances, consisting of words of equal length and matched for how often those words appear in the language in which you are testing; in most cases the language will be English. Music cannot be used either because of things like personal taste, types of music, etc. – one person's music is another person's noise! So, something a bit like music could be used. A steady rhythmic noise played through headphones perhaps.

These factors (things that you need to control for, such as ability in French or music preference) are the extraneous variables, things that *could* influence the dependent variable. For every factor that we fail to control, we become less confident that the IV alone has produced the DV (i.e. whether it was the presence of 'music' that really influenced their ability). There are many different sources of extraneous variables and as many as possible need to be eliminated during the design process. Extraneous variables that we fail to control become confounding variables (i.e. variables that *have* influenced the dependent variable).

In our experiment, then, we cannot use music as an IV and we cannot use verb learning as a DV. Our variables need to be somehow 'neutral'. This means that our hypothesis is going to need a slight change: 'Rhythmic noise played during learning will have a significant effect on subsequent recall'. The IV is whether or not participants have noise played to them whilst learning, and the DV is performance on a word learning task.

Another essential control in an experiment is the use of *standardised procedures*. We must describe every step of our experimental procedure beforehand so that each participant gets an identical experience. This will also include *standardised instructions*, ensuring that participants have the same information. This standardisation will also reduce *researcher bias*, in that it ensures that we do not unconsciously influence the outcome by varying the procedure.

Hopefully it is becoming clear that whilst the logic of an experiment is straightforward enough, it takes a great deal of careful thought and planning to design a good experiment. We've got a bit more to do yet. Even though the question is a simple one, we must be really sure that the way we carry out the experiment will provide us with a useful answer.

	STRENGTHS	LIMITATIONS
Laboratory experiments	1. Provided we have carefully controlled our variables, laboratory experiments allow us to establish cause and effect relationships. That is, we can say with some confidence that the IV has caused the change in the DV. 2. If appropriate care is taken in the design and conduct of the experiment, and if it has been reported accurately, then it allows replication. That is, it allows other researchers to repeat the experiment and achieve the same findings. A piece of research will have far more credibility if it is replicated and supported. 3. Variables are much easier to control in the laboratory than outside in a natural setting. This gives them a real advantage over the natural experiment as we can be more certain that the results have not been confounded by an unknown factor.	1. The more you control behaviour, the less natural it becomes. Because experiments exert a high degree of control it has been argued that they encourage behaviours that are artificial and not like real life (i.e. laboratory experiments lack ecological validity). 2. Not everything of interest to psychologists can be investigated using laboratory experimentation. For example, a psychologist might be interested in understanding the effect that a certain drug has on the developing infant brain but it would not be ethical or practical to do a controlled experiment on this. Therefore, the laboratory experiment's usefulness is limited. 3. Biases introduced through such things as sampling, demand characteristics and experimenter expectancy are almost impossible to eliminate completely. This can reduce confidence in our findings.

Table 3.4: The strengths and limitations of laboratory experiments.

The field experiment

A *field experiment* involves the *direct manipulation of variables* but, unlike the laboratory experiment, this is done in what the participant sees as a natural environment. This makes the study much more *realistic* and it is thus argued that it produces data which are more valid. There is still an independent variable which is being manipulated and a dependent variable which is being measured. A field experiment would be used when it is considered crucial that a natural setting is used to investigate a behaviour. Social psychology makes particular use of the field experiment as it is interested in the behaviour of people in social settings. Since participants should not be aware that they are taking part in a controlled study their behaviour should be natural. An unrealistic example always helps. Imagine you wanted to investigate how people behaved in a typical 'good Samaritan' sort of environment. You might have the idea that people are more 'Samaritan-like' in the north of the country than in the south. You could find yourself a suitable old lady, load her up with shopping, drop her off at the side of a busy road and wait nearby to see what happens. Your IV is whether you are in the north or the south. Your DV is how many people stop to help the elderly, shopping-laden lady across the road.

	STRENGTHS	LIMITATIONS
Field experiments	1. Because of the natural setting there is a greater likelihood of gathering data on natural behaviour, so there is much greater ecological validity with field than with laboratory experiments.	1. There is less control of extraneous variables in a field experiment than there is in a laboratory experiment, meaning that the results are more likely to be confounded in some way.
	2. Because participants are supposed to be unaware that they are taking part in research, demand characteristics should be reduced or even eliminated since the participants will not be able to work out the aim of the study and change their behaviour accordingly.	2. Field experiments are generally more time consuming and expensive to design and run than laboratory experiments.

Table 3.5: The strengths and limitations of field experiments.

Quasi-experiments

A quasi-experiment is one in which the researcher *cannot manipulate the independent variable*. Quasi-experiments lack the control of true experiments. Whilst experimental procedures are used, participants cannot be randomly allocated to conditions. For example, if an experiment is looking at sex difference in an ability such as creativity, then participants are allocated to each condition according to their sex – males in one condition, females in the other. In the example of sex differences in creativity, the IV is the sex difference and it cannot be manipulated by the experimenter. This means that some studies which, on the face of it, appear to be laboratory studies are in fact quasi-experiments.

	STRENGTHS	LIMITATION
Quasi-experiments	1. Quasi-experiments allow us to carry out studies into human behaviour in a setting that can be controlled. This means that we can still control extraneous variables to a certain extent (e.g. noise). 2. Quasi-experiments can be replicated as they are still conducted under controlled conditions. This means that it is easy to repeat the experiment to check for reliability in the findings.	As the experimenter cannot manipulate the IV, it is much harder to say that it is the cause of the effect on the DV.

Table 3.6: The strengths and limitations of quasi-experiments.

Natural experiments

In a *natural experiment*, rather than direct manipulation, the researcher takes advantage of a naturally occurring change in an independent variable. There is no experimental control other than that which is already in place, and there are likely to be extraneous variables that remain uncontrolled. Because participants are not randomly allocated, natural experiments are really quasi-experiments. However, the behaviour is natural and the situations in which natural experiments arise are usually those in which a laboratory or field experiment would not be possible. For example, you might find that a local hospital has changed its policy on post-operative care for patients undergoing brain surgery. This might provide an opportunity to compare the effects of this post-operative care with another hospital that has a more traditional approach. The IV would be the kind of post-operative care offered – this has naturally arisen and is not something that you can possibly have manipulated.

	STRENGTHS	LIMITATIONS
Natural experiments	1. Because it is a natural setting, with naturally occurring changes in the IV, there is high ecological validity. 2. Because the researcher has little or no involvement with the situation, and participants would be unaware that they are taking part in a study, there are likely to be few demand characteristics and reduced researcher bias. 3. This type of method allows the researcher to study real-life problems.	1. Opportunities for natural experiments are rare and when they do occur they are generally unique events. This means that they are virtually impossible to replicate in order to check the reliability and validity of the findings. 2. The possibilities for confounding variables are endless. Experiments may be influenced by any number of things beyond the control of the researcher.

Table 3.7: The strengths and limitations of natural experiments.

OBSERVATIONS

All research begins with some form of observation. Sometimes observations are used as a way of gathering data in other methods, such as experiments. These are *controlled observations*. However, observation is a research method in its own right. The *observational method* involves systematically watching and recording what people say and do. The behaviours observed are those that naturally occur, meaning that no attempt is made to manipulate variables. The main benefit of this is that we get natural behaviour, unchanged by the presence of a researcher or research environment.

Participant and non-participant observation

In observational studies a researcher can be either directly involved in the situation being observed (this is called *participant observation*) or can remain outside and unobserved (called *non-participant observation*).

Both these methods are sometimes called *naturalistic observation*, since people are being observed in their own environment and will thus behave naturally. For example, a participant observation might be one where the experimenter is part of a sports team in which he or she is investigating group behaviour. A non-participant observation might be one where the experimenter is observing the play of children from behind a one-way mirror.

Whilst on the face of it observation seems to be a natural and straightforward method of gathering data, in reality it requires a great deal of thought and careful planning. Imagine that you are interested in whether or not boys are more physically aggressive than girls. You would need an environment in which to observe the natural behaviour of boys and girls, and an obvious choice for this would be the playground of a primary school. Aggression is quite a complex concept and in order to be able

Observation: method or technique?

An important distinction has to be made here between observation as a *research method* and observation as a data-gathering *technique*. For example, in an experiment on aggression a researcher might show one group of participants a film containing only an aggressive scene. The researcher would then observe the participants some time later to see if their behaviour had changed as a result of the film, compared to the group of participants who did not see it. This is a laboratory experiment but the dependent variable is derived through controlled observation.

Controlled observation is also often used in field experiments where the environment has been deliberately altered by the researcher in some way. Observations are then made of any changes in behaviour as a result of the manipulation. For example, drivers and other road users behave in a certain way when there are road signs present. Observing the behaviour and carefully noting down important aspects, such as overtaking frequency and speed, might be of importance to your study. Now, remove all the road signs and repeat the observation. You would look to see if the alteration of the environment had altered the behaviour of the road users.

Observation as a research method is different in that it involves no manipulation of variables by the researcher – the behaviour being observed is free and natural. The control here is in the selection of the situation being observed and the manner in which observations are recorded.

to observe it we must operationalise it. In this case, we are interested in physical aggression, so shouts and other verbal behaviours (which would otherwise be interpreted as aggressive) do not count. We must also use a psychological definition of aggression to clarify our observations further – other people should understand what is meant by aggression in this research. So, if we defined aggression as 'any behaviour in which one person is motivated to cause harm which the victim is motivated to avoid', this would exclude from our observation behaviours such as play fighting and other sorts of rough-and-tumble play.

Choosing the variables to operationalise creates *behavioural categories*. It is these that appear on the checklist that the researcher uses when observing the behaviour. A method of recording observations will need to be devised, probably involving producing an observational checklist. For instance, you might list all the types of physical aggression you are likely to see on a school playground and create a checklist (see Table 3.8). This might be all you need if the only thing of interest is the frequency of types of aggression. The observational checklist would be more complex if you were also interested in the direction and duration of aggression. The key point is that behavioural categories should be self-evident and require no further interpretation by the observers. The more complicated the observation checklist, the more likely there are to be errors in recording.

$\frac{(x - \bar{x})^2}{N}$ **MATHS SKILL:** *Use ratios, fractions and percentages: calculate the percentage of cases that fall into different categories in an observational study.*

BEHAVIOURAL CATEGORY	Push	Kick	Throw object	Spit	Scram	Punch	Poke
FREQUENCY OF BEHAVIOUR							

Table 3.8: An example of an observational checklist containing behavioural categories.

	STRENGTHS	LIMITATIONS
Observations	1. Because observations occur in a natural setting the behaviours occur in their true form. This gives the method high ecological validity. 2. The observational method is a more ethical way of studying behaviour such as aggression which would cause ethical issues if deliberately manipulated under laboratory conditions. 3. There are few demand characteristics in observational studies because people do not know they are being studied.	1. There is a risk of observer bias as it unlikely that researchers will be able to remain completely objective. This reduces the reliability of the data gathered. 2. The lack of control of variables in naturalistic observations means that confounding variables may be introduced. This makes causality difficult to establish and means that replication is going to be more difficult. 3. Observations tend to be rather small scale so the group being studied may not be representative of the population. The findings of the study may therefore be hard to generalise beyond the setting and sample studied.

Table 3.9: The strengths and limitations of observations.

CONTENT ANALYSIS

Content analysis is an observational technique which is used to analyse written or pictorial information. For example, it is used to assess the presence of meanings and concepts in newspapers and books, and can also be used to assess the content of films and television programmes.

At the simplest level, a content analysis is conducted in much the same way as an observational study. The important difference between content analysis and a regular observational study is that in content analysis we produce a *record of the behaviour*, not just an observation of the behaviour. Once the aims of the research have been clarified a sample can be chosen – although, rather than participants, the sample will be of material. For example, if a researcher wanted to find out how women are portrayed in tabloid newspapers he would first read a range of newspapers and devise a checklist of behaviours noted from his research. He would then reread the newspapers using the checklist to gather data. Reliability can be checked in the same way as observations by using more than one rater and investigating if their 'observations' are comparable. This is called *inter-rater reliability*. Findings can be placed into categories and counted to produce quantitative data or can be analysed into themes to produce qualitative data.

	STRENGTHS	LIMITATIONS
Content analysis	1. Content analysis is unobtrusive and it doesn't require contact with people so ethical issues are practically non-existent.	1. Content analysis can be very time consuming. You have to come up with very clearly defined variables that will form the basis of the analysis. You then have to sort through the given material which takes time to do thoroughly.
	2. It is very useful for analysing historical material, especially for documenting trends over time – for example, when looking at changing attitudes of society towards particular issues.	2. Content analysis is a descriptive method. It describes what is in the sample content but may not reveal the underlying reasons. It reveals *what* is happening but does not allow for analysis of *why* something is happening.
	3. Establishing reliability is relatively easy and straightforward in comparison to other methodologies. The materials can usually be made available to other people so replication is easy.	

Table 3.10: The strengths and limitations of content analysis.

Observation

Which of the following are examples of <u>observation as a research method</u> and which are examples of <u>observation as a data-gathering technique</u>? (i) Researchers observe attachment behaviours in children attending a mother and toddler group. (ii) Nursery staff used an observational checklist to measure behaviour of children attending either low or high quality day care. (iii) Researchers investigate whether the more time children spend in day care means the more likely they are to be aggressive during the early primary school years. (iv) A psychologist observes the attachment behaviour of a child from behind a one way mirror. (v) Researchers use the Strange Situation to investigate cultural differences in attachments. (vi) An observation to see whether mothers of premature babies behave differently towards their infants than mothers of full-term infants.

SELF-REPORTS

Self-report techniques are named as such because the information gathered comes directly from the participant. The most common self-report techniques are interviews and questionnaires. Self-report techniques are useful tools when we want to gather in-depth information from an individual's own perspective. In experiments and observations one of the issues we face as researchers is that our data might tell us *what* is happening but it may not always explain *why*. Self-report techniques can give us this information. They allow us to question the motives behind people's behaviour.

Interviews

Interviews and questionnaires are similar in some ways in that they are both based around a set of questions. However, interviews are generally conducted face to face, unlike questionnaires, and the way that information is acquired varies slightly depending on the type of interview. There are many different ways of conducting an interview but the methods are most simply categorised as either *semi-structured* or *unstructured*. The simplest kind of interview to conduct is the *structured interview* but, as with all forms of interview, the sex, personality and skills of the interviewer are extremely important variables that can have significant influences on the interviewee. Training is needed for effective interviewing, and the less structured the interview, the greater the skills and training needed by the interviewer. This means that, wherever possible, researchers lacking this training should opt for a questionnaire method of self-report.

Structured interview

This approach resembles the questionnaire except that rather than write their own responses, participants respond verbally to questions posed by the researcher. The same questions are presented to each participant in the same way and, because of this, it has been described as a 'verbal questionnaire'.

	STRENGTHS	LIMITATIONS
Interviews	1. The kind of data you get from an interview is often rich and varied because interviews offer the opportunity to clarify any questions that the participant doesn't understand and add detail to their answers. 2. The interview can provide a great deal of insight into complicated and difficult individual cases if administered carefully by a skilled interviewer. This can often give clinical psychologists an understanding into complicated and difficult cases with children or adults who may be suffering with psychological abnormalities. 3. Demand characteristics and social desirability may be decreased because it is harder to lie to someone's face than it is on a questionnaire.	1. Interviews can be time consuming and are therefore an expensive way to gather data, especially if interviewers need extensive training in order to ensure that they are able to gather reliable data from their interviewees. 2. Demand characteristics and social desirability can increase with interviews because they are usually done face to face so anonymity is taken away. Participants may not want to give truthful answers because they fear being judged in some way.

Table 3.11: The strengths and limitations of interviews.

Semi-structured interview

There are no fixed questions in a semi-structured interview, and instead the interview is guided by a predetermined set of topics or themes to be covered. The order in which they are covered, or the way in which they are addressed by the interviewer, can vary across participants.

Questionnaires

A questionnaire is a list of prewritten questions. Some aspects of human experience and behaviour (e.g. attitudes) would be impractical to investigate using either experiment or observation. However, a well-designed questionnaire could provide a wealth of useful information. Because people may feel reluctant to complete questionnaires it is important to reduce the perceived cost of taking part. This can be achieved by avoiding asking for personal information, only asking participants when it seems convenient and making the questionnaire appear short and easy. There are two ways to ask questions – closed and open.

Closed questions

Closed questions allow limited responses from participants and may take a variety of forms. There are a variety of closed question formats from which to choose:

1. Rank order questions

This is where participants are asked to rate or rank a range of options. This gives information about preferences, degrees of importance, etc. As ranking long lists is difficult, keep the list to about five items. For example:

> Please indicate in rank order your preferred drink, putting 1 next to your *favourite* through to 5 for your *least favourite*:
>
> Coffee, tea, cola, water, hot chocolate.

2. Likert scale questions

These are statements to which participants are asked to indicate their strength of agreement or disagreement. For example:

> 'Psychology is so much better than mathematics.' Please indicate on the scale the extent to which you agree or disagree with this statement.

3. Checklist questions

This is where a list of items is provided from which participants select those that apply. For example:

> Circle three of the following adjectives that most apply to your personality:
>
> Happy grumpy friendly miserable
>
> sparkly interesting quiet morose sad

4. Dichotomous questions

These are questions offering two choices. For example:

> Did you do any exercise last week?
>
> Yes/No.

5. Semantic differential questions

With this type of question two bipolar words are offered and participants are asked to respond by indicating a point between the two which represents their strength of feeling. For example:

> My home town is ...
>
> Interesting ___:___:___:___:___: Boring
>
> Pretty ___:___:___:___:___: ___: Ugly
>
> Clean ___:___:___:___:___: ___: Dirty

Open questions

Participants are given space to respond more freely with open questions. Allowing participants to express themselves in this way can help the researcher to avoid accidentally biasing a closed question towards a particular point of view and can provide a far richer source of information. However, they can produce qualitative data that is difficult to interpret. For example: 'In the box provided, please describe what it feels like to fall in love.'

Many of the problems of questionnaires come from poorly phrased open and closed questions. The following are some of the things that should be avoided:

1. **Lack of clarity:** Questions should be understandable and mean the same thing to all participants. They should therefore be written in clear language, avoiding ambiguity and unnecessary jargon.

2. **Embarrassing questions:** Questions that focus on private matters should be avoided.

As the questions become more personal, the likelihood of unanswered or wrongly answered questions increases.

3. **Social desirability bias:** Participants will often answer questions in a way that makes them feel better by giving the answers that they think they ought to give, showing them in a better light.

4. **Leading questions:** Leading questions encourage a certain response from participants.

> ## Questionnaires
>
> You have been asked to conduct a survey into how teens spend their leisure time. Write four closed questions (using four different formats) and one open question which could be used in this survey.

	STRENGTHS	LIMITATIONS
Questionnaires	1. Compared to other methods questionnaires can be a cheap, efficient and easy way of collecting large amounts of data. 2. Because the participants can remain anonymous, and therefore perhaps be more willing to express themselves fully, questionnaires are a relatively reliable method of gathering data. 3. Information from closed questions is quantitative and therefore easy to analyse and draw conclusions from. 4. Information from open questions provides rich and detailed data as participants are free to express their opinions and attitudes.	1. There is no guarantee that people will respond truthfully to questions. There are many reasons for this: it might be social desirability, where participants say what they think should be said rather than give their own opinion, or paint a more favourable picture of themselves than is accurate. 2. Open questions generate qualitative data that is hard to analyse. A further method, such as content analysis, may be required to translate the qualitative data into quantitative data and allow conclusions to be drawn.

Table 3.12: The strengths and limitations of questionnaires.

CORRELATIONAL STUDIES

Correlation is a technique that shows whether or not two variables are associated; these are known as *co-variables*. As well as being a research method in its own right, correlation can be used to analyse data gathered from any other research method. For example, data from observational studies and questionnaires might be analysed to see if there is a relationship between two or more factors.

A *positive correlation* means that as one variable increases so does the other. An example might be the relationship between how many hours you spend studying for an exam and how well you do in it. The more time you spend studying, the better your score on the exam.
A *negative correlation* occurs when as one variable increases, the other decreases. An example might be the relationship between stress and memory recall: the more stressed we are the less we recall during this state.
A *zero correlation* is where the two variables are not related at all. In this case you would expect to see a *correlation coefficient* near to zero. There are lots of things that are unrelated – an example might be the relationship between the number of cups of coffee drunk every day and the number of cartoons on the telly between 3 p.m. and 5 p.m. No relationship at all.

Scattergrams are used to depict correlation data. They are also known as scatterplots or scattergraphs. A scattergram is a kind of graph and we'll talk more about these later (see page 149).

Significant correlation coefficients simply indicate that there is a relationship between two variables. It does not say why or how the two things are related. However, care must be taken when interpreting the meaning of correlational data. Correlation does not mean that one

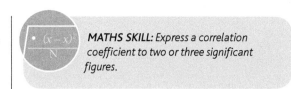

variable *caused* the other to change – only an experiment reveals causal relationships between variables. Causality is only one of three possible explanations for a correlation:

1. The relationship is causal – one variable caused the other to change.

2. The relationship is chance – the two variables just happen to be statistically related.

3. There is a third factor involved – another variable is causing the relationship.

For example, let's say that in a questionnaire study on time management we are interested in whether or not time management habits are related to subsequent exam performance. We could extract the data from the questionnaire which relates to how students manage their time and test performance (e.g. exam grades). Analysis of this data tells us that there is a correlation – the better the time management, the better the grades. We now have to explain this correlation: is it causal, chance or is another variable in operation?

In this instance, it might be that time management caused improved exam grades. However, students who are the best at managing their time are also the most motivated students, so it could be the latter. A third factor explanation might then be the most likely one here – motivation is behind the relationship between time management and exam grades.

Of course, if a causal explanation is suspected to be the most likely one it might be possible to design an experiment to verify this.

	STRENGTHS	LIMITATIONS
Correlations	1. Correlation allows a researcher to measure relationships between naturally occurring variables (e.g. height and intelligence, weight and sleep duration). 2. Correlations can indicate trends which might then lead to further research using experimental means to establish any causal links. They are a really useful and quite simple way of starting off a research project.	1. It is not possible to draw conclusions about cause and effect. A significant correlation does not mean a cause. 2. Extraneous variables which may influence the results are very hard to control. There may be a correlation between two variables but it might be that something else – something you do not know about and have not controlled for – has sneaked into your experiment and 'caused' or influenced the relationship.

Table 3.13: The strengths and limitations of correlations.

CASE STUDIES

A *case study* is a careful and systematic investigation of a single individual or a small group of people such as a family. A researcher studies a single example either because they are rare or unique in some way or because they are a typical example of a type of person. Case studies can take a long time to conduct and a variety of data collection methods can be used, including clinical interviews and laboratory experiments, therefore detailed in-depth information is obtained.

	STRENGTHS	LIMITATIONS
Case studies	1. Case studies produce lots of detail and the depth of understanding acquired through this is useful for understanding the subtleties and complexities of individual behaviour. 2. A case study is sometimes the most sensible and practical method to use. For example, it would not be possible to conduct an experiment into the effects of extremely harsh childhoods, but useful information about this could be gained by carefully constructing a case study.	1. Because case studies relate to one individual the findings from them cannot easily be generalised to others. Even if generalisations are made, they may lack credibility in the eyes of other researchers. 2. Case studies rely on retrospective data – that is, information gathered about past events. This information might not be accurate. People have a habit of forgetting things and our memory for events, especially stressful ones, can be unreliable.

Table 3.14: The strengths and limitations of case studies.

QUANTITATIVE AND QUALITATIVE DATA

Quantitative research produces numerical data, whereas qualitative research produces data that is descriptive. Some research methods produce one or other kind of data, but some can produce both.

Quantitative research

When researchers gather numerical data they are being quantitative – they are assigning numerical values to things. For example, the number of items recalled correctly in a memory test. When these data are collected, statistical techniques are used to analyse them in order to find out if there are any numerical patterns or relationships. Typically, quantitative data is produced by experiments.

Qualitative research

Qualitative research gathers information which is non-numerical. It focuses on a person's experience and feelings, and is more concerned with uncovering the meaning of these things than with measuring behaviour using numbers and statistics. Although this kind of information can be converted into quantitative data, it is often left qualitative and summarised as such. Self-reports (interviews and questionnaires) typically gather qualitative data (e.g. open questions on questionnaires).

Quantitative or qualitative?

Whether or not a quantitative or qualitative approach is selected depends on the nature of the research and the interests of the researcher. For example, a researcher interested in a participant's subjective experience of an event would prefer a qualitative approach to gathering information. On the other hand, a researcher interested in measuring an aspect of human memory might prefer a quantitative approach. Some research methods can actually be used to gather both quantitative and qualitative data (e.g. questionnaires). Qualitative data can also be converted into quantitative data – for example, the number of times an interviewee expressed unhappiness with something could be added up, thus creating a quantity.

	QUANTITATIVE RESEARCH	QUALITATIVE RESEARCH
Advantages	1. It is considered more scientific – because it limits the amount of subjective interpretation it is more objective. 2. The data can be analysed for statistical patterns which can be compared to data from other studies. This improves the reliability and validity of the research.	1. It provides very rich and detailed information about opinions, emotions and attitudes of individuals. 2. It takes the point of view of the participant, since their responses are not restricted in advance by the point of view of the researcher.
Disadvantages	It describes events in numerical form thus reducing the richness of human experience.	1. It is less controlled and structured than quantitative research which makes it more subjective and less scientific. 2. It is difficult and time consuming to analyse, making it hard to see patterns in data that would allow you to draw conclusions.

Table 3.15: The advantages and disadvantages of qualitative and quantitative research.

PRIMARY AND SECONDARY SOURCES

Primary data are those that are gained directly by the researcher. Secondary data are those that have already been collected but which are reused by the researcher.

A case study is a good example of a methodology that uses both primary and secondary sources. For example, primary sources might come from interviews,

> **MATHS SKILL:** *Understand the differences between primary and secondary data, including the ability to recognise whether data collected by a researcher dealing directly with participants is primary or secondary.*

Primary and secondary data

An educational psychologist is constructing a case study of a child who is demonstrating behavioural problems at school. (a) Identify two ways in which primary data could be gathered by the psychologist. (b) Identify two types of secondary data that the psychologist could include in the case study.

assessments and observations of the individual or their family. Examples of secondary data might include school reports, medical records or initial studies of the individual that may have been carried out by other researchers. The type of information collected will depend on what the researcher is trying to investigate. An example of a methodology that solely uses secondary data is a meta-analysis – this is the gathering of data from multiple studies on one topic/area of psychology that is then analysed to draw an overall conclusion about that topic/area.

	PRIMARY SOURCES	SECONDARY SOURCES
Advantages	1. The main advantage of a primary source is that you know the data or information is unchanged and has not been manipulated by another researcher so there is less chance of bias. 2. It allows the researcher to collect data specifically related to the aim of the research, rather than relying on data that might have been collected based on a similar aim or topic.	Secondary sources reduce the amount of work that the researcher has to do on a topic as it's already been covered. This allows you to cover a wider range of information on a topic faster than if you were to design and carry out methods to obtain all the data yourself!
Disadvantages	1. Because you (the researcher) will be collecting and analysing the data, there is the risk of bias in interpreting that data. 2. It is a time consuming technique because it takes time to locate your sample and collect the data; secondary sources will have already done this for you!	It is impossible to know everything about the secondary source as there is always the chance that the original authors left something out or interpreted the data incorrectly, leading to bias.

Table 3.16: The advantages and disadvantages of primary and secondary data.

LOCATION OF RESEARCH

We have seen from the different types of experiments a researcher can conduct that some are carried out in laboratories and others in more natural environments (i.e. in the field). The location of research can have a huge impact on the data that is collected. Table 3.17 summarises the effects that conducting research in different environments can have on the data gathered.

Conducting research online

Conducting research online is still a relatively new concept in psychology, but it began to really take off as a platform for data collection in the early 2000s. There are currently two main ways that researchers can conduct research online:

1. *Questionnaires and surveys* which participants willingly and knowingly complete.

2. *Content analysis* on internet forums – for example, looking at the use of language in relation to a particular topic, studying people's browsing histories or considering the number of people using social media platforms.

The British Psychological Society (BPS) have published ethical guidelines specifically for those conducting research online, to be used in conjunction with the general ethical principles, as there are unique issues that must be addressed. Table 3.18 outlines some of the advantages and disadvantages of conducting research online.

FACTOR	IN LABORATORY ENVIRONMENTS	IN THE FIELD
Ecological validity	Artificial conditions in a laboratory setting mean that behaviour may not be 'natural' or reflect real-life behaviour so ecological validity is low.	Conducting research in the field generally means we have high ecological validity because we have not controlled for extraneous variables (at least to the extent we would in a lab environment) and therefore behaviour is not influenced by researchers.
Reliability	A high level of control over variables means that we can say with more confidence that the changes seen in the DV are because of manipulation of the IV.	Experiments conducted in natural environments are more susceptible to the influence of extraneous variables as there is less control.
Demand characteristics	As participants know they are in a laboratory setting they may alter their behaviour to fit that environment, making the data invalid.	As behaviour is naturally occurring participants are less likely to be aware that they are taking part in a study, lowering the chance of demand characteristics.
Experimenter/ investigator effects	The researcher who is gathering the data is often the researcher behind the experiment. This means there is the risk of investigator effects or researcher bias, where they influence the participant in some way.	The researcher is less likely to be directly involved with participants, especially if the participants are unaware that they are taking part in a study, which reduces the chances of experimenter effects.

Table 3.17: Evaluation of laboratory and non-laboratory research settings.

ADVANTAGES	DISADVANTAGES
People have typically given their consent to take part. You can't force someone to take part in a survey if you aren't with them! The right to withdraw is also less of an issue because people can just close the web browser.	You cannot verify that participants are who they say they are. This is particularly troubling when you have identified a specific target population. For example, if you want to look at women's views on feminism, it is almost impossible to guarantee that everyone who responds to your measure is a woman.
Participants are likely to try to answer the questions honestly as there is no pressure from the presence of a researcher, so validity is increased.	There is little we can do to prevent malicious intent (e.g. deliberately sabotaging the experiment) or multiple submissions (Kraut et al., 2004). This affects the validity of our research as we are not measuring what we intended to measure.
It opens the sample up to a significantly larger population (Kraut et al., 2004) than would ever be possible in a laboratory or field setting. The population validity of our study will increase massively because of this.	Confidentiality may be an issue as participants could be identified through their IP addresses. This risk may lead to some participants not wanting to take part in the research, leading to a biased sample.
Unlike laboratory environments, a researcher does not need to greet or respond to a participant. The instructions and task are all automated (Kraut et al. 2004) and therefore there is less risk of researcher bias.	Acquiring participants to take part in online research can be difficult. For example, where do you advertise for participants? If you advertise on a forum, can you be sure that the sample is not biased in some way?
Participants are under less pressure to appear in a certain way as they are anonymised behind a keyboard. Therefore, their responses may be reflective of their actual thoughts and feelings rather than being censored to suit what is acceptable to society. If you look at 'internet trolls', for example, they are willing to post inflammatory comments that most would not be willing to say in a real-life setting.	Right to withdraw means that even after data has been contributed a participant has the right to pull out of the study and have their data deleted. This is very difficult to do in most online research and impossible in the rest. To avoid this ethical issue researchers would need to make this limitation clear to participants at the outset.

Table 3.18: The advantages and disadvantages of conducting research online.

Location of research

A team of researchers wanted to investigate people's ability to identify emotions from facial expressions. (a) Identify one advantage and one disadvantage of conducting this research in the following locations: (i) laboratory; (ii) in the field; (iii) online. (b) Select one location for this research and justify your choice.

PARTICIPANTS

TARGET POPULATIONS

The people who take part in research are called *participants*. Researchers get their participants from a *population*. A population is defined as all the members of a particular group from which the participants are selected. For example, if you were interested in investigating attitudes to bullying in 14- to 16-year-olds, your *target population* would be 14- to 16-year-olds. You might want to make the population more specific – for example, 14- to 16-year-olds in a geographical area or even 14- to 16-year-olds from a particular school within that area. You might want to see whether there is a bullying problem amongst 14- to 16-year-olds in Cardiff, amongst people of a particular ethnic group. Your *population* in this case would be 14- to 16-year-olds from a particular ethnic group who live in Cardiff. These kinds of decisions are all part of the design process.

Because it is usually impractical for everyone in the target population to take part in a study, researchers need to *select* from the population. This selection of participants is called the *sample*. The main aim of *sampling* is to select a number of people who are typical, or representative, of the rest of the population from which they were chosen. Because the sample is a typical cross section of people, the findings can be safely *generalised* to everyone else in the target population. If the sample is not *representative* then it is *biased*, and *sample bias* is something to avoid if we want to be able to generalise the findings.

SAMPLING FRAMES

Once the target population has been identified, you need to be able to select participants from it. These participants must be accessible in some way so that they are known to the researcher. This will be a listing of all the accessible participants in the population based on a set of characteristics that you are interested in. For example, if you want to investigate people's use of social media, you might access a list of everyone who has a Facebook account. This is known as the *sampling frame*. Another example might be if you wanted to do a phone survey on the general population – you would use a telephone book to choose your sample.

	ADVANTAGE	DISADVANTAGE
Sampling frames	A sampling frame allows you to identify all available members of the target population in a way that is unbiased. By defining the set of characteristics of your target population, you then have the ability to select all of those who fit those criteria.	It is almost impossible to include everyone from your target population in your sampling frame. For example, if you use a telephone book as your sampling frame, not everyone who has a phone is listed in the book.

Table 3.19: The advantages and disadvantages of sampling frames.

RANDOM SAMPLING

In a *random sample*, every member of the target population has exactly the same chance of being selected to participate. There are several ways of doing this. The most straightforward is the 'names from a hat' method, whereby all members of the target population are identified on slips of paper. These are then shuffled in a container and the desired number are selected. Whilst this appears simple, names from a hat is not practical with anything other than a small population, such as the members of an A level class. Fortunately, there are computer programs which can select a random sample from even very large populations, so there is no need to spend hours writing names on hundreds of bits of paper! The simplest program requires each member of a population to be given a unique number. The program randomly generates a series of numbers within the limits set. All we need to do then is match the numbers produced by the computer to the names on the list.

	ADVANTAGES	DISADVANTAGES
Random sampling	1. This method of sampling is unbiased because it is not affected in any way by the researcher and everyone has an equal chance of being selected, regardless of any particular characteristics. 2. As everyone in your target population has an equal chance of being selected, you can conclude with more certainty that your results can be generalised to the general population.	1. The sampling technique relies on all of the target population being available to take part if chosen. If you select participants randomly, and one of those people cannot take part, you will need to replace them – and your random sample is no longer random. 2. The randomly selected sample might end up being biased anyway! For example, there is no guarantee that an equal number of males and females will be selected which may affect the outcome of your results.

Table 3.20: The advantages and disadvantages of random sampling.

OPPORTUNITY SAMPLING

A very common method of sampling is to use anyone you can get hold of (hence the term 'opportunity'). This is very straightforward. The sample selection is based on whoever is willing and available to take part at the time; this is why university students are often used in experiments by their lecturers! Some students of psychology think that just picking people to take part, without any obvious selection criteria, makes it a random sample, but this is not the case at all. Remember, a random sample gives *everyone* in a population an equal chance of being chosen, which will clearly not happen here. If you decide that your target population is all students in a sixth form, and you then set about waiting at a doorway for someone to pass, although you are selecting from your population, you are not doing it randomly since not everyone in the sixth form will walk past the doorway.

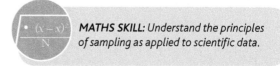

MATHS SKILL: *Understand the principles of sampling as applied to scientific data.*

	ADVANTAGE	DISADVANTAGE
Opportunity sampling	This is the easiest sampling technique because you can just use the first people you find who are willing to take part. It does not take time to locate participants or involve a lengthy selection process.	This technique is much more susceptible to bias, therefore leading to an unrepresentative sample and findings that are harder to generalise to the wider population. It excludes a large proportion of the target population.

Table 3.21: The advantages and disadvantages of opportunity sampling.

SYSTEMATIC SAMPLING

This technique chooses subjects from the target population in an orderly or logical (i.e. systematic) way. The most common way is choosing every *n*th participant from a list. To do this, a starting point and an interval would need to be calculated. This is typically done in one of two ways:

1. The researcher identifies how many participants they need, chooses a starting point (which is less than the total number of individuals in the target population) and an interval that will be the constant difference between the participants selected. For example, the researcher has a population total of 100 individuals and needs 12 subjects. He first picks his starting number, 5, and then he picks his interval, 8. The members of his sample will be individuals 5, 13, 21, 29, 37, 45, 53, 61, 69, 77, 85, 93.

2. The target population is divided by the needed sample size to obtain the sampling fraction. This is then used as the constant difference between subjects. For example, a sample of 100 children from a school of 1,000 would be 1,000 divided by 100 giving every 10th name on a list (which ultimately gives the required sample size).

	ADVANTAGE	DISADVANTAGE
Systematic sampling	The sample obtained should be representative of your target population because the system is objective and it is unlikely that every *n*th participant will be atypical of that population.	In order for this selection to be truly random the starting point should be selected randomly (e.g. by a computer program or a sampling fraction). If it isn't, it means it is not random because you will have selected the first participant.

Table 3.22: The advantages and disadvantages of systematic sampling.

STRATIFIED SAMPLING

With the *stratified sampling* method, the researcher first identifies the different groups of participants within the target population (e.g. gender, age). Participants from each group ('strata') are then randomly selected based on the frequency of occurrence in the general population. For example, if we wanted to see how much revision is done by psychology students in relation to gender, it would not be appropriate to use another method because psychology is still a relatively female dominated area in terms of its students. We may end up with a sample size of all females, which would obviously not be representative of our target population!

For example, a class contains 20% males and 80% females; this is the target population. The sample the researcher uses must then contain the same proportion as the target population (i.e. 20% males, 80% females). To put this into numerical terms, a class might have 200 students; 160 of these will be female and 40 will be male. This is the occurrence of males and females in our target population (psychology students). If we wanted our sample size to be 100 participants we would need 80% females and 20% males, or in other words, 80 females and 20 males. While this may seem biased to females it is actually representative of our target population.

	ADVANTAGE	DISADVANTAGES
Stratified sampling	With this technique, our sample is going to be highly representative of our target population because the frequency of certain types of people in our sample is equal to their frequency in our target population.	1. This method is extremely time consuming as it involves working out the occurrence of different types of people in our target population and then calculating how many we need of each in our sample size. 2. Once we have acquired our sample we still have the issue that some of the selected participants may refuse to take part, and therefore we could still end up with a biased sample.

Table 3.23: The advantages and disadvantages of stratified sampling.

QUOTA SAMPLING

Quota sampling is very similar to stratified sampling. The first stages are exactly the same: the proportions of different groups within the target population are calculated and this will then translate across to the sample you need. As with our previous example of psychology students, we would still need 80 females and 20 males. The difference now would be that we do not randomly select our participants but use another method – most commonly opportunity sampling. For example, the lecturer might stand at the door of their lecture theatre and hand out questionnaires to the first students through the door. Once they have reached their 'quota' of 80 females and 20 males, they would stop. For example, if the quota of 20 males is reached but 80 females isn't, the lecturer would stop collecting data on males but would continue collecting data on females until the quota of 80 is reached. Once one quota has been reached, all participants who come along who meet the criterion (e.g. males or females) would be disregarded.

	ADVANTAGE	DISADVANTAGE
Quota sampling	The sample still has a good chance of being representative of the general population because the rate of occurrence is still the same.	There is the risk that our sample could still be biased as we may only be accessing certain sections of our target population. For example, some of our psychology students might be late to the lecture because of transport issues and therefore would not be available to take part.

Table 3.24: The advantages and disadvantages of quota sampling.

SELF-SELECTED (VOLUNTEER) SAMPLING

It is not uncommon to find, pinned on university noticeboards, appeals for people to take part in a piece of psychological research. Here, either through goodwill, curiosity or financial encouragement (some researchers may pay a small fee to those taking part!), participants are asked to volunteer themselves.

	ADVANTAGES	DISADVANTAGES
Self-selected (volunteer) sampling	1. A simple method, relying only on the correct placement of adverts. 2. It is likely to produce a less biased sample than an opportunity sample as more people will have an opportunity to participate. 3. It allows the researcher to target very specific samples in relation to a population. For example, if the target population was lawyers an advert could be placed in a law journal.	1. People who volunteer may not be typical of members of a population. It has been suggested that some personality types are more likely to volunteer than others. 2. The method of advertisement for volunteers might influence the sample. For example, if a poster is located in a university then psychology students may sign up, and they have a good idea of what the study is about and thus bias the results. 3. It is not necessarily quick as you have to wait for people to respond to your advert. Even then it might take a while to gather sufficient participants.

Table 3.25: The advantages and disadvantages of self-selected (volunteer) sampling.

SNOWBALL SAMPLING

A *snowball sampling* technique is used in research where members of a target population are difficult to locate or are rare. It works by the researcher identifying participants and then asking them to refer or nominate other potential participants who fit the sample profile. It works well as a technique in some circumstances. To illustrate:

Small target population: For example, if someone has a very rare condition or disorder, meaning the target population is very small. A participant may know others with the condition or disorder via a support group and therefore may be able to refer other people.

Keeping identities hidden: For example, people who would rather their true sexuality was not publicly known might be reluctant to respond to advertisements asking for volunteers. However, those few who are willing to participate may know others who might be similarly willing.

Sampling frame not available: For example, if you were doing research into homeless people there would be no available sampling frame – it is very unlikely that there is a list of all the homeless people in any given area! Therefore, you may be able to approach one homeless person who can then nominate or refer other homeless people.

	ADVANTAGE	DISADVANTAGE
Snowball sampling	It allows us to study issues or topics that may be unavailable to us through using other sampling techniques. It is often the only way to get a sample in circumstances such as those described on page 141.	The sample is likely to be biased because it relies on people's connections and therefore you may not get a representative sample of the target population.

Table 3.26: The advantages and disadvantages of snowball sampling.

OBSERVATIONAL SAMPLING TECHNIQUES

Unless we are able to film proceedings for later analysis it is impossible to record everything in an observation. We have to be selective in what we observe. In other words, we have to take a sample of behaviours to observe. There are two basic sampling techniques we could use.

Time sampling involves making observations for short intervals within a given period of time. For example, if we were conducting a study on aggression in boys and girls, we could watch children for 3 minutes out of every 15, using the intervening time to clarify our observations and make notes.

Most observations use *event sampling*, where all clearly defined relevant behaviours are recorded each time they occur. This is why operationalising variables is so important. An example of this might be observing the behaviour of a child each time it is left at the nursery by its mother. This is an event which only occurs once each day.

	ADVANTAGE	DISADVANTAGE
Time sampling	This technique allows us to write detailed notes that can be clarified almost immediately after the event. This can reduce observer bias and the chance of missing something important.	We might miss something important if it isn't in our time frame, which might bias observations. For example, if we are assessing child behaviour for aggression and this behaviour occurs outside the time frame we may erroneously conclude that children are not aggressive.

Table 3.27: The advantages and disadvantages of observational time sampling.

	ADVANTAGES	DISADVANTAGES
Event sampling	1. This technique allows us to record everything that we have operationalised and therefore gives us an overview of all behaviours that we are interested in. 2. If we record everything we see it gives more credibility to our results as we have not been biased in what we record (as long as the variables have been fully operationalised).	1. As we are recording everything we see there is the possibility that we might miss something while we are making notes on a previous event. This is only preventable if we film the observed event which raises ethical issues of consent and confidentiality. 2. There is always the risk of observer bias. Even if we have taken every possible step to operationalise our variables, what one observer might view as aggressive another might not, leading to poor reliability.

Table 3.28: The advantages and disadvantages of observational event sampling.

EXPERIMENTAL DESIGN

Research design refers to way that participants in experiments are allocated to conditions. Sometimes the design will be decided for us depending on what we are investigating. **For example, if we wanted to see the difference between the behaviour of men and women, they would only be able to take part in one condition because they cannot take part in both the men and women conditions!**

REPEATED MEASURES DESIGN

In a *repeated measures design*, each of our participants carries out the experiment twice – once in each of our conditions. In the experiment outlined in the section on laboratory experiments we described an experiment with two conditions: one condition involved performing a memory task in silence and the other condition involved repeating the same memory task while listening to sound. If repeated measures was used then all participants would complete the first task followed by the second task.

Overcoming order effects

To overcome order effects we would have to use *counterbalancing*. Half of the participants could do no noise followed the next day by noise (i.e. the control condition followed by the experimental condition). The other half could do noise on the first day and no noise on the next day (experimental condition followed by control condition). In this way, order effects would appear in both conditions and, in effect, balance themselves out.

	ADVANTAGE	DISADVANTAGES
Repeated measures design	As the same people are used in two conditions, individual differences (e.g. in age, gender, ability) are eliminated from influencing the results. In effect, participants act as their own 'control'.	1. As participants take part more than once there is a greater chance of demand characteristics, where the participant guesses what the experiment is about and alters their behaviour to fit. 2. There may be order effects. For example, improvement in a second task might be due to experience with the first task. This kind of order effect is called a practice effect. On the other hand, performance on the second task could worsen due to tiredness or boredom. This type of order effect is called a fatigue effect.

Table 3.29: The advantages and disadvantages of repeated measures design.

INDEPENDENT GROUPS DESIGN

In an *independent groups design* we use different people in each experimental condition – each participant is randomly allocated to one condition. In our experiment, one half of the sample would be allocated to the control condition and do the memory test in silence, whilst the other half of participants would be put into the experimental condition and do the test whilst listening to a noise.

	ADVANTAGES	DISADVANTAGE
Independent groups design	1. There are no order effects with this design so factors like practice or fatigue will not confound the results. 2. The risk of demand characteristics is reduced because there is less chance of the participants being able to guess what is being measured and manipulated as they only experience one condition.	Individual differences between participants could influence the results. For example, it could be by chance that a few people with extraordinary memories are allocated to one condition. In this case, the difference between the two conditions might not be due to the independent variable at all but to the contribution of several 'unusual' participants.

Table 3.30: The advantages and disadvantages of independent groups design.

MATCHED PAIRS DESIGN

Matched pairs design involves having two separate groups of participants who are matched on some important variable in order to make them as similar as possible. The ideal participants in a matched pairs design would be identical twins, with one twin in each condition, as they are as matched as two individuals could ever be. If it was always practical, this is the ideal compromise between the independent groups design and repeated measures design, as it avoids most of the problems with both and has all their advantages. However, the problems associated with matching (or finding sufficient numbers of twins to participate!) means that this design is rarely used.

	ADVANTAGES	DISADVANTAGES
Matched pairs design	1. Because the participants are matched there is less confounding caused by individual differences. 2. The design is really an independent measures design with practically identical people in each group, so there are no order effects.	1. Matching participants is very difficult and time consuming, especially if you try to match participants on every possible variable that could cause a problem for your results. 2. Even with identical twins individual difference is not eliminated. They will be genetically identical but one twin may be better at maths – a difference that could have an important impact on your results.

Table 3.31: The advantages and disadvantages of matched pairs design.

Experimental designs

	REPEATED MEASURES DESIGN	INDEPENDENT GROUPS DESIGN
Condition A		
Condition B		

With repeated measures design, the same participants take part in both conditions of the experiment. With independent groups design, different participants take part in each condition of the experiment.

Experimental designs

Identify the type of designs used in experiments with the following hypotheses:

(i) Females are less likely to administer an electric shock to a woman than to a man.

(ii) The greatest attachment problems are experienced by children fostered after 12 months.

(iii) Leading questions have a greater influence on children's recall of a story than an adult's recall.

(iv) Performance is better on memory tasks in those remembering by rote than those using another technique.

(v) Obedience increases according to the status of the authority figure.

(vi) Witnesses of violent crimes recall more details than witnesses of less violent crimes.

MATHS SKILL: *Understand the differences between quantitative and qualitative data and explain how qualitative data can be converted into quantitative data.*

 *Some researchers have suggested that whether an adult is secure or insecure in their adult relationships depends on the quality of the emotional bond they formed with their caregivers early in life. A psychologist decided to test this idea using a questionnaire.*

(a) What is meant by the term 'quantitative data'? (1 mark)

(b) Give an example of one possible question that the psychologist could have included which would produce quantitative data. (1 mark)

(c) Questions producing qualitative data were also included. Suggest a question for inclusion that would generate qualitative data and give one advantage of asking such questions. (4 marks)

(d) The researchers had their questionnaire printed in a local newspaper and invited readers to complete and return it.

(i) What name is given to this sampling technique? (1 mark)

(ii) Outline one problem with this kind of sampling technique. (2 marks)

(iii) Describe an alternative way in which the psychologist could have selected participants and explain how this would have avoided the problem outlined in (ii). (4 marks)

(e) Identify one potential ethical issue arising from this research and explain how it could be dealt with. (3 marks)

(f) What method other than a questionnaire could the psychologist have used in this research? State one advantage and one disadvantage of this alternative method. (4 marks)

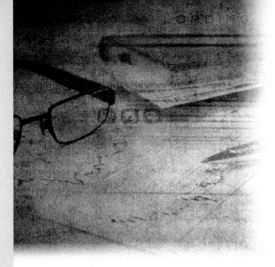

LEVELS OF MEASUREMENT

There are four types of measurement you can make in psychological research. Each measurement has its own mathematical properties which limit the kind of analysis you can use it for.

NOMINAL DATA

Data that can be classified into categories is known as *nominal data*. By this we mean that if something is in one category, it cannot also be in another category. For instance, if you make a trip to a safari park to carry out a survey of animals, you may want to count the number of monkeys you see and the number of hippos. You cannot have a monkey that is also a hippo – they exist as discrete categories. If your data is like this, it is described as nominal level data or discrete data.

ORDINAL DATA

The clue for this one is in the name – *ordinal* suggests that there is an order. Horse racing is a good example: horses are recorded as finishing first, second, third, fourth and so on. The order in which they finish is the important thing, not the distance between them. It doesn't matter if the horse that finishes first finishes before the horse in second by 10 minutes or by 10 seconds. If your data is like this, in some kind of order or rank, then it is described as ordinal level data.

INTERVAL DATA

If you are measuring something on a scale, perhaps the height of something or the time it takes someone to do something, then you are using an *interval scale*. Time, temperature, weight and height are all examples of interval level data.

RATIO DATA

Ratio data means that whatever variable we are measuring has an absolute zero (a point where none of the quality being measured exists). It means that we can make comparisons such as being 'twice as big' or 'half as much'. It is very similar to *interval data* except that the distances between points are equivalent to one another (otherwise you wouldn't be able to make a meaningful comparison). For example, weight is a ratio variable – 2 kg is half of 4 kg. Reaction time can also be a ratio variable – although reaction time is always greater than zero, we conceptualise a zero point in time to measure from, so that we can state that a response time of 30 seconds is twice as long as a 15-second response time.

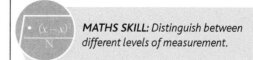

MATHS SKILL: *Distinguish between different levels of measurement.*

GRAPHICAL REPRESENTATION

In order to communicate data to others we could represent the data pictorially on a *graph*. The whole point of a graph is to convey information clearly. If this is not done then the purpose of a graph is lost, therefore care should be taken not only in choosing the right graph to use but also in how the graph is drawn. For example, always label and title graphs and avoid those that put looking good above being clear and simple.

Data should not be presented in ways that are misleading. For example, the distances between points on a vertical axis should be equal and the scales carefully chosen so that the data are not exaggerated and distorted by the look of the graph. Since graphs are intended to *summarise* data, it is not appropriate to use individual participant scores unless you are constructing a scattergram.

If data are gathered using experimental methods then it is a usual convention to plot the dependent variable on the vertical axis and the independent variable on the horizontal axis. So, if your study investigates the type of vehicles using a road outside a local school, then convention says you plot 'categories of vehicle' (car, lorry, motorbike, bus, etc.) along the bottom (the *x* axis) as it is your independent variable, and the 'number' along the side (the *y* axis) because that is the one you measure – your dependent variable – the number of each category of vehicle.

> Tip: when drawing graphs, remember SALT! *Scale* (appropriate to the data), *axis* (scaled), *labels* (for the axis and a key if appropriate) and *title* (to tell people what your graph shows).

FREQUENCY TABLES

A *frequency table* is used to display raw data that is easy to understand and interpret. It tells us at a glance how often a certain score occurred, or was frequent, in a given set of scores. For example, if we conducted a test on memory to see how many items out of 15 our 30 participants could recall, we might end up with these scores:

9, 8, 4, 5, 7, 10, 13, 5, 9, 4, 2, 6, 7, 8, 4, 10, 11, 9, 8, 5, 3, 2, 7, 3, 10, 15, 4, 7, 10, 10

The frequency table would look like this:

Items recalled	Frequency
0	0
1	0
2	2
3	2
4	4
5	3
6	1
7	4
8	3
9	3
10	5
11	1
12	0
13	1
14	0
15	1

As you can see, a frequency table is much easier to understand than a long list of numbers! In addition, it is also an easy way to help us calculate descriptive statistics. For example, the table shows us without too much work on our part that 10 is the most commonly occurring frequency which would therefore make it our *mode* (see page 153). Frequency tables then allow us to construct appropriate graphs (usually a histogram – see below).

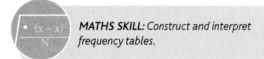

MATHS SKILL: *Construct and interpret frequency tables.*

LINE GRAPHS

Line graphs are used to present relationships between quantitative variables when the independent variable has, or is organised into, a relatively small number of distinct levels. Each point in a line graph represents the mean score on the dependent variable for participants at one level of the independent variable. They are used with interval and ratio data. Line graphs can be used to display data or information that changes continuously over time and allows us to see overall trends, such as an increase or decrease in data over time. For example, if we were to keep repeating our memory test (like the one we used to calculate our frequency table) every month for the next year, we could use a line graph to show our mean score over that time period.

BAR CHARTS

Bar charts use data which come in categories. Each item or factor you count for these data can only fit into one category. We call this nominal, or discrete, data. For example, on a trip to a safari park or on holiday in Africa, you may collect data on how many of each animal you see (e.g. elephants, giraffes, lions). Each time you see one of the three you add it to the appropriate column. The data are discrete – a lion can only be a lion, it cannot belong to one of the other categories.

When drawing a bar chart, the vertical axis should show the score of a variable – for example, the mean or frequency (how often something occurred), whilst the horizontal axis should show the individual categories, or variables, you measured. The bars on the horizontal axis should be drawn separately with equal widths and gaps.

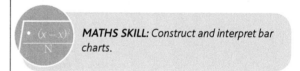

MATHS SKILL: *Construct and interpret bar charts.*

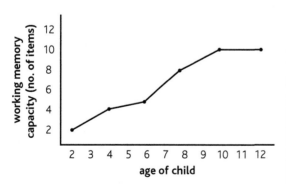

Figure 3.1: Line graph showing the working memory capacity of children at different ages.

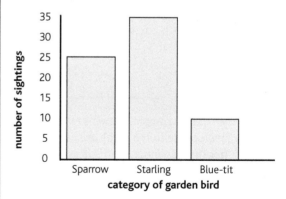

Figure 3.2: Bar chart showing sightings of different garden birds in a domestic garden, spring 2007.

HISTOGRAMS

Because *histograms* are similar to bar charts they are sometimes confused. However, whilst bar charts deal with discrete data, histograms use continuous data. This means that the variable on the horizontal axis is a scale of something, such as length or mass. For instance, in our example of a frequency table, the most appropriate graph to use would be a histogram because our data is continuous (items that can be recalled – all participants were given 15 items). A histogram is also used with ordinal data that we can put in order – our graph wouldn't make sense if we didn't order the data! If we used our frequency table example again, we would start with the minimum number of items that can be recalled and end with the maximum – it wouldn't make sense to start with 7 and then go back to 0. When drawing a histogram, we join the bars to illustrate the continuous nature of the variable on the *x* axis.

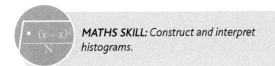

MATHS SKILL: *Construct and interpret histograms.*

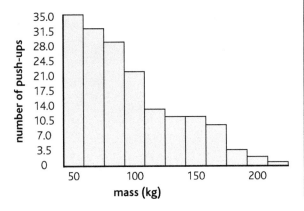

Figure 3.3: Histogram showing the number of push-ups possible at different masses.

PIE CHARTS

A *pie chart* shows the differences in frequencies or percentages amongst categories of a nominal (i.e. the rates of frequency within a given category) or ordinal variable (i.e. the rates of frequency in order of our variable). The categories are displayed as segments of a circle whose pieces add up to 100% of the total frequencies. In a pie chart the frequency or percentage is represented both visually and numerically, so typically it is quick for readers to understand the data and what the researcher is conveying. We could use this for our memory example from the frequency table because it would discount any data with a 0 frequency and therefore only show data that occurred.

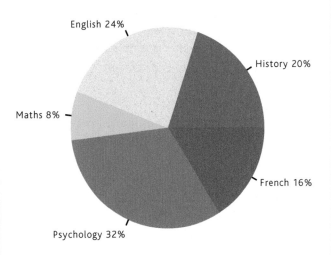

Figure 3.4: Pie chart showing the favourite A level subjects voted for by students.

SCATTER DIAGRAMS

Scattergraphs (or *scattergrams* or *scatterplots*) are used to display data when the study is correlational. This means that a relationship between two variables is being investigated. Drawing a scattergraph involves plotting two scores – one score is measured along the horizontal axis and another along the vertical one. Where the two plots intersect on the graph an 'x' (plotting point) is placed.

Sometimes a *line of best fit* is added after all the scores have been plotted. This straight line is drawn to show a trend in the plots – it is an estimated line and it doesn't have to pass through any particular number of x's (plotting points). For example, it might not be entirely clear what type of correlation the graph is showing, so a line of best fit clarifies this. Generally speaking, unless there is a specific need to draw attention to this line of best fit it is better to just leave it out.

The pattern of the points plotted on a scattergraph represents particular kinds of correlation.

Positive correlation

As one variable increases, so too does the other. The more the points resemble a straight line, the stronger the positive correlation.

Negative correlation

As one variable increases, the other decreases. As with positive correlation, the tighter the points cluster around a single straight line, the stronger the negative correlation.

Zero correlation

With *zero correlation*, there appears to be no relationship between the variables.

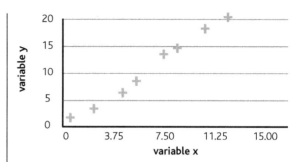

Figure 3.5: Strong positive correlation.

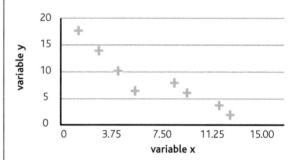

Figure 3.6: Strong negative correlation.

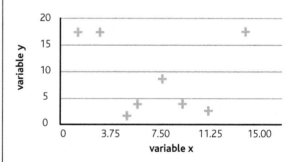

Figure 3.7: Zero correlation.

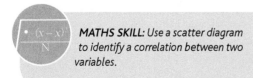

MATHS SKILL: *Use a scatter diagram to identify a correlation between two variables.*

DESCRIPTIVE STATISTICS

Whatever you do in research, you always end up with loads of numbers and a huge amount of information. **You can't expect others to spend hours trying to make sense of this 'raw data', so you need to do something with it to make everybody else's life much easier and bring out the main points in your data.**

Just as you can summarise a book or story in a few words, researchers use descriptive statistics to summarise their findings. Let's use an improbable example! Let's imagine we've given an intelligence test to everyone in the whole world. The postman arrives with a large sack of responses and we need to summarise the huge amount of data we have. Descriptive statistics allow us to boil down the data and squeeze it into a few handy numbers, so others will not have to spend their time reading all the raw data to try to understand our results.

Descriptive statistics can't do everything! The clue here is in the name – descriptive statistics. They simply describe the raw data. They do not tell us what you did or whether your findings are reliable (i.e. whether they would be the same if you did the experiment again), and they do not explain the result, the type or the size of the relationship you may have found. They simply allow you to describe the raw data and reduce them to just a few numbers that are easier to manage.

MEASURES OF CENTRAL TENDENCY: MEAN, MEDIAN AND MODE

Measures of central tendency are sometimes referred to as averages. To find an average of a set of numbers is to calculate a single value that

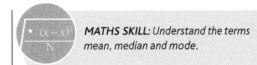

MATHS SKILL: *Understand the terms mean, median and mode.*

is representative of the whole set. That is, the average is said to be a score which is typical of the rest of scores – they are 'central'.

There are three measures of central tendency: *mean*, *median* and *mode*.

Mean

The mean is the best measure of central tendency and is calculated by adding all the scores in a set of scores together and dividing by the number of scores. The formula looks like this:

$$\frac{\sum x}{n}$$

For example, take the following raw data where we've measured the height of five people.

Height (cm): 153, 146, 151, 170, 160

Step 1: Add up all the heights to find the

Total: (153 + 146 + 151 + 170 + 160) cm = 780 cm

Step 2: Divide the *total* by the number in your sample (in this case 5): 780 cm divided by 5 (780 / 5) = 156 cm

The mean height of this sample is 156 cm.

The mean height is quite typical of the heights of your sample. Three people are shorter and two are taller. It is pretty much in the middle. A good 'typical' mean.

Evaluation of the mean

The mean is the most powerful measure of central tendency because it is the only one which uses all the numbers in its calculation. However, this is also its weakness. Because the calculation uses all your numbers, one rogue number has a huge effect on your mean. For example, imagine if one of your people was 234 cm in height. You now have six people in your sample.

> *Step 1*: Add up all the heights to find the *total* (153 + 146 + 151 + 170 + 160 + 234) cm = *1014 cm*
>
> *Step 2*: Divide the *total* by the number in your sample (now 6) 1014 divided by 6 (1014 / 6) cm = *169 cm*

The mean height is now 169 cm.

The new mean height is not really typical of the heights of your sample. Five out of six of the people have heights that are lower than the mean. This is why it is a good idea, when using a mean, to also give some indication of how spread out your scores are by including a *measure of dispersion*, particularly the *standard deviation* (see page 154).

Another weakness is that occasionally a mean is calculated that does not make sense in the context of the set of numbers. Imagine you are interested in how many children a typical family has in Britain. You would collect a load of raw data which would show how many children each family has. If you calculated a mean you might end up with a number like 2.4 children. How can someone possibly have 2.4 children? That's two whole ones and almost half of another one, just their legs perhaps! It just doesn't make much sense. In this case, another measure of central tendency might be preferable.

Median

The median is the central number in a set of scores. In order to find the median, all the numbers in a set of scores need to be put in order and the mid-point found. If there is an odd number of scores (Example 1) then the number in the centre of the set, once you have put them in order, is the median. If there is an even number of scores (Example 2) then the median is the number midway between the two central numbers.

Example 1:

Ages of employees/years: 21, 56, 44, 34, 29

Put them in order (youngest to oldest, or oldest to youngest, it doesn't matter which!):

21, 29, 34, 44, 56

The one in the middle is 34 years

The median age of the employees is *34 years*

Example 2:

Ages of employees/years: 21, 56, 48, 44, 34, 29

Put them in order (youngest to oldest, or oldest to youngest, it doesn't matter which!):

21, 29, 34, 44, 48, 56

Even number in the sample – two in the middle are 34 and 44 years

The median age of the employees is the midpoint of the two: *39 years*

Evaluation of the median

The main strength of the median is that it is less affected by extreme scores than the mean. When put in order extreme scores will be at either end of the list. Being at the centre of the list, the median is likely to be affected only by the extreme scores shifting the centre point slightly. However, it is not suited to being used with small sets of data, especially when these contain widely varying scores. For example:

7, 8, 9, 102, 121

The median here would be 9, which is neither central nor typical. A central number might be something between 9 and 102, maybe 60. In cases like this, the median does not provide us with a very good measure of central tendency.

Mode

The mode is the most frequently occurring number in a set of scores. It's the score that appears most often in your data. For example, if our data is 'days off work because of sickness', we might have a set that looked like this:

3, 5, 6, 6, 6, 8, 9

Here, the mode would be 6 as it occurred most often (three times in total).

Sometimes a set of numbers gives us two modes, in which case the data are said to be *bimodal*. More than two modes would make the data *multimodal*. For instance, let's enlarge our 'days off work because of sickness' data set:

3, 3, 3, 5, 6, 6, 6, 8, 9

In this case, the numbers 3 and 6 occur just as often as each other. The data is bimodal, which means it has two modes, 3 and 6.

Evaluation of the mode

The mode is useful when you want to know how often something occurs. For instance, we might want to know how many days off due to sickness most people take. The mode is usually unaffected by occasional extreme scores because they (usually) only occur once, and so will not be the most typical number and will not affect your assessment of the mode. However, the mode does not always provide a typical score – for example, in a small set of numbers when the most frequent number occurs at either end

of a set of scores and is thus far from the central score. For instance, take this set of data showing the number of holiday days taken:

1, 1, 1, 23, 24, 26, 27, 30, 33

The mode here is 1 day. Not really a 'central' measure and not really informative about the whole set of data. Also, sometimes a set of scores doesn't actually have a most frequent score – for example, everyone may take a different number of days off for sickness or holidays. In these cases there is no mode. The mode is therefore best used when there are lots of numbers in the set of data and there are likely to be lots of tied scores.

Correlation

The following are correlations. For each:

(a) State the kind of correlation each represents (i.e. positive or negative).

(b) Give an explanation for the correlations (i.e. causal, chance, or third factor).

(c) Rewrite the statement as the opposite correlation (e.g. if positive, rewrite as negative).

(i) The more time spent studying for an exam, the better the grade.

(ii) There is increased conflict and stress at home when workers are overloaded at work.

(iii) The more quality time a child has with its parents the greater their social competence.

(iv) People who are good at managing time do better in assessments.

(v) The less in control someone feels at work, the more stress they experience.

(vi) People who spend more time cycling are better at balancing a ball on their nose.

MEASURES OF DISPERSION: RANGE AND STANDARD DEVIATION

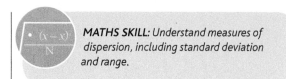

MATHS SKILL: *Understand measures of dispersion, including standard deviation and range.*

Whilst measures of central tendency give us a typical value, *measures of dispersion* tell us something about the spread of scores or how diverse they are. Whenever you give the measure of central tendency, you should also give a measure of dispersion, as both scores together tell us more about our numbers than either one alone does. For example, the mean height of everyone in a large college might be 153 cm. This does not tell us anything about how spread out the heights are. If we just give the mean value, we are hiding the true nature of the data. We want to give an idea of how spread out the heights are – how much shorter than 153 cm people might be and how much taller.

Range

The *range* is the simplest measure of dispersion and is calculated by finding the lowest and highest scores in the data and subtracting the smallest from the biggest.

For example, if the smallest person in the college is 135 cm and the tallest is 165 cm, the range is (165 – 135) cm = 30 cm.

Evaluation of the range

Using only two numbers, the range is a very easy figure to calculate. It also takes into consideration extreme scores. However, these are also its main weaknesses: in simply using only two scores the majority of scores are ignored. These two scores could also be particularly extreme thus distorting the range.

For example, the mean height may well be 153 cm, but the tallest may be 190 cm and the shortest may be 110 cm. Your range here would come out as (190 – 110) cm = 80 cm. This is not really a true reflection. The majority of the heights, which cluster more closely around the mean of 153 cm, are ignored; they provide nothing to the range. The range tells us very little about the actual spread of scores – for example, how spread out or clustered they are.

Standard deviation

The *standard deviation* tells us the mean distance of scores from the mean of a set of scores. A large standard deviation tells us that scores are widely spread out above and below the mean, suggesting that the mean is not very representative of the rest of the scores. If there is a small standard deviation then the mean is representative of the scores from which it was calculated.

For example, take two sets of data, set A and set B:

> The mean of set A is 72.
>
> The mean of set B is also 72.

But:

> The standard deviation of set A is 14.2.
>
> The standard deviation of set B is 3.2.

What does this tell us? Whilst the mean scores are the same, the standard deviation tells us something about the quality of the mean in terms of how well it represents the rest of the scores. The first mean has a standard deviation of 14.2 compared to 3.2, showing that there is a greater spread of scores around this mean. It is therefore less representative than the mean with a standard deviation of 3.2.

The following formula is used to calculate the standard deviation.

$\sqrt{} $ = square root

$\sum$ = sum of

$\bar{x}$ = mean

x = a data point

^{2} = squaring the data point

n = the number of data points in your data set

Just take a closer look at this. It's not that complicated actually – it just seems alarming! What it means, in words, is this.

Step 1: Calculate the mean. This is written as an x with a line over it. Mathematicians call this the x-bar ($\bar{x}$).

Step 2: Get a sheet of paper. In the first column (column 1), write down each value in your data set (in maths, each data value is referred to as x) Subtract the mean ($\bar{x}$) from it and write this value in the next column (column 2).

Step 3: Multiply each value in column 2 by itself (^{2}) and write the result next to it in column 3. This procedure is called *squaring* the value.

Step 4: Add up everything in column 3 ($\sum (x - \bar{x})^2$).

Step 5: Divide the value you get in step 4 by the number in your data set (n).

Step 6: Finally! Take the square root of the value you get from step 5. That's your standard deviation!

An example:

Data set: 1, 2, 3, 4, 5, 6, 7, 8, 9, 10

$\bar{x}$ (mean) = 5.5

n (number of data points in data set) = 10

x	$x - \bar{x}$	$(x - \bar{x})^2$
1	−4.5	20.25
2	−3.5	12.25
3	−2.5	6.25
4	−1.5	2.25
5	−0.5	0.25
6	0.5	0.25
7	1.5	2.25
8	2.5	6.25
9	3.5	12.25
10	4.5	20.25
	$\sum (x - \bar{x})^2 = \sum (x - 5.5)^2$	82.5
	$\dfrac{\sum (x - \bar{x})^2}{n = 10} = 82.5$	8.25
	$\sqrt{\dfrac{\sum (x - \bar{x})^2}{n}} = \sqrt{8.25}$	2.87

From this, we can see that our data deviates from the mean by 2.87 so the spread of scores is relatively low.

Evaluation of the standard deviation

The standard deviation is the most sensitive measure of the spread of scores as it uses every score in its calculation and it is not heavily distorted by extreme scores. The standard deviation is closely related to the mean. Indeed, the mean is part of the standard deviation calculation. *It is therefore the measure of dispersion to use whenever the mean is used as the measure of central tendency.* However, even though it only involves relatively simple mathematics, it is still relatively laborious to calculate.

Which measure of dispersion to use with a measure of central tendency?

A measure of central tendency should always be accompanied by at least one measure of dispersion. The choice of which to use is really down to a careful consideration of the raw data that have been gathered. However, Table 3.32 presents a simple rule of thumb which can be followed – but remember, it is only a rule of thumb! Sometimes more than one measure of dispersion is a good idea and sometimes more than one is asked for!

Summary

Each measure of central tendency and dispersion has its good and bad points. A strong descriptive statistic is generally one that takes in a good deal of the raw data in its calculation, so bear that in mind when thinking about which one is most suitable. The strengths and weaknesses of each are described in Table 3.32. It's not really useful to ask which of the measures is best and which is worst. Each is appropriate in different circumstances, depending on the data you have and what you are looking for in your research.

	MEAN	MODE	MEDIAN	STANDARD DEVIATION	RANGE
Strength	Most powerful measure of central tendency as it uses all of the data.	The best measure to use if you want to know how often things happen.	Not heavily influenced by rogue scores.	Uses every value in the data set, not heavily distorted by extreme values and the most sensitive.	Takes extreme scores into consideration and is simple to calculate.
Weakness	One rogue score (large or small) can heavily influence it.	Sometimes a data set does not have a most common value and sometimes it has lots of common values.	Not good for using with small data sets.	The most laborious of the measures of central tendency to calculate.	If either of the two scores are extreme, the range will be distorted. It tells us little about how spread out or clustered together the data are.

Table 3.32: The strengths and weaknesses of measures of central tendency and dispersion.

Populations and samples

(a) Identify the target population in the following studies and (b) suggest an appropriate sampling technique for selecting participants. (i) A study investigating whether there are gender differences in aggression amongst participants under 19 years of age. (ii) A study to see whether children brought up with nurses show weaker attachments to their mothers. (iii) A study into the effectiveness of cognitive-behavioural therapy for reducing exam stress. (iv) A study to see if children with siblings are more socially skilled than children without siblings. (v) An investigation into whether watching television talent shows causes teens to erroneously believe that they too have talent.

RELIABILITY

In terms of psychological research, reliability refers to *consistency*. **What this means is that if the evidence gathered by research is reliable, then anybody else doing the study using the same method would get the same findings. Reliability is very important in psychological research as it gives a degree of confidence in both the method of data collection and the findings.**

Some research methods are more reliable than others, therefore the reliability of studies will vary to some degree according to the method used to gather the data. More important, perhaps, is that it will vary according to the design and conduct of the study. For example, a laboratory experiment, which involves tight control of variables, is considered a more reliable research method than an observational study, which employs less control and relies more on the perception of individual observers.

There are a number of techniques available for assessing and improving reliability and they are all based on the same principle – *replication*. For example, if two observers rate a behaviour in the same way then their observations are consistent (or reliable); if an experiment is carried out more than once with the same results then it is consistent (reliable). In other words, if we can replicate something, we can be more certain of the reliability of the study.

INTERNAL RELIABILITY

Internal reliability refers to the extent to which something is consistent within itself. For example, if you wanted to do a questionnaire on how happy someone is, all the questions should be measuring happiness in the same way. A way to test for internal reliability is to do a split-half measure. This is where the questions are divided into two halves and the results of each are correlated with one another. If the correlation is close, we can say with some confidence that both halves of our questionnaire are measuring the same thing.

EXTERNAL RELIABILITY

External reliability refers to the extent to which something is consistent over several different occasions. For example, if we gave our happiness questionnaire to someone and then gave it to them one week later, we would expect the score for happiness to be similar each time. If it isn't, then our measure may be unreliable.

WAYS OF DEALING WITH ISSUES OF RELIABILITY

If we do have issues with reliability, then there are steps we can take to try to increase it. If we have low internal reliability, we can seek to change or remove items from our measure that are lowering it. For example, in our happiness questionnaire we may have a question that asks, 'What type of pizza topping do you like?' This question is obviously not related in any way to whether someone is happy or not and so may be reducing our internal reliability. By removing it we may increase reliability.

If our external reliability is low, we must try to identify why this might be. The timing of the test is important. If the duration between tests is too brief, the participants may recall information from the first test which could bias the results. If the duration is too long, the participants could have changed in some important way which could also bias the results (e.g. they may have started university and therefore view themselves as happier now).

One way to try to rectify both internal and external reliability is to do a *pilot study*. This is a small-scale version of the real study and is done on a limited sample of participants in order to

iron out any issues. For example, before giving out our happiness questionnaire to our target population, we may give it to a smaller sample and test for the internal and external reliability. It also allows researchers to ask the participants if there were any items on the questionnaire that they didn't think were measuring happiness (internal reliability) or if there is anything that would be affected by the timing of the questionnaire (external reliability). For example, one of the questions may be, 'How many times have you been out with friends in the last week?' This could be affected by a number of factors other than happiness, such as when someone gets paid! Therefore, if there are any issues we can rectify them before the full study is carried out.

QUESTION TIME?

The Great Holtodo has a world-renowned memory. He really is something special, and can remember the order of up to 500 cards that have been professionally shuffled. Holtodo claims that the key to his superb memory is taking regular exercise and drinking water derived only from melted Welsh snow. For some time now psychologists have been closely investigating Holtodo and developing a detailed knowledge of his amazing talents and claims.

(a) (i) What kind of study is this? (1 mark)

(ii) State one weakness of the research method identified in (i). (2 marks)

(b) The team designed a laboratory experiment to investigate the possible benefits to memory of drinking this special water. The results are recorded in the table below:

Memory score after drinking different amounts of water

PARTICIPANT NUMBER	1 CUP	2 CUPS	3 CUPS
1	10	13	12
2	13	15	25
3	9	9	30
4	12	15	17
5	4	8	12

(c) Identify the independent variable and the dependent variable in this experiment. (1 mark)

(d) Identify the experimental design used here and give one limitation of this kind of design. (3 marks)

(e) Identify one possible extraneous variable in this study. (1 mark)

(f) Assuming that they used the mean as a measure of central tendency, what would be an appropriate measure of dispersion for these data? (1 mark)

(g) What type of graph would you use to display these data? (1 mark)

(h) Sketch a graph of this data and suggest what the graph tells us about the effects of the special water on memory. (3 marks)

VALIDITY

Validity refers to the extent to which a test actually tests what it claims to. In other words, validity means that the data collected give an accurate, or 'true', picture of what is being studied. We can be fairly sure that tools used in the physical sciences, such as thermometers, really are testing what they claim to test – in this instance, thermometers are valid tools for measuring temperature.

However, in psychology we are often far less sure. For example, IQ (Intelligence Quotient) tests are used to measure intelligence. The problem is that there is considerable debate about whether or not IQ tests really do test intelligence – their validity is questioned. This is not a unique case. The nature of the phenomena which are of interest to psychology means that they can only be brought to light by the methods used to test them. For example, psychologists demonstrate aspects of human memory through the response of participants to particular kinds of memory task. If the test is flawed then it follows that the assumptions which are drawn from the results of the test must also be suspect. The issue of validity is a crucial one for psychology.

A further complication is that a test can be reliable without being valid. For example, a personality test might give consistent results but it might not be measuring what we think it is measuring. We might hope it is measuring how confident someone is, or how shy, but really it might just be measuring how good they are at doing that particular personality test!

Whilst there are numerous methods used for assessing the validity of a test, most researchers rely on their theoretical knowledge of the research area to make a judgement as to whether a test is valid. Added to this is educated common sense – on the face of it, does the test look as though it is doing what it is supposed to? This kind of assessment of validity is called *face validity*.

INTERNAL VALIDITY

Internal validity refers to the study itself and whether the researcher has measured what they intended to. For example, carrying on from our example of the happiness questionnaire, we would say that our questionnaire is valid if it does actually measure if someone is happy, rather than if they like to go out drinking (not necessarily a behaviour of just happy people). In an experiment, it refers to whether the independent variable was really the cause of the effect on the dependent variable, or whether the dependent variable was caused by some other variable (i.e. confounding variables).

Improving internal validity
Anything that influences the dependent variable other than our independent variable reduces the internal validity of our research. In general these things are described as extraneous variables.

If an extraneous variable (such as fatigue or practice) influences our findings, then internal validity is reduced. One of the most important aspects of research design is to minimise the influences of extraneous variables. Improved internal validity comes from better resistance of your research to the influence of extraneous variables. This is best achieved by very careful research design and planning.

EXTERNAL VALIDITY

External validity refers to how well the findings of the study can be generalised outside of the study itself. There are different types of external validity:

Ecological validity
This is the most commonly known type of external validity. It refers to how well the findings of the study can be generalised outside of that setting. It essentially means how life-like or realistic the study was. A laboratory experiment is typically a highly controlled setting and therefore lacks ecological validity because we wouldn't experience those things in everyday life. A field or natural experiment is higher in ecological validity because we do not control variables as tightly as in a laboratory experiment.

Population validity
This refers to how well the results can be generalised outside of the sample of participants used in the study. This is why choosing an appropriate sampling technique is so important.

Temporal validity
This refers to how well the findings of a study can be generalised to different time periods. It can be affected by the changing attitudes and laws of society.

Improving external validity
Improving ecological validity
Where possible research should be conducted in a natural setting (field or natural experiment or an observation). This means that the behaviour that is recorded is more natural and can be generalised outside of the research setting.

Improving population validity
The sampling technique needs careful consideration. You are trying to generalise your findings to your target population, so you need to select a sampling technique that allows you to do this with greater confidence. You must take into account all relevant factors, such as age, gender, culture, etc.

Improving temporal validity
Conduct the experiment or study at a different point in time. If the results are similar, the time validity is high.

WAYS OF DEALING WITH ISSUES OF VALIDITY

A pilot study can be used to test the validity of our research and ensure that the variables have been appropriately operationalised (therefore allowing them to be measured accurately). A pilot study also provides an ideal opportunity to talk to a small sample of participants about their experience of taking part. Such feedback can provide vital information about demand characteristics, investigator bias and the design of the study in general. After a careful check of the procedures and findings, problems can be ironed out and the research design amended, where necessary, before the study begins for real.

SPECIFIC VALIDITY ISSUES

Researcher bias and investigator effects
Because the researcher is aware of the hypothesis they may give cues to the

participants on how to respond. For example, they may alter the procedure slightly or change their language to indicate something to the participant in ways that might influence the investigation. It affects the validity of our research because it means the findings are not a direct result of our independent variable but result from the researcher's behaviour. The age, gender or ethnicity of the researcher can also influence the behaviour of participants.

It should also be remembered that researchers will have put a great deal of time and effort into their research and may unconsciously interpret ambiguous situations in ways which are favourable to their point of view. The amount of influence that a researcher has on the research will vary to some degree according to the research method used, but *investigator effects* are an issue in all types of research. They have to be identified early on in the research design and, as far as possible, eliminated.

Overcoming researcher bias/investigator effects

A researcher could recruit assistants to run their study for them. If these assistants are unaware of the aim and hypothesis of the study, then they are unable to give any cues to the participants about how they would like them to behave that could bias the findings. This is called a *double-blind* procedure, where both the participants and the researchers involved in gathering data are kept unaware of the research aims.

Demand characteristics

Psychological research often involves a direct interaction between researcher and participant – it is a social situation. Since people generally alter their behaviour when around others, it is reasonable to assume that behaviour will change in a research situation. Participants may be aware that they are being observed or may think that they are being personally assessed or evaluated in some way. This might motivate them to attempt to find clues in the research

environment or procedure as to what the study is about and to alter their behaviour accordingly. These features of research, which participants use to change their behaviour, are called *demand characteristics*.

Demand characteristics can seriously affect the findings of research. However, the extent to which this is a factor varies according to the research method used and the way the study is designed and conducted. For example, demand characteristics are going to be much more of an issue when people know that they are taking part in a study, such as is the case with a laboratory experiment.

Overcoming demand characteristics

Although often impossible to eliminate entirely, well-designed research will try, as much as possible, to minimise demand characteristics. For example, if there is to be communication between the researcher and the participant, then the verbal and non-verbal content of this communication needs to be controlled by using standard instructions. The setting of the study will also need to be carefully considered, especially since some participants may be familiar with the research area.

It is almost inevitable that the solution to reducing demand characteristics will involve some kind of *deception* – keeping the participants in the dark about the aims of the research. If the participants are not told the aims of the research, they are less likely to be able to work out what the researchers are expecting to find, thus reducing demand characteristics. This is called a *single-blind* procedure.

Social desirability

Social desirability is when someone alters their behaviour or responses to portray themselves in a way that is desirable to society. It can involve either maximising 'desirable' behaviour or minimising 'undesirable' behaviour. For example, in a questionnaire on aggression, participants might not be truthful about how aggressive they are because they think that society views aggression in a negative way. However, what could be being measured by this questionnaire is how the participant responds when asked about their aggression, not how aggressive they actually are. Social desirability can therefore affect the validity of our research because it stops us from measuring what we claim to be measuring.

Overcoming social desirability

This is perhaps one of the hardest validity issues to overcome because it is very difficult to ensure that people won't do what they think is desirable in the eyes of society! However, we can try to avoid it by ensuring confidentiality. In this way, if participants know their private data won't be made public, they may be more likely to show their natural behaviour. Another way to overcome social desirability is to try to conduct research in a natural setting when people aren't aware that they are being observed. They are therefore more likely to react to situations as they would normally.

Demand characteristics and researcher bias

Identify one potential demand characteristic and one potential source of researcher bias in each of the following pieces of research.

(i) A study investigating whether child behaviour is related to physical punishment.

(ii) A study looking at whether workers with supportive managers experience greater job satisfaction and reduced stress.

(iii) A study to see whether individuals below a certain intellectual measure have the mental capacity to vote during elections.

(iv) A study to see whether homework benefits boys more than girls.

(v) A study investigating whether the early childhood relationship with the mother is related to later happiness in adult relationships.

(vi) A study investigating whether children would benefit academically from not having long summer breaks from school.

QUESTION TIME

It has been suggested that humans are not constantly vigilant and often simply don't remember details of events happening around them. To test this, psychology students conducted a study in a nearby town centre. Working in pairs, one student approached a passer-by and asked for the time. A few minutes later the second student approached the same passer-by and asked him or her to describe the person who had just asked them the time.

(a) State the aim of this study. *(2 marks)*

(b) The students are conducting a field experiment. In the context of this study, give **one** advantage of a field experiment. *(2 marks)*

(c) How does a field experiment differ from a natural experiment? *(2 marks)*

(d) Explain why might it have been a good idea for the students to have conducted a pilot study. *(2 marks)*

(e) What kind of sample was used in this study? Give one disadvantage of this kind of sample. *(2 marks)*

(f) Identify one ethical issue arising from this research and explain how the students might deal with it. *(3 marks)*

ETHICS

The breadth of the subject matter studied within psychology makes it unique amongst the sciences. Psychology might be described as the study of the experiences of living, feeling organisms and, as such, special care must be taken.

There is the potential for participants to be affected by their experiences of taking part in psychological research. For instance, investigating the relationship between emotion and memory may require the researcher to bring about certain emotional states in the participant. This is often achieved by showing the participant a short film which makes them feel happy or perhaps a little sad. Generating an emotional state such as happiness is much more acceptable, and less likely to lead to any kind of damage, than generating an emotional state such as fear or terror. For this reason, it might not be acceptable to show a clip of a horror film to participants because of the potential damage it might cause. Researchers have to be constantly aware that it is both morally wrong and professionally unethical to engage in research which in any way violates the dignity of participants and their right not to be treated in this way.

Ethical issues

For each study (a) identify one ethical issue, (b) explain why it is an ethical issue and (c) suggest a way of dealing with it.

(i) An experiment to investigate whether 3- to 4 year-olds are more likely to forget a list of words than adults.

(ii) A study to investigate whether people will hurt someone when they are told to do so by an authority figure.

(iii) An experiment to see whether strict parenting makes children less happy.

(iv) An experiment to investigate whether anxiety influences thinking.

(v) A study to see whether workplace stress increases the likelihood of heart attacks.

(vi) A study to investigate whether taking vitamins improves school performance.

What is an 'ethical issue'?

Ethical issues arise from the tension between what a researcher needs to do to conduct research and the rights of participants. To resolve these tensions the British Psychological Society (BPS) have produced guidelines for the conduct of psychologists.

'In all circumstances, investigators must consider the ethical implications and psychological consequences for the participants in their research. The essential principle is that the investigation should be considered from the standpoint of all participants; foreseeable threats to their psychological well-being, health, values or dignity should be eliminated.' (BPS, 2001, p. 9)

ETHICAL ISSUES AND WAYS OF DEALING WITH THEM

Because of the broad subject matter of psychology, a very wide range of ethical issues could arise. There is often no simple right or wrong answer, so dealing with these ethical issues is frequently a matter of judgement, for example weighing up the costs and benefits of the research. Table 3.33 summarises some ethical issues and ways of dealing with them.

ETHICAL ISSUE	WAYS TO DEAL WITH THE ETHICAL ISSUE
Confidentiality: Participants have a right to confidentiality and anonymity. Their participation and performance in research is private and not open to public scrutiny. Participants have the same moral and legal rights to confidentiality as everyone in our society, and this is set out in government legislation in the Data Protection Act (1998).	Do not record names or any irrelevant personal information about participants; instead use numbers to refer to participants. Store data securely, according to the Data Protection Act. Ask permission (consent) to use any information (e.g. publish a case study, release a film clip/image of a participant).
Deception: Deception means that participants are in some way deliberately misled or misinformed. This usually involves withholding information about the aims of the study so they are not fully informed before consenting to take part. Most studies in psychology cannot happen without at least low levels of deception.	Seek permission from an ethics committee to check that the level of deception is both necessary and acceptable. Use debriefing with participants after the study to inform them of the aim of the research.
Risk of stress, anxiety, humiliation or pain: Some experiments might need to induce stress, anxiety, humiliation or pain to fulfil the aim. The experimenter must be able to justify this and it should not exceed the minimum amount needed. All reasonable steps must be taken in all research to ensure that you are protecting your participants from undue physical and psychological harm.	Make the right to withdraw very clear at the start of the study so if a participant feels anxious or stressed they may leave. Any rewards/benefits that are available for taking part should still be given if the participant withdraws. Ensure harm does not exceed that which would be experienced in everyday life.
Risk to values, beliefs, relationships, status or privacy: Researchers must take all reasonable steps to ensure that their research protects participants from any damage to their values, beliefs, relationships, status or privacy. Investigations should not seek to damage these in any way, unless absolutely vital and fully justifiable by the research. Researchers must respect individual, cultural and role differences, including age, disability, education, ethnicity, gender, language, nationality, religion, race, sexuality and socioeconomic status.	Seek permission from an ethics committee to ensure that any risks or are acceptable. Stop the study as soon as the risk becomes too high to justify. Use debriefing and provide support if necessary. Ask at first contact if there are any factors that might lead to a risk of harm (e.g. if the experiment involves being in a room alone with a male researcher, a female Muslim will not be able to partake as this is a violation of the Islamic faith).

ETHICAL ISSUE (continued)	WAYS TO DEAL WITH THE ETHICAL ISSUE
Valid consent: Participants must be fully informed about the study before they agree to take part. This need not involve disclosing every single detail of the study, but certainly anything that might influence a person's willingness to take part must be revealed to potential participants. In this way, their decision to take part is based on an understanding of the consequences and what their contribution means.	Get participants to give formal consent (e.g. signing something) beforehand where possible. Seek retrospective consent by asking participants if it is okay to use their data once the study is over and they have been debriefed. Use presumptive consent. Instead of asking participants directly seek opinions from people similar to the participant. It is assumed that because they are similar they will feel the same way.
Working with vulnerable individuals: If children are to be used in research, then consent must be sought from their parents or carers. This rule might also apply to some adults – for example, people who have certain kinds of mental illness or who have learning difficulties, or elderly patients suffering with certain kinds of dementia which may influence their ability to make informed decisions. If the participant might be considered 'vulnerable' in any way, the researcher must proceed very carefully.	Make the right to withdraw very clear at the start of the study. Any rewards/benefits that are available for taking part should still be given if the participant withdraws. Gain consent from a relevant individual (e.g. a parent or carer). Ensure harm does not exceed that which would be experienced in everyday life. Seek permission from an ethics committee. Stop the study as soon as the risk of harm becomes too high to justify. Use debriefing which is appropriate to the needs of the individual and provide support if necessary.
Working with animals: The ethical guidelines drawn up by the BPS contain guidance about working with animals, but there is an entire document dedicated to those who use animals in their research. The guidelines say that anyone who conducts research using animals must: 'observe the highest standards of animal welfare, including reduction to the minimum of any pain, suffering, fear, distress, frustration, boredom, or lasting harm' and 'avoid the infliction of any of these conditions which cannot be strictly justified, in adherence to the Society's published Guidelines for Psychologists Working with Animals' (British Psychological Society, 2012).	Provide evidence that alternatives to using animals have been considered. Obtain a licence to show that you are trained to work with animals. Use the minimum number of animals. Inflict the least amount of harm. Euthanise animals in the kindest possible way. Keep the study as short as possible. Keep up to date on the latest developments in knowledge of species and animal welfare. Use the support of professionals (e.g. qualified vets) for advice on animal welfare and euthanasia.

Table 3.33: The key ethical issues in psychology.

WAYS OF DEALING WITH ETHICAL ISSUES

Ethical guidelines

Researchers in psychology are guided by a set of ethical principles designed to prevent research from infringing on the rights of participants. Drawn up by the BPS, these guidelines state that:

> In all circumstances, investigators must consider the ethical implications and psychological consequences for the participants in their research. The essential principle is that the investigation should be considered from the standpoint of all participants; foreseeable threats to their psychological well-being, health, values or dignity should be eliminated. (British Psychological Society, 2001)

Ethical guidelines must be adhered to and the failure of psychologists to maintain professional standards can lead to serious reprisals. Psychologists may be ejected from the Society or have any licences revoked. The value of their research will be questioned and they will no longer be able to carry out legitimate work. This could mean that employment will be hard or impossible to find and other researchers may not want to be associated with them.

Ethics committees

Before a researcher can begin a study of any kind they must apply to an *ethics committee*, which will review their application and decide whether there are any ethical issues that must be dealt with before the study can go ahead. This applies to any level of research at and above undergraduate level. You won't have to apply to do experiments at AS and A level, but it is important that any research you carry out is done ethically. A research ethics committee will be responsible for:

- Reviewing all research involving human participants.
- Ensuring that the ethics review is independent, competent and timely.
- Protecting the dignity, rights and welfare of participants.
- Considering the safety of the researcher(s).
- Considering the legitimate interests of other stakeholders.
- Making informed judgements of the scientific merit of proposals.
- Making informed recommendations to the researcher if the proposal is found to be unethical in any areas.

Debriefing

One of the key techniques that psychologists use to overcome ethical issues is to *debrief*. Even if the study lacks informed consent, causes harm, deceives the participants and takes away the right to withdraw, it could potentially still be justified if the researcher provides an adequate debrief.

After the data have been collected, the researcher debriefs the participant. The full aims of the research are revealed and the participant is given the opportunity to ask any questions. If a participant reports any reaction or distress because of taking part in the research, then the researcher is responsible for correcting these consequences. This might require no more than discussing the rationale for the study and reassuring the participant about confidentiality. Sometimes, however, more lengthy procedures are needed to ensure that participants are left no worse for their experience. This can include a referral to see someone who is more qualified to deal with the issues being experienced by the participant, such as a therapist.

SOCIAL PSYCHOLOGY: MILGRAM (1963)

> Milgram, S. (1963), Behavioral study of obedience. *Journal of Abnormal and Social Psychology*, 67, 371–378

Aim

Milgram wanted to investigate if people would obey a *legitimate authority* figure even when asked to do something morally wrong – that is, injure another person.

Method and procedure

Milgram recruited his participants by advertising for volunteers to take part in a study at Yale University to see how punishment influenced learning (false aim). They would receive payment for taking part and even if they withdrew, participants would still be paid. Forty males took part, ranging from 20 to 50 years old, all from New Haven. Milgram also employed two confederates (someone working on behalf of the experimenter): one played the role of the 'experimenter' and was dressed in a white lab coat, and the other played the role of the 'learner'. The participants believed they were randomly allocated to be the 'teacher' or the 'learner' but the roles were always fixed so that the participant would be the teacher. They saw the learner being wired to a shock generator and also experienced a slight shock themselves (45 volts) to show that the shocks were real. The participants sat in a room adjacent to the learner and had to ask them a question. Every time they got an answer wrong, they were asked to administer a shock that increased in voltage with every wrong answer. The voltage ranged from 15 to 450 volts and increased in 15 volt increments; underneath the switches were labels – 'slight' to 'danger' to 'XXX'. The learner remained quiet until the shocks reached 300 volts, at which point they would bang on the wall between the two rooms and not give a response to the next question (this was to be taken as an incorrect answer). When the participants asked to stop the experiment, the experimenter would step in and say, 'You have no choice', 'You must go on' or 'It is essential that you go on'.

Findings

Some 65% of participants went to the maximum voltage of 450 volts, which was clearly marked as dangerous. Only 12.5% of participants stopped at the 300 volt level when the learner began to object.

Conclusion

Milgram concluded that if a person appears to have legitimate authority, people would obey their demands even if those demands are clearly morally wrong. He also said that evil acts are not always committed by evil people but that the situation can also play a part. While someone's disposition can contribute to their decisions, their actions depend on whether an authority figure has given them what they believe to be a legitimate order. The experimenter was wearing a white lab coat and the study took place at Yale University, so this probably also contributed to the legitimacy of the study.

Another conclusion that can be drawn from the study is the idea of *graduated commitment* (also known as gradual commitment). This is when someone tells you to do something small,

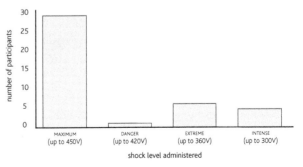

Figure 3.8: The results of Milgram's 1963 study of obedience.

which doesn't seem like a big deal, and then gradually tells you to do bigger and bigger things. In the study, Milgram started off at 15 volts, which doesn't seem like much (especially as the participants themselves experienced a 45 volt shock). When told to increase the shocks, the participants were willing to do so because it was gradual (i.e. only increasing by 15 volts rather than by 100 volts). This graduated commitment made it more difficult to refuse the commands as the experiment went on, because the increase in voltage was the same as it had always been.

Evaluation of Milgram (1963)

External validity

The study may lack ecological validity as it was in a controlled setting and is therefore not something that is experienced in everyday life. This may explain the extreme levels of *obedience* observed. However, other studies conducted in real-life settings support Milgram's study. Hofling et al. (1966) found that 95% of nurses were willing to administer a medication that exceeded the safe dosage when asked to do so by a fictitious doctor who phoned them. This is supporting evidence that the obedience seen in Milgram's study may also be found in real life.

Demand characteristics

One of the arguments put forward by Milgram's critics is that the participants didn't really believe they were giving real shocks. This would suggest that they may have been showing demand characteristics when they continued to administer them. However, in videos of the participants, they appear to be genuinely distressed so this is a questionable issue.

Limited sample

Only males took part in the experiment so the sample may lack generalisability (would the same levels of obedience be found in women?). There may also be a cultural bias as only Americans were used (might some cultures be more obedient than others?). While research has been conducted in other countries, the methods used were different from Milgram's and therefore it is hard to compare the results.

Ethical issues

Protection from harm

The videos of Milgram's participants show them experiencing extreme levels of distress. They showed signs of stress through sweating, shaking, biting their nails and three had full-blown seizures and had to be withdrawn from the experiment. The study may also have damaged their self-esteem; before they may have believed they were incapable of harming another person, but afterwards this belief was shattered. However, Milgram defended his study by stating that he did not expect to find the results he did, and when his participants were interviewed a year later, 80% said that they didn't regret taking part and showed no signs of long-term damage.

Deception

The participants were deceived by being told a false aim (i.e. that the allocation to the role of learner and teacher was random when it was fixed) and by being told that the generator administered real shocks when it didn't. However, if the participants weren't deceived, they would probably have shown demand characteristics and the results would lack validity.

Informed consent

As participants were deceived, they couldn't have given informed consent as they didn't know what they were agreeing to.

Right to withdraw

Although Milgram made it clear when recruiting participants that they could withdraw at any stage, the prompts by the experimenter to continue may have made them feel like they couldn't. This could explain why so many continued to the highest shock level.

DEVELOPMENTAL PSYCHOLOGY: KOHLBERG (1968)

Kohlberg, L. (1968). The child as a moral philosopher. *Psychology Today, 2*, 25–30

Aim

To investigate the moral development of children.

Method

Kohlberg was interested in the emergence of moral understanding (i.e. what is right and wrong) in children. He recruited 75 American boys aged 10–16 at the start of the study and followed them at three-year intervals until the ages of 22–28 (making this a longitudinal study). Moral development was also studied in boys of other cultures including Great Britain, Canada, Taiwan, Mexico and Turkey to allow for cross-cultural comparisons. Participants were presented with hypothetical moral dilemmas, in the form of short stories, to solve to determine

The Heinz dilemma

One of the most famous stories used in Kohlberg's research was the story of Heinz.

Heinz's wife was dying from a particular type of cancer. Doctors said a new drug might save her. The drug had been discovered by a local chemist and Heinz tried desperately to buy some, but the chemist was charging 10 times the money it cost to make the drug and this was much more than Heinz could afford.

Heinz could only raise half the money, even after help from family and friends. He explained to the chemist that his wife was dying and asked if he could have the drug cheaper or pay the rest of the money later. The chemist refused saying that he has discovered the drug and was going to make money from it. The husband was desperate to save his wife, so later that night he broke into the chemist's and stole the drug.

The participants would be asked things like, 'Should Heinz have stolen the drug?'

LEVEL	STAGE	MORAL REASONING SHOWN
1. Pre-conventional	1. Punishment and obedience orientation	Rules are kept to avoid punishment.
	2. Instrumental-relativist orientation	'Right' behaviour is that which ultimately brings rewards to oneself.
2. Conventional	3. Good boy–good girl orientation	'Good' behaviour pleases others – conformity to goodness. Behaviour is judged by intention (e.g. 'he means well').
	4. Law and order orientation	Doing one's duty and obeying laws is important.
3. Post-conventional	5. Social contract orientation	'Right' is what is democratically agreed upon; the 'legal point of view'.
	6. Universal principles orientation	Moral action is taken based upon self-chosen principles.

Table 3.34: Kohlberg's stages of moral development.

each participant's stage of moral reasoning for 25 moral concepts/aspects (see box 'The Heinz dilemma' for an example of a moral dilemma used by Kohlberg). For example, to test for the 'value of human life', they would be asked, 'Is it better to save the life of one important person or a lot of unimportant people?' and 'Should the doctor "mercy kill" a fatally ill woman requesting death because of her pain?' This was altered for different cultures, such as asking Taiwanese participants, 'A man's wife is starving to death but the store owner won't give the man any food unless he can pay, which he can't. Should he break in and steal some food? Why?' These responses were then analysed in relation to the boys' moral development.

Findings

From his analysis of the responses, Kohlberg was able to construct a six stage theory of moral development. This staged theory states that all children will go through the stages in the same order, without missing out any steps or returning to previous ones (e.g. no participants in stage 4 had been through stage 6, but all stage 6 participants had gone through stage 4). However, children progress at different rates and not all children reach the sixth stage.

Kohlberg also found that when a child at an earlier stage of development is confronted with the views of a child one stage further along than them, they tend to move forward a stage and prefer it.

In terms of culture, participants from Mexico and Taiwan showed the same results except that development was a little slower. However, at the age of 16, stage 5 thinking was much more salient in the United States than either Mexico or Taiwan. When looking at social standing, middle class children were found to be more advanced in moral judgement than matched lower class children and moved faster and further through the stages. In terms of religion, no important differences were found

in the development of moral thinking amongst Catholics, Protestants, Jews, Buddhists, Muslims or atheists.

Conclusion

From his empirical research, Kohlberg concluded that all children develop morally following the same stages as each other and that this moral development is not significantly affected by different social, cultural or religious conditions. The only thing that is affected is the rate at which individuals progress through the stages.

Evaluation of Kohlberg (1968)

Reliability

Some psychologists have criticised the fact that Kohlberg interviewed children at different ages to gather his data rather than following children of the same age. However, Colby et al. (1983) tested 58 male participants of Kohlberg's original study six times over 27 years and found support for Kohlberg's conclusion. This provides corroboration for the reliability of Kohlberg's assertion that we all pass through the stages of moral development in the same order.

Sample bias

The sample was all males and therefore the results may not be generalisable to women; it's androcentric. Gilligan (1977) states that men's morality is based on abstract principles of law and justice, while women's is based on principles of compassion and care, and therefore the stages may be different.

Culture bias

Even though Kohlberg did test participants from different cultures, the moral dilemmas he used may have been unintentionally biased to make Westernised children appear more morally developed. As they were conceived in the United States, it is difficult to claim that they weren't culturally biased because the moral dilemmas that might be experienced in one culture could be perceived in a very different way in another culture, and this would affect the moral judgements made by the participants.

Validity of the theory

Kohlberg claims that there are distinct stages in moral development but the evidence does not always support this. For example, a person who justified a decision using post-conventional reasoning in one situation might fall back on conventional reasoning in another. It seems that moral reasoning depends more on the situation than on general rules (e.g. of the stages). There is also the issue that individuals do not always progress through the stages – for example, Rest (1979) found that 1 in 14 actually slip backwards in the stages. The evidence for distinct stages to moral development is very weak and some argue that the theory is based on a culturally biased belief that American values are superior to those of other cultures and societies.

QUESTION TIME?

People often have difficulty carrying out more than one task at a time, especially when they are quite similar tasks. To investigate this, researchers presented groups of participants with telephone numbers to remember and recall. There were six participants, three in each group. Group 1 were given the numbers 0123456789 to learn in 30 seconds, in silence. Group 2 were given the numbers 0756382496 to learn in 30 seconds, whilst at the same time listening to a recording of a conversation (which they would also be tested on later).

(a) The hypothesis that was tested was: 'Fewer numbers will be recalled in the right order when a person also listens to a conversation.'

  (i) Is this a directional or non-directional hypothesis? *(1 mark)*

  (ii) What is the operationalised independent variable? *(1 mark)*

(b) Which type of experimental design is used in this experiment? *(1 mark)*

(c) Identify a flaw in this experiment and explain how the investigator might have avoided it. *(3 marks)*

(d) The data are presented in the graph.

  (i) What type of graph is this? *(1 mark)*

  (ii) What is the main finding indicated by the graph? *(1 mark)*

(e) Outline limitations of locating research in laboratory environments. *(4 marks)*

(f) The target population was 240 sixth-form students. Explain how you would obtain a systematic sample from this population for this study. *(3 marks)*

(g) Give one advantage of using systematic sampling. *(2 marks)*

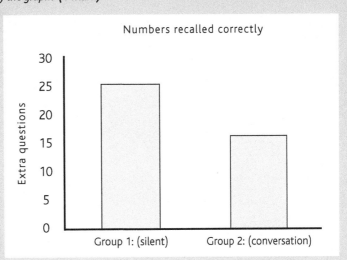

Numbers recalled correctly

Your AS Level

The AS specification is divided into two units:

COMPONENT	UNIT 1 PSYCHOLOGY: PAST TO PRESENT	UNIT 2 PSYCHOLOGY: USING PSYCHOLOGICAL CONCEPTS
Content	Compulsory questions relating to five psychological approaches and classic pieces of research	*Section A: Contemporary debates* One question on any of the debates. *Section B: Principles of research* Compulsory questions on the theory of psychological research (including social and developmental psychologists). *Section C: Application of research methods to a novel scenario* Compulsory questions requiring a response to a piece of research that has not been seen.
Assessment	Written exam: 1 hour 30 minutes	Written exam: 1 hour 30 minutes
Marks	80	80
% of AS qualification	50%	50%

ASSESSMENT OBJECTIVES

Throughout the course, you will be demonstrating your ability to meet the following assessment objectives (AOs).

You will hear a lot about AOs on internet forums, in textbooks, from the WJEC and from your teachers. However, the reality is that, other than telling you about the range of skills you will demonstrate in an exam, *they have very little relevance to you as a student doing an AS level examination!* Nigel and Rob have spent years and years advising teachers to develop the three skills (of course, they're really important) but to dump the jargon. Focus on learning and enjoying the psychology. Put the effort into becoming a good student of psychology rather than a dodgy examiner.

AO1	AO2	AO3
Demonstrate a knowledge and understanding of scientific ideas, processes, techniques and procedures.	Apply knowledge and understanding of scientific ideas, processes, techniques and procedures: • In a theoretical context. • In a practical context. • When handling qualitative data. • When handling quantitative data.	Analyse, interpret and evaluate a range of scientific information, ideas and evidence, including in relation to issues to: • Make judgements and reach conclusions. • Develop and refine practical design and procedures.

YOUR EXAMINATION

You have two examinations, each one covering different parts of the specification but assessing the same range of skills.

Unit 1: Psychology: Past to Present

This exam paper will never contain more than eight questions totalling 80 marks. These questions will range from short answers (2 or 3 marks) to longer answers (16 marks maximum). There are a wide range of questions you could be asked which will cover:

- Assumptions of the approaches.
- Evaluation of the approaches.
- Formation of relationships as explained by the approaches.
- Description and/or evaluation of classic evidence (studies).
- Description and/or evaluation of therapies.

Unit 2: Psychology: Using Psychological Concepts

This exam paper will contain a range of questions totalling 80 marks. There may be several questions requiring a longer written response, and one of these will be a contemporary debates question (up to a maximum of 20 marks). Questions will cover:

- Definitions of key psychological terms.
- Description and evaluation of social and/or developmental research.
- Data interpretation and analysis.
- Application of psychological terminology to a given scenario.
- Advantages and disadvantages of different aspects of psychological research.

HINTS AND TIPS

The exam papers largely consist of short answer questions – the questions are written to elicit skills, so by just answering the questions you *will* demonstrate the AOs. Amazing – the secret of exam success is revealed! There is one exception to this: the longer written response questions (e.g. 16 or 20 marks). You will need to show more than one skill with these questions but the clue is always in the question wording. With commands like 'identify', 'describe', 'outline' and 'evaluate', the requirement is clear enough – do what the command says. Longer answers, however, will use a command like 'discuss'. These kinds of command feel different – it is not obvious from the word itself what you have to do (like it is from 'outline'). Remember with these questions to give a balance of descriptive and evaluative skills. Don't just describe or you will lose a bunch of marks.

One other key thing to be aware of: if the question uses the word 'including', you *must* cover this in your answer. For instance, 'Explain the assumptions of the biological approach, including neurotransmitters.' If the question says 'for example', you have the option so you *may* include this in your answer (e.g. 'Explain the assumptions of the biological approach, for example neurotransmitters.'). These are the kinds of skills your teacher will impart – listen carefully, practice and learn. Success follows effort.

GLOSSARY

Age of witness The accuracy of the memory of an event (the *eyewitness testimony*) may be influenced by the age of the witness. The accuracy of the elderly or children may be questionable.

Aggression Intentional or unintentional harm directed towards others.

Aim The aims of a research project describe the reason for carrying out the research. They indicate what the research intends to investigate or find out.

Antidepressant Drugs used to treat mood disorders, particularly depression.

Antipsychotic Drugs used to treat the symptoms of psychotic disorders (e.g. schizophrenia), including hallucinations and disturbed thinking.

Anxiety The physical tension associated with feeling stressed. A factor that may influence the accuracy of an *eyewitness testimony*.

Anxiolytic Drugs used to treat feelings of anxiety, common examples of which are *benzodiazepines*.

Attachment An emotional bond between the child and the principal caregiver.

Aversion therapy A behaviourist therapy that aims to create a new stimulus–response bond that supresses the undesirable behaviour.

Bar chart Use data which come in categories (*nominal data*); these data can only fit into one category. The vertical axis should show the score of a *variable*, whilst the horizontal axis should show the individual categories, or *variables*, you measured.

Behavioural approach A *psychological approach* which sees abnormal behaviour as learned through a conditioning process, in much the same way as normal behaviour.

Behavioural category When engaging in any observation, categories of behaviour are decided upon for observing and recording. Behavioural categories might include things like 'aggression towards peers' or 'aggression towards carers' in a study where children's behaviour is being observed.

Benzodiazepines Drugs used in the control of *stress*. They work by affecting levels of *neurotransmitters*.

Biological approach Mental health problems are regarded as illnesses with identifiable physiological symptoms, origins and treatments.

Biological therapies Designed to alter the physical state of the body. These include *drug therapy*.

Blank slate A behaviourist assumption that we are born with basic drives (e.g. hunger) but we are not born with any innate characteristics, traits or behaviours.

Bowlby John Bowlby applied the principles of imprinting to the human infant–caregiver relationship and is regarded as the major thinker in the study of human *attachment*.

British Psychological Society (BPS) The professional body that governs the professional activity of psychologists in Britain.

Case study A detailed investigation, usually of a single individual with a particularly interesting or unusual psychological problem. An example of a case study includes Freud's Rat Man.

Classical conditioning Learning happens because we learn associations between things. For instance, Pavlov said that the dogs in his experiments associated the sound of footsteps with the stimulus of food. When they heard footsteps they began to salivate in anticipation of food. A similar relationship between stimuli and responses might be said to happen when infants and caregivers become attached.

Code of ethics What should and should not be done to ensure that research is carried out ethically.

Cognitive approach A *psychological approach* which considers abnormality to be a result of faulty thinking.

Cognitive-behavioural therapy (CBT) A *psychological therapy* within the *cognitive approach*. CBT aims to identify errors and distortions in thinking that give rise to problems and help clients to find alternative ways of thinking to overcome them.

Cognitive interview A technique employed by the police to carefully help a witness recall the events of an often stressful event or experience.

Cognitive triad According to Beck, depressed patients typically think negatively about themselves, the world and the future; the three things make up the cognitive triad.

Computer analogy A *cognitive approach* that compares the human mind to a computer; information is processed through input, storage and retrieval.

Condition A word used in research methods to describe different manipulations of the *independent variable*.

Confidentiality An *ethical issue*; *participants'* details and performance in research is private and not open to public scrutiny.

Confounding variable A confounding variable is one that interferes with ('confounds') the relationship between the two *variables* we want to study and can lead us to an incorrect conclusion.

Content analysis A method of data collection that takes information from the content of things like newspapers, magazines, television programmes or recorded conversations.

Correlation A technique used to show whether two *variables* are related. A *positive correlation* includes the relationship between, for example, the amount of time spent revising and the exam mark (the more revising you do, the better your mark will be). A *negative correlation* might be, for example, the number of DVDs purchased from your savings and the amount of money in your savings account (the more DVDs you buy, the less money you have left).

Correlation coefficient A statistic that describes the *correlation* data. It varies between −1 and +1. A *positive correlation* has a correlation coefficient of between 0 and +1. A *negative correlation* has a coefficient of between 0 and −1. A *zero correlation* will have a coefficient of 0. Coefficients closest to 1 are strongest.

Co-variable A term used in correlational research. Co-variables both vary and they are both measured; they are never set or manipulated by the researcher. Co-variables tend to have a relationship with each other.

Debriefing A method used to overcome *ethical issues*.

Deception An *ethical issue*; *participants* are in some way deliberately misled or misinformed.

Demand characteristic Details in the conduct of a study that give *participants* some idea of how the researcher wants them to respond.

Dependent variable (DV) The attribute the researcher measures that depends on the *independent variable*. For instance, if the research is concerned with how fast we can run while carrying different weights, then the *independent variable* might be the different weights and the attribute that depends on this (the dependent variable) is the running speed. It is this that the researchers record as their data.

Directional hypothesis A *hypothesis* that sets out a particular prediction of what the research will find. For instance, the *hypothesis* that 'Girls are better at science than boys' is directional; it predicts that girls will get higher scores in science tests than boys will. Sometimes called a one-tailed hypothesis.

Distress A negative kind of *stress*; caused by stressors that we feel we cannot cope with.

Dream analysis A method used in psychodynamic therapy where the therapist interprets a client's dreams. In the *psychodynamic approach*, the content of the dream is regarded as having meaning, since it is in dreams that hidden unconscious thoughts are freely expressed.

Drug therapy A physiological method of *stress* management that involves taking medications to reduce the physical symptoms of stress. They include *benzodiazepines*. It may be palliative (the symptoms of abnormality are suppressed) or curative (the mental health problem is cured).

Ethical guidelines A set of ethical principles designed to prevent research from infringing on the rights of *participants*.

Ethical issue Issues that must be considered in the design of research if it is to be regarded as ethically sound. These include informed consent, *deception*, *debriefing*, the right to withdraw, *confidentiality* and protection from harm.

Ethics committee A committee that oversees psychological research to ensure it is conducted ethically.

Event sampling All clearly defined relevant behaviours are recorded each time they occur.

Evolution A theory made famous by Charles Darwin. It describes how species develop over generations and evolve to live in the world around us and cope with the demands placed upon them by their environment. The mechanisms by which we do this include *natural selection* and sexual selection.

Experimental design The process of designing experiments – that is, whether or not the same or different *participants* are used in

all *conditions* of the experiment. There are a number of different general design options open to the researcher, each with their own strengths and weaknesses (e.g. *repeated measures design*).

Experimental method A description of how research is carried out in psychology.

External reliability The extent to which something is consistent over several different occasions.

External validity How well the findings of a study can be generalised outside of the study itself.

Extraneous variables Factors other than the *independent variable* that might influence the *dependent variable*. These need to be avoided or controlled at all costs.

Eyewitness testimony (EWT) The report of what happened in a crime or an event by someone who has seen or witnessed it.

Field experiment Research that involves the direct manipulation of *variables* in a natural environment (i.e. not in a laboratory).

Free association A method used in psychodynamic therapy where the therapist attempts to access the subconscious. Words are presented to the client, who replies with the first word that comes to mind. An example might be 'carrot' associated with 'rabbit'. The responses of the client allow the therapist to draw conclusions about the client's subconscious.

Free will The ability to make our own choices without the interference of fate.

Frequency table Used to display raw data that is easy to understand and interpret; it shows how often a certain score occurred or was frequent in a given set of scores.

Graph A visual, pictorial method of presenting data.

Histogram Similar to *bar charts* but use continuous data rather than discrete data; the *variable* on the horizontal axis is a scale of something.

Hormone Chemicals released into the bloodstream by the endocrine system that travel rapidly to different parts of the body. Some have a general effect on the body and some influence specific organs or glands.

Hypothesis The hypothesis is central to research. It is a formalised version of the *aims* of the research and is set out as a statement that the research attempts to test. It may be *directional* or *non-directional*.

Independent groups design Also known as independent samples. An *experimental design* whereby *participants* are allocated to different groups. Each group does something slightly different in the experiment, and the performance of the different groups is then compared.

Independent variable (IV) The *variable* manipulated by the researcher. Ideally, the only thing you want to influence is the *dependent variable*.

Individual differences The things that make people different from one another. This may include the study of such things as *personality*, gender and abnormality.

Internal reliability Refers to the extent to which something is consistent within itself.

Internal validity Refers to the study itself and whether the researcher has measured what they intended to.

Inter-rater reliability A comparison of two or more observations of the same event to see if there is consistency.

Interval data Data that is measured on a scale (e.g. height).

Interview A method of data collection whereby a researcher asks a *participant* questions. The interview can take a number of forms – for example, it may be structured or unstructured.

Investigator effect A situation in research where an investigator unintentionally encourages a *participant* to behave in a certain way.

Laboratory experiment Research that is carried out in controlled conditions in a laboratory. Typically, in psychology, a laboratory is a quiet room where people will not be disturbed and where sights and sounds can be carefully controlled.

Legitimate authority People are more likely to obey others whom they regard as having legitimate authority. These people might include police officers, doctors or maybe even teachers and lecturers!

Line graph Used to present relationships between quantitative *variables* when the *independent variable* has, or is organised into, a relatively small number of distinct levels.

Localisation of brain function The theory that particular areas of the brain are specialised for certain functions or tasks.

Matched pairs Like an *independent groups design* but members in each of the groups are matched (for age, gender, etc.) with people in the other group. The best matched pair to use is identical twins.

Mean A *measure of central tendency*. The sum of all the values divided by the number of values that there were.

Measure of central tendency A *summary statistic*. The 'average' value. There are three averages: the *mean*, the *mode* and the *median*.

Measure of dispersion A *summary statistic* that describes how spread out the data are.

Median A *measure of central tendency*. When the data are put in order, smallest value to largest value or largest to smallest, the median is the central number if there are an odd number of values. If there are an even number of values then the media is the mean of the two numbers in the middle.

Milgram Stanley Milgram designed a series of experiments in the early 1960s to investigate *obedience* to authority.

Mindfulness A positive approach therapy that aims to develop a sense of 'here and now' in an individual, so the focus of a person's attention is on what is happening in their mind and environment in the present moment.

Misleading information Information that encourages witnesses to recall events in ways in which they did not happen. For instance, asking, 'You did see a young boy in a white hooded top, didn't you?', may lead the memory of the witnesses and encourage them to answer yes even though they had not seen such a person.

Mode A *measure of central tendency*. The most common value in the data set. If there are two numbers that are equally common then we say that there are two modes – bimodal. If there are more than two numbers that are equally common then we can say that the data are multimodal.

Natural experiment A little like a *field experiment* but in this case the *variables* are not manipulated. Rather, researchers take advantage of naturally occurring changes to observe natural behaviour. For instance, if a city centre changes its roads to one-way, then the behaviour of road users before and after the change (a naturally occurring change) can be monitored.

Natural selection A central principle of *evolution*. Animals produce many young and not all can survive. Those that do because of cunning, strength, etc., are 'naturally selected' to pass on their genetic material to the next generation.

Naturalistic observation A technique whereby the behaviour of people in their natural environment is observed.

Negative correlation A *correlation* which suggests that as one *variable* increases, the other decreases. For example, the number of DVDs purchased and the amount of money in our bank account: the more DVDs we buy, the less money we have left.

Nervous system A system of billions of *neurons* communicating using *neurotransmitters*.

Divided into two parts, the central nervous system (CNS) and the peripheral nervous system (PNS).

Neurons Specialised nerve cells that make up the *nervous system*.

Neuroscience The study of the function of the brain and nervous system to understand the impact of these structures on our behaviour and cognition.

Neurotransmitter A chemical used in transmitting information between *neurons* in the brain, examples of which include dopamine and serotonin. Imbalances in neurotransmitters may lead to abnormal feelings or behaviours. Addressing imbalances using *drug therapy* can reduce symptoms of mental health disorders.

Nominal data Data that can be classified into categories; if something is in one category, it cannot also be in another category.

Non-directional hypothesis A *hypothesis* that does not set out a precise prediction of what the research will find. For instance, the hypothesis, 'Ability at science depends on whether you are a girl or a boy', is non-directional because it does not predict that girls will be better or worse than boys. Rather, it states that there will be a difference between the genders. Sometimes called a two-tailed hypothesis.

Non-participant observation Where a researcher remains outside and unobserved during the observation.

Null hypothesis A *hypothesis* (written as H_0) which predicts that what we find in our research happened by chance.

Obedience A direct form of social influence where people do as they are told by an authority figure.

Observational method A research method that involves observing people, usually in their natural environment, and systematically recording what they say and do.

Observational technique A data-gathering technique used in a number of different research methods.

Online research Research that is conducted on the internet, either through questionnaires, surveys or content analysis.

Operant conditioning Learning happens because we are rewarded (or reinforced) for our behaviour, or the way we feel, or because we are punished for it. For instance, a child may learn that smiling is rewarded by loving kind words so he or she may repeat the behaviour more often.

Operationalise To make something measurable. For instance, if our *dependent variable* is 'memory score', then we can operationalise it by saying, 'Memory score on a 10 item list'.

Opportunity sampling A method of *sampling* whereby *participants* are chosen to take part because they are convenient. An example might be asking people who happen to be sitting in a local cafe.

Ordinal data Data that have an order or rank.

Participant observations An observation where a researcher is directly involved in the situation being observed (this is called participant observation) or can remain outside and unobserved (called *non-participant observation*).

Participant One who takes part in research.

Personality A collection of characteristics or traits that make us who we are.

Pie chart Shows the differences in frequencies or percentages amongst categories of a nominal or ordinal *variable*. The categories are displayed as segments of a circle whose pieces add up to 100% of the total frequencies.

Pilot study A brief version of the full research that is quicker, perhaps less controlled, and involves fewer *participants*. The pilot experiment is useful to iron out any unforeseen problems and also to give the researchers an idea of what might happen. Sometimes researchers may change their design or their *hypothesis* because a pilot study has suggested that they should.

Positive approach Martin Seligman described positive psychology as the scientific study of optimal human functioning that aims to help people prosper and lead healthier and more satisfactory lives.

Positive correlation A *correlation* that suggests that as one *variable* increases, so too does the other. For instance, the amount of food eaten is positively correlated with how full we feel; the more food eaten, the more full we feel.

Primary source Primary data are those that are gained directly by the researcher.

Progressive relaxation A technique where people learn how to relax the tension in their muscles that accompanies their feelings of anxiety. It is often part of *systematic desensitisation*, a behavioural therapy for abnormality.

Psyche In the *psychodynamic approach* to abnormality, the psyche is the name given to the mind.

Psychoanalysis A *psychological therapy* within the *psychodynamic approach*. Developed by Freud in the 1890s, it can involve dream analysis or free association. The goal of the therapy is to reveal unconscious, hidden thoughts that hold the origin of the person's abnormality.

Psychodynamic approach A *psychological approach*. The mind (*psyche*) is seen as being influenced by powerful and changing (dynamic) unconscious forces. Most closely associated with Sigmund Freud.

Psychological approach Mental health problems, resulting from abnormal thoughts, feelings and behaviours have their origins in our psychology.

Psychological therapies Therapies that are based on the assumptions of *psychological approaches*. These include *psychoanalysis*, *systematic desensitisation* and *cognitive-behavioural therapy*.

Psychosurgery A *physiological therapy* that aims to alleviate the symptoms of mental illnesses or disorders by destroying areas of the brain or interrupting the functioning between particular areas that may be the cause of the behaviour.

Qualitative Research that focuses on collecting data in the form of opinions.

Quality of Life Therapy A positive approach therapy that aims to help clients identify and meet their goals and wishes in life.

Quantitative Research that generates data in the form of numbers.

Questionnaire A pen-and-paper (or, more often than not these days, online) selection of different types of questions, the answers to which allow researchers to address the aims of their research.

Quota sampling Quota sampling is very similar to *stratified sampling*. The first stages are exactly the same: the proportions of different groups within the target population are calculated and this will then translate across to the sample you need. Once one quota has been reached, all *participants* who come along who meet the criterion would be disregarded.

Random sampling A method of *sampling* whereby all *participants* in a population have an equal chance of being selected to take part in the study. An example might be random generation of names by a computer or drawing names out of a hat.

Range A *measure of dispersion*. The simplest measure, given by subtracting the smallest number in the set from the largest.

Ratio data Ratio data means that whatever *variable* we are measuring has an absolute zero (a point where none of the quality being measured exists), which allows us to make comparisons (e.g. twice as much).

Rational emotive behaviour therapy (REBT) A cognitive therapy that seeks to replace irrational cognitions with rational thoughts so that behaviour will change in the long term.

Reciprocal inhibition In *systematic desensitisation*, the client's stress response to a stimulus becomes inhibited because it is incompatible with another behaviour. For instance, if the client is in deep relaxation, and the stressful stimulus is brought to mind, then the usual feeling of anxiety is inhibited because one cannot feel anxious and relaxed at the same time.

Reconstructive memory We don't store exact records of events in memory. This means that when we recall information we change it – for example, according to logic and common sense. Memories that are reconstructed might therefore not resemble the actual event.

Reinforcement In *learning theory*, something that increases the likelihood of a behaviour occurring again.

Reliability Another name for consistency. A reliable study is one that, if repeated, would return the same result. In observational research, where different people 'rate' behaviours, you might measure *inter-rater reliability* so as to check whether the different researchers agree with one another.

Repeated measures design An *experimental design* in which each *participant* takes part on more than one occasion. Results are a comparison of the person's performance under each of the *conditions*. For instance, if the experiment aimed to investigate whether running speed is influenced by the amount of weight carried, the *independent variable* would be 'weight carried'. Under a repeated measures design, each person would run carrying one weight, then the same person would run carrying another weight and so on.

Researcher bias The notion that researchers could behave in ways that might influence the investigation. For example, they may give cues, such as the use of language, that signify something to the participant that may affect the validity of the results.

Sampling The act of choosing *participants* to take part in the study.

Sampling frame The method used to select *participants* from the target population based on characteristics. This is usually from a list of all the accessible *participants* in the population.

Scattergram Also known as a scatterplot or scattergraph. A graph that plots a person's score on one *variable* on one axis and their score on another value on the other axis. The *scattergram* is used to depict correlation data.

Schema A collection of ideas for people, places and activities.

Secondary sources Secondary data are those that have already been collected but which are reused by the researcher.

Self-report A method of collecting data from people where the *participants* present the information themselves, such as in a *questionnaire* or an *interview*.

Self-selected sampling See *volunteer sampling*.

Semi-structured interview There are no fixed questions in a semi-structured interview; instead the *interview* is guided by a predetermined set of topics or themes to be covered. The order in which they are covered, or the way in which they are addressed by the interviewer, can vary across *participants*.

Separation anxiety An infant's suspicion and possible fear at the approach of someone unfamiliar (a stranger).

Snowball sampling Used in research where members of a target population are difficult to locate or are rare. It works by the researcher identifying *participants* and then asking them to refer, or nominate, other potential *participants* who are similar in some way.

Social desirability When someone alters their behaviour or responses to portray themselves in a way that is desirable to society.

Standard deviation A *measure of dispersion*. Calculated using a mathematical formula, it describes the 'average' distance that each value in the data is away from the *mean*.

Stratified sampling The researcher identifies the different groups of *participants* within the target population (e.g. gender, age). *Participants* from each group (strata) are then randomly selected based on the frequency of occurrence in the general population.

Stress The body's way of responding to a demand placed on it. Some stress is positive, and motivates and drives us – this is eustress. When we cannot cope with stress because it is either too much, or too little (leading to boredom and apathy), it is called *distress*.

Structured interview The same questions are presented to each *participant* in the same way. Sometimes referred to as a verbal questionnaire.

Summary statistics Numbers that include a *measure of central tendency* and a *measure of dispersion*, which provide a useful summary of the data.

Systematic desensitisation A psychological therapy within the *behavioural approach*. It is based on *classical conditioning* and is designed to reduce feelings of anxiety. A person is first taught relaxation techniques, and then the therapist exposes him or her to increasingly more stressful stimuli in an anxiety hierarchy, at each stage helping the client to relax and cope. Eventually the client is able to deal with the focus of the anxiety alone.

Systematic sampling This technique chooses subjects in a systematic (i.e. orderly or logical) way from the *target population*. The most common way is choosing every *n*th *participant* on a list of names.

Table A method of presenting data or *summary statistics* as numbers in an organised grid.

Target population A target population is defined as all the members of a particular group from which *participants* are selected.

Time sampling Making observations for short intervals within a given period of time.

Tripartite personality Freud's theory that the adult *personality* is made up of three components: the id, ego and superego.

Valid consent An *ethical issue*; *participants* must be fully informed about the study before they agree to take part.

Validity If the research investigates what it says it will investigate then it is said to be valid. Similarly, if a tool used in research is valid then it measures what it is supposed to. For instance, a technique for measuring *attachment* is the Strange Situation which is regarded as being valid for that purpose. Using a thermometer to measure *attachment* is not valid.

Variable Something that is changed or controlled in research. These include *extraneous*, *independent* and *dependent variables*.

Volunteer sampling A method of *sampling* whereby *participants* volunteer to take part, perhaps by responding to a notice requesting volunteers.

Zero correlation *Correlation* data which suggests that there is no relationship between the two *variables* at all. For instance, the number of apples on an apple tree and the amount of time you spend watching TV.

REFERENCES

Aharoni, E., Vincent, G., Harenski, C., Calhoun, V., Sinnott-Armstrong, W., Gazzaniga, M. and Kiehl, K. (2013). Neuroprediction of future re-arrest. *Proceedings of the National Academy of Sciences USA*, 110(15), 6223–6228.

Alberto, P. and Troutman, A. (2012). *Applied Behaviour Analysis for Teachers* (2nd edn). Upper Saddle River, NJ: Pearson Education.

Bancroft, J. (1992). *Deviant Sexual Behaviour*. Oxford: Oxford University Press.

Beck, A. T. (1976). *Cognitive Therapy and the Emotional Disorders*. New York: International Universities Press.

Blackburn, I. and Moorhead, S. (2000). Update in cognitive therapy for depression. *Journal of Cognitive Psychotherapy*, 14(3), 305–311.

Bowlby, J. (1944). Forty-four juvenile thieves: their character and home-life. *International Journal of Psychoanalysis*, 25, 19–52.

Bowlby, J. (1951). *Maternal Care and Mental Health*. Geneva: WHO; London: HMSO.

Bowlby, J. (1958). The nature of the child's ties to his mother. *International Journal of Psychoanalysis*, 39, 350–371.

British Association for Counselling and Psychotherapy (2010). *Ethical Framework for Good Practice in Counselling and Psychotherapy* (rev edn). Lutterworth: BACP.

British Psychological Society (2001). *Code of Conduct, Ethical Principles, & Guidelines*. Leicester: BPS.

British Psychological Society (2012). *Guidelines for Psychologists Working with Animals*. Leicester: BPS.

Brophy, J. (1996). *Enhancing Students' Socialization: Key Elements*. Urbana, IL: ERIC Clearinghouse on Elementary and Early Childhood Education.

Buss, D. M. (1989). Sex differences in human mate preferences: evolutionary hypotheses tested in 37 cultures. *Behavioral and Brain Sciences*, 12, 1–49.

Buss, D. M. (1995). Evolutionary psychology: a new paradigm for psychological science. *Psychological Inquiry*, 6, 1–30.

Butler, R. J. (2004). Childhood nocturnal enuresis: developing a conceptual framework. *Clinical Psychology Review*, 24, 909–931.

Campbell, A. (2002). *A Mind of Her Own: The Evolutionary Psychology of Women*. Oxford: Oxford University Press.

Cassidy, J. (1999). The nature of the child's ties. In J. Cassidy and P. R. Shaver (eds.), *Handbook of Attachment: Theory, Research, and Clinical Applications*. New York: Guilford Press, pp. 3–20.

Ceci, S. J. and Friedman, R. D. (2000). The suggestibility of children: scientific research and legal implications. *Cornell Law Review*, 86, 34–108.

Choy, Y., Fyer, A. J. and Lipsitz, J. D. (2007). Treatment of specific phobia in adults. *Clinical Psychology Review*, 27, 266–286.

Colby, A., Kohlberg, L., Gibbs, J. and Lieberman, M. (1983). A longitudinal study of moral judgment. *Monographs of the Society for Research in Child Development*, 48(1–2), serial no. 200.

Comer, R. J. (2006). *Abnormal Psychology*. New York: Worth.

Crocker, J. and Major, B. (1989). Social stigma and self-esteem: the self-protective properties of stigma. *Psychological Review*, 96, 608–630.

D'Astous, M., Cottin, S., Roy, M., Picard, C. and Cantin, L. (2013). Bilateral stereotactic anterior capsulotomy for obsessive-compulsive disorder: long-term follow-up.

Journal of Neurology, Neurosurgery and Psychiatry, 84(11), 1208–1213.

David, D., Szentagotai, A., Lupu, V. and Cosman, D. (2008). Rational emotive behavior therapy, cognitive therapy, and medication in the treatment of major depressive disorder: a randomized clinical trial, posttreatment outcomes, and six-month follow-up. *Journal of Clinical Psychology*, 64 (6), 728–746.

Davidson, R. J., Kabat-Zinn, J., Schumacher, J., Rosenkranz, M., Muller, D., Santorelli, S. F. and Urbanowski, F. (2003). Alterations in brain and immune function produced by mindfulness meditation. *Psychosomatic Medicine*, 65(4), 564–570.

DeRubeis, R. J., Hollon, S. D., Amsterdam, J. D., Shelton, R. C., Young, P. R., Salomon, R. M., O'Reardon, J. P., Lovett, M. L., Gladis, M. M., Brown, L. L. and Gallop, R. (2005). Cognitive therapy vs. medications in the treatment of moderate to severe depression. *Archives of General Psychiatry*, 62, 409–416.

Devlin, Honourable Lord Patrick (chair) (1976). Report to the Secretary of State for the Home Department of the Departmental Committee on Evidence of Identification in Criminal Cases [Devlin Report]. London: HMSO.

Diener, E. and Seligman, M. E. P. (2002). Very happy people. *Psychological Science*, 13(1), 81–84.

Diener, E. and Seligman, M. E. P. (2004). Beyond money: toward an economy of well-being. *Psychological Science in the Public Interest*, 5, 1–31.

Diener, E., Sandvik, E., Seidlitz, L. and Diener, M. (1993). The relationship between income and subjective well-being: relative or absolute. *Social Indicators Research*, 28, 195–223.

Diener, E. and Biswas-Diener, R. (2008). *Happiness: Unlocking the Mysteries of Psychological Wealth*. Oxford: Wiley-Blackwell.

Doll, C., McLaughlin, T. F. and Barretto, A. (2013).The token economy: a recent review and evaluation. *International Journal of Basic and Applied Science*, 2, 131–149.

Elkin, I., Shea, M. T., Watkins, J. T., Imber, S. D., Sotsky, S. M., Collins, J. F., Glass, D. R., Pilkonis, P. A., Leber, W. R., Docherty, J. P., Fiester, S. J. and Parloff, M. B. (1989). National Institute of Mental Health Treatment of Depression Collaborative Research Program: general effectiveness of treatments. *Archives of General Psychiatry*, 46, 971–982.

Ellis, A. (1962). *Reason and Emotion in Psychotherapy*. New York: Lyle Stuart.

Evans, M. D., Hollon, S. D., DeRubeis, R. J., Piasecki, J. M., Grove, W. M., Garvey, M. J. and Tuason, V. B. (1992). Differential relapse following cognitive therapy and pharmacotherapy for depression. *Archives of General Psychiatry*, 49, 802–808.

Eysenck, H. J. (1952). The effects of psychotherapy: an evaluation. *Journal of Consulting Psychology*, 16, 319–324.

Fawley, P. J. and Smith, J. W. (1990). Chemical aversion therapy in the treatment of cocaine dependence as part of a multimodal treatment program: treatment outcome. *Journal of Substance Abuse Treatment*, 7(1), 21–29.

Feeney, B. (2007). The dependency paradox in close relationships: accepting dependence promotes independence. *Journal of Personality and Social Psychology*, 92(2), 268–285.

Filcheck, H. A., McNeil, C. B., Greco, L. A. and Bernard, R. S. (2004). Using a whole-class token economy and coaching of teacher skills in a preschool classroom to manage disruptive behavior. *Psychology in the Schools*, 41, 351–361.

Fisher, R. P., Chin, D. M. and McCauley, M. R. (1990). Enhancing eyewitness recollection with the cognitive interview. *National Police Research Unit Review*, 6, 3–11.

Fisher, S. and Greenberg, R. P. (1996). *Freud Scientifically Reappraised: Testing the Theories and Therapy.* New York: John Wiley.

Fontaine, N. M. G., McCrory, E. J. P., Boivin, M., Moffitt, T. E. and Viding, E. (2011). Predictors and outcomes of joint trajectories of callous-unemotional traits and conduct problems in childhood. *Journal of Abnormal Psychology*, 120(3), 730–742.

Foulkes, S. H. (1964). *Therapeutic Group Analysis.* London: George Allen & Unwin.

Frisch, M. B. (2013). Evidence-Based Well-Being/Positive Psychology Assessment and Intervention with Quality of Life Therapy and Coaching and the Quality of Life Inventory (QOLI), *Social Indicators Research*, 114, 193–227.

Frisch, M. B. (2006). *Quality of Life Therapy.* Hoboken, NJ: Wiley.

Geiselman, R. E., Fisher, R. P., MacKinnon, D. P. and Holland, H. L. (1986). Enhancement of eyewitness memory with the cognitive interview. *American Journal of Psychology*, 99, 385–401.

Gilligan, C. (1977). In a Different Voice: Women's Conceptions of Self and of Morality, *Harvard Educational Review*, 47(4), 481–517.

Gonzalez, J. E., Nelson, J. R., Gutkin, T. B., Saunders, A., Galloway, A. and Shwery, C. S. (2004). Rational emotive therapy with children and adolescents: a meta-analysis. *Journal of Emotional and Behavioural Disorders*, 12(4), 222–235.

Greist, J. H., Marks, I. M., Baer, L., Parkin, J. R., Manzo, P. A., Mantle, J. M., Wenzel, K. W., Spierings, C. J., Kobak, K. A., Dottl, S. L., Bailey, T. M. and Forman, L. (1998). Self-treatment for obsessive compulsive disorder using a manual and a computerized telephone interview: a US–UK study. *MD Computing*, 15, 149–157.

Grünbaum, A. (1993). *Validation in the Clinical Theory of Psychoanalysis: A Study in the Philosophy of Psychoanalysis.* New York: International Universities Press.

Hensley, P. L., Nadiga, D. and Uhlenhuth, E. H. (2004). Long-term effectiveness of cognitive therapy in major depressive disorder. *Depression and Anxiety*, 20, 1–7.

Hill, K. and Hurtado, A. M. (1996). *Ache Life History: The Ecology and Demography of a Foraging People.* New York: Aldine.

Hofling, C. K., Brotzman, E., Dalrymple, S., Graves, N. and Pierce, C. M. (1966). An experimental study in nurse-physician relationships. *Journal of Nervous Mental Disease*, 143, 171–180.

Hölzel, B. K., Carmody, J., Vangel, M., Congleton, C., Yerramsetti. S. M. and Gard, T. (2011). Mindfulness practice leads to increases in regional brain gray matter density. *Psychiatry Research: Neuroimaging*, 191, 36–43.

Hrdy, S. B. (1999). *Mother Nature: A History of Mothers, Infants, and Natural Selection.* New York: Pantheon Books.

Huppert, F. and Johnson, D. (2010). A controlled trial of mindfulness training in schools: the importance of practice for an impact on well-being. *Journal of Positive Psychology*, 5(4), 264–274.

Jung, H. H., Kim, S. J., Roh, D., Chang, J. G., Chang, W. S., Kweon, E. J., Kim, C. H. and Chang, J. W. (2015). Bilateral thermal capsulotomy with MR-guided focused ultrasound for patients with treatment-refractory obsessive-compulsive disorder: a proof-of-concept study. *Molecular Psychiatry*, 20, 1205–1211.

Kabat-Zinn, J. (2003). Mindfulness: the heart of rehabilitation. In E. Leskowitz (ed.), *Complementary and Alternative Medicine in Rehabilitation.* St Louis, MO: Churchill Livingstone, pp. xi–xv.

Keller, H. (2003). Socialization for competence: cultural models of infancy. *Human Development*, 46(5), 288–311.

Kendall, P. C. (1993). Cognitive-behavioural therapies with youth: guiding theory, current status and emerging developments. *Journal of Consulting and Clinical Psychology*, 61(2), 235–247.

Kim, M. C., Lee, T. K., and Choi, C. R. (2002). Review of long-term results of stereotactic psychosurgery. *Neurologia Medico-chirurgica (Tokyo)*, 42, 365–371.

Kohlberg, L. (1968). The child as a moral philosopher. *Psychology Today*, 2, 25–30.

Kraut, R., Olson, J., Banaji, M., Bruckman, A., Cohen, J. and Couper, M. (2004). Psychological research online: report of board of scientific affairs' advisory group on the conduct of research on the internet. *American Psychologist*, 59(2), 105–117.

Kupfer, D. J. and Frank, E. (2001). The interaction of drug- and psycho-therapy in the long-term treatment of depression. *Journal of Affective Disorders*, 62, 131–137.

Langston, C. A. (1994). Capitalizing on and coping with daily life events: expressive responses to positive events. *Journal of Personality and Social Psychology*, 67, 1112–1125.

Loftus, E. F. (2003). Our changeable memories: legal and practical implications. *Nature Reviews: Neuroscience*, 4, 231–234.

Loftus, E. F. and Ketcham, K. (1994) *The Myth of Repressed Memory*. New York: St. Martin's Press.

Loftus, E. F. and Palmer, J. C. (1974). Reconstruction of automobile destruction: an example of the interaction between language and memory. *Journal of Verbal Learning and Verbal Behavior*, 13, 585–589.

Massie, H, and Szajnberg, N. (2002). The relationship between mothering in infancy, childhood experience and adult mental health. *International Journal of Psychoanalysis*, 83(1), 35–55.

McClure, S. M., Li, J., Tomlin, D., Cypert, K. S., Montague, L. M. and Montague, P. R. (2004). Neural correlates of behavioral preference for culturally familiar drinks. *Neuron*, 44, 379–387.

Meehan, C. L. (2005). The effects of maternal residential locality on parental and alloparental caregiving among the Aka foragers of central Africa. *Human Nature*, 16, 62–84.

Milgram, S. (1963). Behavioral study of obedience. *Journal of Abnormal and Social Psychology*, 67, 371–378.

Miller, D. W. (2000). Looking askance at eyewitness testimony. *Chronicle of Higher Education*, 25 February.

Montoya, R. M. (2007). Gender similarities and differences in preferences for specific body parts. *Current Research in Social Psychology,* 13 (11), 133–144.

Myers, D. G. and Diener, E. (1995). Who is happy? *Psychological Science*, 6(1), 10–19.

Paul, G. L. (1966). *Insight versus Desensitization in Psychotherapy: An Experiment in Anxiety Reduction*. Stanford, CA: Stanford University Press.

Pavlov, I. P. (1897). *The Work of the Digestive Glands*. London: Griffin.

Peterson, C. (2006). *A Primer in Positive Psychology*. Oxford: Oxford University Press.

Raine, A., Buchsbaum, M. and LaCasse, L. (1997). Brain abnormalities in murderers indicated by positron emission tomography. *Biological Psychiatry*, 42(6), 495–508.

Raine, A., Mellingen, K., Liu, J., Venables, P. and Mednick, S. A. (2003). Effects of environmental enrichment at ages 3–5 years on schizotypal personality and anti-social behaviour at ages 17 and 23 years. *American Journal of Psychiatry*, 160, 1627–1635.

Rest, J. R. (1979). *Development in Judging Moral Issues*. Minneapolis, MN: University of Minnesota Press.

Rodrigue, J. R., Baz, M. A., Widows, M. R. and Ehlers, S. L. (2005). A randomized evaluation of Quality of Life Therapy with patients awaiting lung transplantation. *American Journal of Transplantation*, 5(10), 2425–2432.

Schaffer, H. R. and Emerson, P. E. (1964). The development of social attachment in infancy. *Monographs of the Society for Research in Child Development*, 29(3), serial no. 94.

Schou, I., Ekeberg, Ø., Sandvik, L., Hjermstad, M. J. and Ruland, C. M. (2005). Multiple predictors of health-related quality of life in early stage breast cancer: data from a year follow-up study compared with the general population. *Quality of Life Research*, 14(8), 1813–1823.

Segerstrom, S. C. and Sephton, S. E. (2010). Optimistic expectancies and cell-mediated immunity: the role of positive affect. *Psychological Science*, 21(3), 448–455.

Seligman, M. E. P. (2011). *Flourish*. New York: Simon & Schuster.

Seligman, M. E. P. (2002). *Authentic Happiness*. New York: Simon & Schuster.

Singh, D. (1993). Adaptive significance of female physical attractiveness: role of waist-to-hip ratio. *Journal of Personality and Social Psychology*, 65(2), 293–307.

Skinner, B. F. (1948). Superstition in the pigeon. *Journal of Experimental Psychology,* 38, 168–172.

Smith, J. E., Meyers, R. J. and Delaney, H. D. (1997). Community reinforcement approach with homeless alcohol-dependent individuals. *Journal of Consulting and Clinical Psychology,* 66, 541–548.

Smith, J. W. (1988). Long term outcome of clients treated in a commercial stop smoking program. *Journal of Substance Abuse Treatment,* 5(1), 33–36.

Steeves, J. A., Thompson, D. L., Bassett, D. R., Fitzhugh, E. C. and Raynor, H. A. (2012). A review of different behavior modification strategies designed to reduce sedentary screen behaviors in children. *Journal of Obesity*, 2012. Article ID 379215, 16 pages.

Tang, Y-Y., Ma, Y., Wang, J., Fan, Y., Feng, S., Lu, Q., Yu, Q., Sui, D., Rothbart, M. K., Fan, M. and Posner, M. I. (2007). Short-term meditation training improves attention and self-regulation, *Proceedings of the National Academy of Sciences of the United States of America*, 104(43), 17152–17156.

Thibaut, J. W. and Kelley, H. H. (1959). *The Social Psychology of Groups*. New York: Wiley.

Thorndike, E. L. (1911). *Animal Intelligence*. New York: Macmillan.

van Golde, C. (2011). Fact Sheet: Child Eyewitnesses. *European Association of Psychology and Law – Student Society Publication*. Available at: http://itssimple.ca/forensicgroup/wp-content/uploads/Factsheet_Child_Eyewitnesses.pdf.

Vollen, L. and Eggers, D. (2005). *Surviving Justice: America's Wrongfully Convicted and Exonerated*. San Francisco, CA: McSweeney's.

Waddington, P. A. J. and Bull, R. (2007). Cognitive interviewing as a research technique. *Sociology at Surrey Social Research Update*, Issue 50.

Watson, J. B. (1913). Psychology as the behaviorist views it. *Psychological Review*, 20, 158–178.

Watson, J. B. and Rayner, R. (1920). Conditioned emotional reactions. *Journal of Experimental Psychology*, 3(1), 1–14.

Weiner, M. W., Aisen, P. S., Jack, C. R., Jagust W. J., Trojanowski, J. Q., Shaw, L., Saykin, A. J., Morris, J. C., Cairns, N., Beckett, L. A., Toga, A., Green, R., Walter, S., Soares, H., Snyder, P., Siemers, E., Potter, W., Cole, P. E. and Schmidt, M. (2010). The Alzheimer's Disease Neuroimaging Initiative: Progress report and future plans. *Alzheimers Dement*, 6(3), 202–211.

Weisner, T. S. and Gallimore, R. (1977). My brother's keeper: child and sibling caretaking. *Current Anthropology*, 18, 169–190.

Yalom, I. D. with Leszcz, M. (2005 [1967]). *Theory and Practice of Group Psychotherapy*. New York: Basic Books.

Yuille, J. C. and Cutshall, J. L. (1986). A case study of eyewitness memory of a crime. *Journal of Applied Psychology*, 71(2), 291–301.

INDEX

V

validity, of research 133, 136, 159, 162, 184
validity, types of
  ecological 54, 123, 126, 135, 160, 161, 168
  external 49, 64, 160, 168, 178
  internal 49, 64, 159, 179
  population 160
  temporal 160
Vollen and Eggers (2005) 107

W

Waddington and Bull (2007) 106
Watson (1913) 40

Watson and Rayner (1920) 48, 49
Weisner and Gallimore (1977) 97
Wernicke, Carl 11
Wernicke's area 11
World Wide Alzheimer's Disease Neuroimaging
  Initiative (WW-ADNI) 91, 92

Y

Yalom (2005) 34
Yuille and Cutshall (1986) 106, 108

Z

zero correlation 131, 150, 184

IMAGE CREDITS

Lightning Source UK Ltd.
Milton Keynes UK
UKOW07f0350040816

279947UK00001BA/4/P